MAKING HER MARK

~

FIRSTS AND MILESTONES
IN WOMEN'S SPORTS

ERNESTINE GICHNER MILLER

Contemporary Books

Chicago   New York   San Francisco   Lisbon   London   Madrid   Mexico City
Milan   New Delhi   San Juan   Seoul   Singapore   Sydney   Toronto

Library of Congress Cataloging-in-Publication Data

Miller, Ernestine G.
    Making her mark : firsts and milestones in women's sports / Ernestine
Miller.
        p.   cm.
    ISBN 0-07-139053-7
    1. Sports for women—Records—United States.   2. Sports for
women—United States—History.   3. Women athletes—Rating of—United
States.   I. Title.

GV709.18.U6 M53   2002
796'.082'021—dc21   2002022407

Contemporary Books

*A Division of The **McGraw·Hill** Companies*

ISBN 0-07-139053-7

This book was set in Caslon and Trade Gothic
Printed and bound by Quebecor Martinsburg

Cover and interior design by Monica Baziuk
Except where noted, interior photos provided by the author.

Cover photographs, clockwise from top: Serena Williams at the Estyle.com Classic,
© Tom Hauk/Allsport; Team USA Soccer celebrating their win at the 1996 Olympic
Games, © David Cannon/Allsport; Julie Krone, the winningest female jockey and
only one to take a Triple Crown race, © Bill Janscha/AP Wide World Photo; pitcher
Amanda Freed of the USA Women's softball team pitching against Australia in the
Olympic Cup, © Donald Miralle/Allsport.

McGraw-Hill books are available at special quantity discounts to use as premiums
and sales promotions, or for use in corporate training programs. For more
information, please write to the Director of Special Sales, Professional Publishing,
McGraw-Hill, Two Penn Plaza, New York, NY 10121-2298. Or contact your local
bookstore.

This book is printed on acid-free paper.

To the patience and fortitude of the women athletes of past generations, who in spite of continuous hardships stayed on the playing field. Their courage and spirit have left an enormous imprint on women's sport history, and today's girls and women in many new arenas are benefiting from these unselfish efforts. Here's to fans everywhere knowing their names, their sports, and their legacies—the recognition is long overdue.

Contents

Organizations, Leaders, and Other Milestones   391

Bibliography   401

Foreword

ERNESTINE MILLER IS a woman with a mission! From the first time I met her, I was impressed with her devotion to the process of revealing, especially to an unknowing public at large, the long and rich history of women and sport.

If laypeople know anything concerning the heroines in the development of a sport, it is knowledge that seems to begin with Title IX of the Higher Education Act of 1972, or even later. Her extraordinary collection of women's sports memorabilia features women participating in many sports, and it exhibits the health and vitality of the "modern women" of the early 20th century. Miller knows well the long and colorful history of women in sport. In this book, she takes steps to make comprehensible—and comprehensive—the people, places, events, and accomplishments that combine to create women's sport, being perhaps the most progressive and pervasive of human efforts of the 20th century in the United States. Those of us who share the passion and devotion to maintain and propel advances of girls and women salute this remarkable publication.

The first national-level professional-development experience for me was in 1965: the National Institute on Girls' and Women's Sport, which focused on basketball and volleyball and was cosponsored by the National Association of Girls and Women in Sports (NAGWS) and the U.S. Olympic Committee. It is difficult today to re-create the terror of those times so that obstacles faced by women that Miller documents can be made clear. Apart from the deficits in resources, both human and monetary, to my mind the worst of it was the numbing disinterest of the surrounding community. In the face of each young woman's shining dream for herself as an athlete, the social reply ranged from "Really, why?" to active disapproval.

In my years as commissioner of national championships in the precursor organization to the Association for Intercollegiate Athletics for Women (AIAW) and as the first president of AIAW, I saw dedication, organization, and advocacy change the face of collegiate sport. This strong, enduring, coordinated effort had to be exerted, inexorably, in each sport context, over most of the years of the 20th century. These are the stories and events about which Ernestine Miller writes. It should be clear, as well, that the advance is not complete. Progress is not automatically maintained. There is still a need for those who advocate and those who dream of accomplishment on the field of play.

The evolution of progress in more than 50 sports is featured here. It is must reading for parents of women athletes, coaches, and administrators wanting their charges to understand the history of women's participation. It is also for women's sport advocates who wish to chart how far we have come, as well as how far there is yet to travel.

—CAROLE OGLESBY
Professor Emeritus, Temple University
First President of AIAW and NAGWS
Winner of the Billie Jean King Award
from the Women's Sports Foundation

Acknowledgments

WITH GRATEFUL APPRECIATION to Maggie Barnett for her "marathon job" in assisting me during this project. Maggie is a golfer and basketball player in her junior year at New York University.

A special thank-you to Beth Rasin, lawyer and marketing executive whose knowledge and passion for women's sports were invaluable in helping me with this book.

List of Contributors

Gary Abbot, director of communications, USA Wrestling; Beth Anders, field hockey coach, Old Dominion University; Kim Barlag, motorcycling; Tim Boggan, table tennis historian; John Falzone, president, Professional Women's Bowling Association; Matt Fitzgerald, *Triathlon* magazine; Desirae Freiherr, USA Archery; Sandie Hammerly, assistant executive director, Resource Department, U.S. Field Hockey Association; Doug Haney, USA Canoe/Kayak; Wendy Hilliard, former rhythmic gymnastic champion and director of Sports NYC 2012; Paula Hunt, journalist and ice hockey historian; Rena "Rusty" Kanokogi, pioneer in women's judo; Bill Kellick, USA Boxing; John Kessel, USA Volleyball; Ann King, sports information director, College of New Jersey; Sarah A. Krainert, manager of communications, USA Bowling; Betsy Liebsch, U.S. Taekwondo Union; Carole Lowe, Water Skiing Hall of Fame; Shari LeGate, Women's Shooting Sports Foundation; Sue Lubking, associate professor of kinesiology, West Chester University, and past president of the U.S.

Women's Lacrosse Association; Jon Lundin, U.S. Luge Association; Peggy Manter, U.S. Olympic Committee, Media and Public Relations Division; Mark Merderski, executive director, Motorcycle Hall of Fame; Jim Moorhouse, director of communications, U.S. Soccer; Nick Paulenich, U.S. Speed Skating; Bill Plummer III, Amateur Softball Association; Joanne Potts, race director, Iditarod Trail Committee; Sally Ratcliff, U.S. Lacrosse; Jirina Ribbens, figure skating historian; Paul Robbins, freelance ski journalist who has covered the World Cup since 1978; Chip Rogers, athletic media relations, University of Virginia; Scottie Rogers, NCAA Basketball Division I; Kelli Servizzi, U.S. Diving; Allison Swickard, media and public relations coordinator, U.S. Rugby; Jenepher Shillingford, U.S. Field Hockey Association and Bryn Mawr College; Kathy Keeler, former Olympic rower and coach.

Introduction

THEY ARE MILESTONES in women's sports—two events that dramatically and forever changed society's perception of female athletes. On September 20, 1973, Billie Jean King defeated Bobby Riggs in the famous "Battle of the Sexes" tennis match. Watched by millions of people around the world, no other sporting event had an impact of such magnitude. Twenty-six years later, on the afternoon of July 10, 1999, the final game of the Women's World Cup in soccer took place in Pasadena, California. The U.S. National team beat China, 2–1, in a dramatic shoot-out. This win came before 90,185 fans—the largest crowd ever to attend a women's sporting event—and millions of viewers. These triumphs sent messages that were instantly clear and pivotal moments in the evolution of women's sports.

Today these historic achievements and many other significant people and events are responsible for women's mixing sport with life as never before. On playing fields around the country, whether for the sheer benefit of exercise, for the pleasure of recreation, or for the purpose of athletic competition, women are engaged in sports in record numbers. At the highest level, women athletes are breaking records, receiving heightened media coverage, and, at long last, earning increased prize money. These assertive and committed competitors are gaining the spotlight in sports and have become role models for a whole new generation of young girls.

Yet, while many significant advances have been made in the last decades, especially since the passage of Title IX (the first federal law to prohibit sex discrimination in any educational institution receiving federal aid) in 1972, it is important to remember that not long ago women interested in sports were considered an oddity and were more often the object of catcalls and jeers than of praise and cheers. Being competitive and aggressive with their bodies was something most of society thought improper in a woman—surely overstepping the boundaries of "ladylike" behavior.

Making Her Mark: Firsts and Milestones in Women's Sports takes a step back in time and builds to today, focusing on the legends, heroes, events, and milestones that have advanced the cause of women's athletics on a broad scale. In comprehensive time lines covering more than 50 disciplines, the book pays homage to lesser-known and underappreciated women and events as well as the more famous athletes in many types of competitions. Each entry is linked to a carefully chronicled aspect of the sport that sheds light on the impetus and groundwork for what has emerged today.

Making Her Mark also helps shape a new perspective of the past. At the turn of the 20th century, women were starting to question their role in society. While the emergence of the sportswoman was dismissed by most men and the majority of women, other women, by sheer force of will, defied social restrictions, endured ridicule, and took part in sports despite the obstacles in their way. These women welcomed the challenge and held the hope that the admirable qualities of female athletes would soon override the current views of what women *could* and *should* do. Over the years, they helped form clubs and organize tournaments, but for the most part, they received little recognition from the world at large.

Many of the early sports programs were developed at women's colleges. In the early 1900s, Smith, Wellesley, Radcliff, Mount Holyoke, Vassar, and other schools emphasized physical education in their curricula to counter claims of physical incapability of women. Well-equipped gymnasiums and playing fields were built on campuses, and when a given sport received a certain degree of popularity, competitions between colleges were held, becoming a major sign not only of the seriousness of sports but also of the reality that academic successes and athletic skill were a workable combination. Tournaments in tennis, golf, swimming,

ARCHERY

Archery is one of the country's oldest sports for women, with records of women archers dating back before the 19th century. Target archery is the best-known form of competition. It requires the archer to shoot a set number of arrows from various distances at a five-color target. The target has 10 scoring rings, and scoring consists of 10 points for hitting the center (the bull's-eye), on down to 1 point for the outside ring.

1870 One of the first all-women's archery clubs, the Crescent City Archery Club of New Orleans, was formed.

1879 The National Archery Association (NAA) was established as a co-ed organization, with championships for both men and women.

1879 On August 12–14, the first U.S. National Archery Association championship was held in Chicago. Twenty women competed, and Mrs. Spalding Brown took the title with 110 hits and a score of 548.

1883 At the national championships, the double nationals and the double Columbia rounds were shot by women for the first time.

1900 Archery was first included in the Olympic Games in Paris, with Lydia Scott Howell winning the gold medal. It was an Olympic sport again in 1904 and 1908 but then was canceled due to inconsistencies in international rules.

1904 At the Olympics in Saint Louis, the U.S. women swept the double Columbia rounds. This three-day event consists of two rounds of 21 arrows shot at a distance of 30 yards, 24 arrows shot at 40 yards, and 24 arrows shot at 50 yards. Lydia Howell took the gold; Emma Cook took the silver; and Jessie Pollock received the bronze. Archery was also in the Olympics in 1908 and 1920 and then was dropped until international rules could be established. It wasn't until 1972 that it was reinstated.

1907 Lydia Scott Howell, of Cincinnati, Ohio, won 17 U.S. National Archery Association championships between 1883 and 1907. She also won two Olympic gold medals in 1904. Howell set a scoring record in 1895 that stood until 1931.

1916 Cynthia Wesson, of Cotuit, Massachusetts, won the national championship in Jersey City, New Jersey.

1931 The Federation Internationale de Tir (FITA) was formed to standardize rules and govern international competition.

1931 Dorothy Smith Cummings, of Newton Centre, Massachusetts, came the closest to Lydia Howell's national title record with seven NAA championships from 1919 to 1931. She also won 11 Eastern Archery Association championships.

1931 The first world championships for women took place in Lvov, Poland. No American was a finalist.

1950 On July 30, Jean Lee became the first American woman to win a medal at the world championships, taking the gold in Copenhagen, Denmark.

1955 Ann Weber-Hoyt became the first woman to win both the national target and field championships.

1959 Ann Weber-Hoyt won 15 Eastern target championships and five National Field Archery Association championships between 1940 and 1959. In 20 years of competition in national and world tournaments, Weber-Hoyt finished first eight times, second seven times, and third three times.

1961 At the world target championships, American Nancy Vonderheide won the gold medal; in '63, Victoria Cook won the gold.

1967 Lois Ruby, of Michigan State University, was the first female U.S. Collegiate Champion.

1969 Doreen V. Wilber won her first national championship. In 1974, she won her fourth national championship.

1971 Ann Weber-Hoyt, who had retired in 1960, came out of retirement and subsequently won the Professional Division of the National Archery Association championship four times. Hoyt competed in a total of 23 national archery championships, the most by any woman. She was inducted into the Archery Hall of Fame as part of the inaugural group of archers in 1972.

1972 Archery became a medal event again in the Olympics in Munich, Germany. In competition, two FITA rounds are shot at four distances: 70, 60, 50, and 30 meters. Doreen Wilber won the gold medal, setting a world record of 2,424 points.

1976 Luann Ryon broke the world record with 2,499 points, winning the gold at the Olympics in Montreal.

1982 The Shenk Award, named after former NAA president Clayton Shenk, was established. It is given annually to the male and female archers with the highest accumulated scores from the U.S. indoor and national target championships. Ruth Rowe won the award in '82 and '83.

1988 The U.S. team won the bronze medal at the Olympics in Seoul, South Korea. Denise Parker was the only individual medal winner for the United States, capturing the bronze. She also won national championships in 1990 and '91 and won a bronze at the world championships in 1989. In 1995, she earned four gold medals and a silver at the Pan American Games. From the late '80s to the '90s, she won seven U.S. national titles.

1991 Judi Adams, who won the intercollegiate championship in 1981, was a member of 11 U.S. teams between 1982 and 1991.

1993 At the world indoor championships, Glenda Penaz won the compound bow competition. This event uses a bow that incorporates cables and pulleys to draw the string.

1994 Carol Pelosi, beginning in 1973, notched a total of 22 national crossbow target titles and 20 indoor championships. The crossbow is a short, powerful bow that uses a trigger to launch the arrow.

1995 At age 13, Angela Mascarelli became the youngest archer on a U.S. gold medal team. She won the world title in the compound bow at the world target championships and the world indoor championships.

1998 At the national indoor championships, Amber Dawson set a world record in the Junior Division with 538 points in compound bow.

1998 Janet Dykman won her third consecutive FITA U.S. national target championship in the Olympic bow.

1999 Sally Wunderle won her second consecutive and fourth career compound bow national championship. Her other titles came in '92, the inaugural year of compound bow, and '96. Wunderle is the only archer ever to win this event multiple times.

2000 Legendary archer Ann Weber-Hoyt set a U.S. record in 10 categories at the FITA 2000 national tournament in the Master 60 Division. Hoyt still holds the U.S. 70-meter record in the Professional Division, which she set in 1979.

2000 Janet Dykman finished first at the Olympic trials. She placed second at the 2000 U.S. indoor championships. In the '95 Pan American Games, Dykman won individual and team gold and silver at 50 meters and 30 meters.

2000 Susan Kell, of Massachusetts, set two U.S. records at the indoor national championships in single and double longbow with 341 points and 671 points, respectively.

2000 Actress Geena Davis drew additional attention to the sport when she passed the first round of the Olympic trials.

2000 At the Olympics in Sydney, Janet Dykman, Denise Parker, and Karen Scavotto combined to place fifth in the team competition—a big improvement over the U.S. team's 13th place finish at the 1996 games in Atlanta.

2001 At the U.S. indoor national championships, Elizabeth Norckauer set two U.S. records in the Master 70 Division with 448 points in the single 18 meter and 845 points in the double 18 meter.

2001 The 2001 world championships were held September 15–22 in Beijing, China. This marked Janet Dykman's seventh world championships, but the U.S. did not medal.

2001 Donna Packard set a record in the 18-meter single division of the Master 60+ Division with a score of 479.

2001 Carol Bitner, a Master Compound shooter, set records in the single round 60 meter and in the single round 30 meter.

AUTO RACING

THE INDIANAPOLIS 500 is not only one of the world's most famous races; it is one of the world's toughest—200 laps around a 2.5-mile track. In 1976, after racing for 13 years, Janet Guthrie passed her rookie test at Indianapolis; but her car developed mechanical problems, and she couldn't compete. Dejected but not discouraged, Guthrie headed for Charlotte, North Carolina, to compete in the NASCAR (National Association for Stock Car Auto Racing) Grand National. In a car she had never seen before and without a relief driver, she finished the 600-mile endurance race in 15th place against a field of 40 top male drivers, marking the first time a woman had competed against men in a major U.S. stock car race. The next year at Indianapolis, she not only qualified but also stunned her disapproving competitors by finishing nineth against 33 of the world's most famous drivers. Guthrie fits the accolade "You go, Girl!"

1909 The Women's Motoring Club organized the first all-women auto race. Twelve competitors took up the challenge.

1944 The Sports Car Club of America (SCCA) was founded by a group of amateur motor sports enthusiasts. Their amateur racing circuit is called club racing.

1951 The National Hot Rod Association (NHRA) was established in the U.S. to create racing rules and safety standards.

1964 Donna Mae Mins became the first woman to win an SCCA championship, beating 31 men in the Class II production category for imported two-seaters.

1965 Margaret Laneive "Lee" Bradlove set a land speed record for a woman of 308.65 miles per hour on the Bonneville Salt Flats in Utah.

1974 Shirley Muldowney became the first woman to qualify in a top-fuel dragster event. These cars can go 0 to 100 mph in less than one second and can reach speeds of 250 mph in just 660 feet.

1975 Karen Stead became the first girl to race to victory at the world championship in gravity racing at the All-American Soap Box Derby.

1975 Shirley Muldowney became, at age 35, the first woman to be licensed by the NHRA to operate a top-fuel dragster. In 1976, Muldowney won the Spring Nationals in Columbus, Ohio, making her the first woman to win an NHRA event title. Also in 1976, she became the first woman to break the 6-second barrier, clocking 5.705 seconds to win the Gator Nationals in Gainesville, Florida. In a 33-year career, Muldowney won 17 NHRA titles on the top-fuel dragster circuit, a first for women, and more than any other driver of either sex except for her archrival, Don Garlits.

1976 Janet Guthrie, a licensed commercial pilot, became the first woman to compete in a NASCAR Winston Cup; at the Charlotte World 600, Guthrie finished 15th after starting in 27th place. She drove the entire 600 miles without a relief driver. In 1976, she drove in four NASCAR and four United States Auto Club (USAC) races.

1976 On May 29, at the 61st Indianapolis 500, Janet Guthrie became the first woman to qualify for, and race in, the Indy. The call was heard at the Indianapolis Motor Speedway, "In company with the first lady ever to qualify at Indianapolis—gentlemen, start your engines." Guthrie's average speed during the qualifying round was 188.403 miles per hour.

1978 Janet Guthrie became the first woman to complete the Indianapolis 500. Her ninth-place finish remains the highest ever by a woman.

1980 Shirley Muldowney won 11 races, including her second NHRA Top Fuel World Championship. In that race, driving her trademark pink car, she became the first driver to win the world title more than once.

1982 Shirley Muldowney set a drag racing record of 5.57 seconds in the quarter mile to win the U.S. Nationals in Indianapolis, her first nationals championship. In the same year, she also won her third top-fuel Winston world championship.

1983 Lyn St. James became the first woman to win a solo North American professional road race, at Watkins Glen, New York. She also became the first woman to average more than 200 miles per hour on an oval track, at the Talladega Super Speedway in Alabama in 1985. She reached 204.233 miles per hour in a Ford Mustang prototype.

1987 Tanis Hammond is the second woman to break into the 200-mph club at the Bonneville Salt Flats in Utah. She clocked speeds of 301 mph in a Bonneville Lakester, Number 77. In 2001, at age 52, she was still competing and has set five land speed records over 200 mph.

1988 In June, at the AC Delco 100 Dash Division NASCAR race in Asheville, North Carolina, Shawna Robinson became the first woman ever to win a major NASCAR event.

1989 Patty Moise was the first woman to qualify for pole position in the ARCA 200 race, sponsored by the Automobile Racing Club of America. She also holds the distinction of being the first woman to reach 74-plus career starts in the Grand National series.

1992 Lyn St. James, at age 45, was the oldest rookie to qualify for the Indianapolis 500, finishing 11th. She also was the second woman to race on the Indy Car circuit and the first to win Rookie of the Year honors.

1994 In Atlanta, Shawna Robinson became the first woman to win the pole position at a Grand National NASCAR race. (Grand National Division cars have eight-cylinder engines and reach speeds of 200 mph).

1997 On May 25, Lyn St. James started in her sixth Indy 500. She was the first woman to compete full-time on the Indy circuit and the first woman to start in seven Indianapolis 500 races.

1999 In January, the first Women's Global GT Series was held in Georgia. Leading drivers raced the 2.6-mile road course in preparation for a full field of 32 in identically equipped Esperantes.

1999 On April 22, at the age of 82, Louise Smith became the first woman inducted into the International Motor Sports Hall of Fame at Talladega Super Speedway in Alabama. Smith was the only woman on the circuit from 1945 through the mid-'50s, achieving 38 victories and attracting crowds at races up and down the East Coast.

2000 Shawna Robinson became the first woman to run a full season in a national stock car series. She took ARCA Rookie of the Year honors after placing sixth in the Automobile Racing Club of America Series and winning a pole at the Michigan International Speedway with a record-setting lap of 184.606 miles per hour, finishing 34th in the race.

2000 May 29 marked the first time that more than one woman raced in the Indianapolis 500. Lyn St. James, 53, and Sarah Fisher, 19, competed in the event as the oldest and youngest in the 33-driver field.

2001 At age 20, Sarah Fisher, of Commercial Point, Ohio, placed second at the Infinite Grand Prix of Miami. This was the highest finish by a woman in Indy Car racing history.

2001 Angelle Savoie, at age 31, completed her 19th career victory, breaking Shirly Muldowney's record as the NHRA's winningest female.

AVIATION

FROM THE time of the Wright brothers' first flight in 1903, women have been attracted to aviation and have accomplished remarkable feats both in distance and as daredevils. American barnstormer Harriet Quimby, with her trademark purple flying suit, was one of the first people to draw attention to women who like to soar through the skies. But it was pilot Amelia Earhart who, three-quarters of a century ago, gained international fame by setting early aviation records that became the subject of numerous newspaper and magazine stories. In an open-cockpit biplane that posed many hazards, Earhart became the first woman to fly solo across the country. She strongly believed women should challenge traditional roles.

1910 Blanche Scott, of Dayton, Ohio, was the first woman to pilot an airplane solo. She was also a stunt pilot and became famous for her death dive—a stunt that sent her flying straight toward the ground.

1911 Harriet Quimby, of Coldwater, Michigan, started off as a journalist, but her enthusiasm for airplanes and her determination to fly them outweighed the lure of her writing career. On August 1, she became the first American woman and only the second woman in the world to be granted a pilot's license from the Federation Aeronautique Internationale. Her greatest achievement came in 1912 when she became the first woman to pilot a plane across the English Channel.

1913 A year after earning her pilot's license, Ruth Law became the first pilot to fly at night, when she took a moonlight flight over Staten Island, New York. She soon became famous with her nighttime exhibitions and spectacular air shows, which included death-defying stunts and earned her $9,000 a week. Law's fame grew in 1916 when floodlights were thrown on the Statue of Liberty for the first time and she performed her stunts for President and Mrs. Wilson. She tried to enlist in the military in World War I but was rejected because of her sex. Law later flew as an official recruiter for the U.S. Army and Navy.

1915 On July 18, Katherine Stinson, a fearless stunt pilot, thrilled a crowd by looping the loop, becoming the first woman to perform the feat. In 1917, Stinson flew 606 miles from San Diego to San Francisco, setting an American nonstop distance record.

1921 Laura Broomwell looped the loop 199 times in 1 hour and 20 minutes, setting a women's record for consecutive loops.

1921 Bessie Coleman became the first African American to earn a pilot's license. In 1922, she became the first woman to earn an international aviation license from the Federation Aeronautique Internationale. "Brave Bessie" also had a short but successful career as a stunt pilot on the barnstorming circuit. She hoped to establish a flight school for black pilots but died while practicing a stunt on April 30, 1936, in Jacksonville, Florida.

1924 Aviator Eleanor Smith was the first woman pictured on a Wheaties box.

1928 Only a year after Charles Lindbergh's solo flight across the Atlantic, Amelia Earhart was chosen to be the first female passenger in a transatlantic flight. Also in 1928, she became the first female to make a round-trip solo flight across the United States.

1929 The Ninety-Nines, the first club for licensed women pilots, was formed. Amelia Earhart served as the first president of the club, which had 99 original members and subsequently became a worldwide organization. The Ninety-Nines sponsored air derbies and served as judges for the National Intercollegiate Flying Association competitions.

1929 The first Women's Air Derby was held by the Ninety-Nines. It was the first competitive cross-country event held for women. The race started in Santa Monica, California, and finished in Cleveland, Ohio. The race took a week to complete and featured 40 solo flyers. Louise Thaden, at age 23, won the event and the $2,500 prize.

1932 Amelia Earhart, a daring woman who became enormously popular with the public, was the first woman and only the second person to fly the Atlantic Ocean solo and nonstop. She completed the flight from

Newfoundland to Ireland in less than 15 hours. Prior to this, in 1922, after taking lessons from pioneer woman pilot Neta Snook, Earhart set a women's altitude record of 14,000 feet. In 1928, she became the first woman to fly from the Atlantic Ocean to the Pacific Ocean and back. In 1935, Earhart became the first person to fly solo from Hawaii to California. She never completed her final record-breaking trip around the equator, which would have logged her 29,000 miles. Her plane crashed in the Pacific on July 2, 1937, and Earhart and the wreckage have never been found.

1934 Jacqueline Cochran was the first woman to compete in the London-to-Melbourne air race, and in 1935, she was the first woman to take part in the Bendix Trophy transcontinental race.

1934 At age 25, Helen Richey became the first female pilot to fly regularly scheduled airmail. She had logged nearly a thousand hours in the air prior to her mail flights between Washington, D.C., and Detroit.

1935 The first woman to fly nonstop east to west across North America was Laura Ingalls, whose flight occurred in July.

1942 The Army Air Force appointed Nancy H. Love the commander of the newly created Women's Auxiliary Ferrying Squadron. The unit was renamed the Women Airforce Service Pilots (WASP). In 1977, after continuous lobbying of Congress, members of the WASP unit finally achieved military active-duty status for their service.

1953 Jacqueline Cochran became the first woman pilot to break the sound barrier, flying at a speed of 652.337 miles per hour over the California desert. In 1964, at the age of 57, she set a women's airspeed record of 1,429 miles per hour piloting a Lockheed F104-6 Super Star fighter. Cochran set a total of 33 national and international airspeed records in her career.

1964 Geraldine Mock was the first woman to fly around the world solo. She began the trip on March 16, made 21 stops, and flew a total of 22,858.8 miles in her single-engine Cessna named *The Spirit of Columbus*. The flight took the 37-year-old Mock twenty-nine and one-half days.

1973 Emily Howe Warner, of Denver, was the first female pilot to fly for a commercial U.S. airline, Frontier Airlines. She was admitted to the Airline Pilots Association.

1974 Lieutenant Sally Murphy was the first female pilot trained by the U.S. Army. The U.S. Navy followed suit and selected its first noncombatant female pilots. It was not until 1977 that the air force selected its first group of females for pilot training.

1977 Patricia Undall and Nan Gaylord arrived in Tampa, Florida, from Palm Springs, California, in a Cessna 177 to win the 30th and last women's continental race known as the Powder Puff Derby.

1978 On March 23, Captain Sandra M. Scott of the U.S. Air Force became the first woman pilot to fly an alert duty in strategic command in a KC-135 tanker. Also in March, 40 USAF women officers began to train as crew operators on Titan intercontinental ballistic missiles.

1978 The first female astronaut candidates were chosen by NASA. The group included Anna L. Fisher, M.D.; Shannon W. Lucid, Ph.D.; Judith A. Resnick, Ph.D.; Sally K. Ride, Ph.D.; Rhea Seddon, M.D.; and Kathryn D. Sullivan, Ph.D.

1983 Sally Ride was the first American woman to fly in space.

1984 On June 17, Captain Lynn Ripplemeyer became the first woman to fly a Boeing 747 on a transatlantic flight, piloting a People Express flight from Newark, New Jersey, to London's Gatwick airport.

1984 On October 5, NASA astronaut Kathy Sullivan left Earth for eight days and became the first woman to float in space.

1986 The first woman to fly nonstop around the world without refueling was Jeana Yeager. She and copilot Dick Rugan set a record with their 26,000-mile flight and received the Presidential Citizen's Medal from Ronald Reagan.

1987 Frontier Airlines deployed the first all-women cockpit crew. Captain Emily Warner and first officer Barbara Cook were at the controls from Denver to Lexington, Kentucky.

1990 The First Annual Women in Aviation Conference was held in Prescott, Arizona. In 1993, Women in Aviation International was established with the help of Peggy Baty, Ph.D.

1991 The first woman to win the U.S. National Aerobatic Championships was Patty Wagstaff, who went on to win the next three years.

1995 Lieutenant Colonel Eileen Collins of the U.S. Air Force became the first woman to pilot a space shuttle, on February 5. Collins, NASA's first female pilot, was the copilot of the space shuttle *Discovery*.

1999 In Houston, Lieutenant Colonel Eileen Collins, the first woman shuttle commander of a U.S. space mission, successfully landed the space shuttle *Columbia*.

2000 At NASA, nearly one-third of the workforce were women, as were 25 percent of NASA's astronauts and 16 percent of the scientists and engineers.

BADMINTON

BADMINTON, ONE of the oldest racket sports, is played with a shuttle-cock made of cork and feathers, which is hit back and forth over a five-foot net. Women's single games are played to 11 points, and doubles and mixed doubles are played to 15 points. A match consists of winning two out of three games. In 1992, badminton became an Olympic sport with women's singles and doubles events. In 1996, a third event—mixed doubles—was added, making badminton the only Summer Olympic sport with a mixed event.

1878 The first badminton club in the United States, the Badminton Club of the City of New York, was formed.

1899 The All-England Championships were viewed as the unofficial world championships until 1979, when the official World Badminton Championships were established.

1937 The American Badminton Association held the first U.S. National Badminton Championships at the Naval Armory Pier in Chicago on April 1. Bertha Barkhuff, of Seattle, defeated New York's Wanda Bergman, 11–4, 11–1, for the women's singles title. Barkhuff also won the doubles with Zoe G. Smith and the mixed doubles with Hamilton Law. The following year she won the singles and mixed titles before retiring from the game.

1941 Thelma Kingsbury, an early pioneer of the game in the late 1930s and early 1940s, won the singles and doubles titles at the U.S. Nationals. After World War II she went on to win four more doubles titles.

1942 Badminton was broadcast on national television on July 24, as players on the East Coast competed for the CBS Silver Bowl.

1947 Ethel Marshall won the first postwar women's singles title and then went on to win the next six titles—giving her an astonishing seven titles in a row.

1947 The first U.S. Junior Nationals were held in Los Angeles.

1949 Patsy Stephens and David Freeman became the first U.S. world mixed doubles champions.

1951 The R.S.L. Carlton plastic shuttlecock was introduced in the United States, making the sport more affordable for many Americans.

1953 Ethel Marshall was the first person to win seven consecutive national championship titles, covering the years 1947 to 1953. Judy Rankin Harkman subsequently went her one better, winning eight straight titles from 1956 to 1963.

1954 Judy Devlin became the first U.S. woman to win an All-England Championship.

1957 International team competition for women began with the creation of the Umber Cup, played every three years in England during March. The U.S. team, captained by Margaret Varner, won the inaugural cup with a 6–1 defeat of Denmark. The U.S. women's team also won the next two meets, in 1960 and 1963. The competition is now staged every other year and is known as the Thomas Cup Championships.

1967 Judy Devlin Hackman won her record 10th All-England women's title in singles. The previous year marked her seventh All-England doubles title. Also in 1967, she won her 12th U.S. Nationals singles title as well as her 12th doubles title. During her 15-year career, she won 56 national championships.

1970 The first women's National Collegiate Championships were held at Tulane University (New Orleans). Diane Hales, of Cal Poly Pomona University, was the first singles champion, and the team of Judy Brodhun and Hester Hill captured the doubles championship.

1974 Arizona State University offered three athletic scholarships for women's badminton, a first for the sport.

1977 The first world championship in badminton was held.

1978 The American Badminton Association changed its name to the United States Badminton Association.

1992 Badminton became a medal event at the Barcelona Olympics, with medals awarded in four events: men's and women's singles, and men's and women's doubles.

1995 Badminton was included for the first time in the Pan American Games, held in Buenos Aires, Argentina, March 12–16.

1996 The Olympics in Atlanta added a third event to badminton, mixed doubles, making badminton the only Summer Olympic sport with a mixed event.

1997 At the U.S. National Badminton Championships, Cindy Shi defeated Yeping Tang to garner the women's title. Shi and Tang teamed to win the doubles, giving Shi two U.S. titles in three days.

1998 Helen Noble "Kelly" Tibbetts was active in playing and promoting badminton for 61 years, until her death in 1998. In 1969, she was the U.S. doubles champion, and in 1952 and 1971, she was the national adult mixed doubles champion.

2000 In Orange, California, Yeping Tang won her third consecutive singles U.S. Open. That victory marked her seventh U.S. championship in three years: in 1998 and '99, Tang teamed with Cindy Shi to win the U.S. Open doubles championship and with A. Chong to win the U.S. Open mixed doubles championship.

2001 The USA team won two medals in the women's competition at the Pan American Games in Lima, Peru. Meiluawati won the gold in women's singles and Cindy Shi won the silver.

BASEBALL

THE EARLIEST records of American women playing team sports include accounts of baseball. Many of the women's colleges in the East fielded teams in the late 1800s. The first league—the All-American Girls Baseball League—began during World War II and lasted until 1954. The league comprised teams from the Midwest.

One of the league's outstanding players was Sophie Kurys, the short-stop of the Racine (Wisconsin) Belles. Kurys, one of the all-time greatest base stealers, male or female, was a threat whenever she reached first base. She displayed not only remarkable speed but also extraordinary nerves. In both 1944 and '45, she stole a league-leading 115 bases, and she continued to lead the league in all eight years of her playing career. In 1946, she attempted a phenomenal 203 steals and succeeded in 201. What is most phenomenal is that Kurys executed all of her sliding skills while bare-legged and wearing a skirt.

1866 The Laurel Base Ball Club, with 12 members, and the Abenakis Base Ball Club, with 11 members, were founded at Vassar College (Poughkeepsie, New York). The first nine-member college team was the Vassar Resolutes. Team members wore traditional attire for the day—long skirt, long-sleeve blouse with a high neck, and a band around the waist with "Resolutes" on it—a uniform not exactly conducive to batting, running, and fielding.

1867 Girls began playing in prep schools such as Miss Porter's, in Connecticut, where the Tunxis Base Ball team was formed.

1875 On September 11, in Springfield, Illinois, the first game of baseball ever played for money between two women's teams took place. Two barnstorming teams, the Blondes and the Brunettes, played six innings and gained widespread publicity.

1879 Intramural teams formed at Smith College (Northampton, Massachusetts), and in the spring, the freshmen beat the sophomores by a score of 29–9. Vassar had seven teams that competed against each other and eventually against other women's colleges: Smith, Mount Holyoke, Wellesley, and Barnard.

1880 The first U.S. women's baseball team was organized by Harry Freeman, of New Orleans.

1898 Lizzie Arlington was the first woman to sign a minor-league contract. She pitched for two Pennsylvania teams.

1905 Amanda Clement, of Hudson, South Dakota, became the first woman to umpire a men's baseball game, when the umpire for her brother's team in a semipro league failed to show up. Clement called the balls and strikes and was so good that other men's teams began to request her. She umpired through 1911 for semipro teams in the Dakotas, Nebraska, Minnesota, and Iowa.

1907 Alta Weiss, a pitcher for the semipro Vermillion Independents, was one of the most popular players of her day. Weiss, who played mostly in Ohio, attracted fans from all over the state and was dubbed "the Girl Wonder."

1911 Former star player Maud Nelson and her husband, John, formed several barnstorming teams, including the Western Bloomer Girls and the American Athletic Girls. Maud loved to manage and promote, and her teams of six women and three men flourished, playing throughout the 1920s, which helped to increase opportunities for women. "Bloomer

Girl" teams were popular in several areas of the country from the late 1800s through the 1930s. The teams were composed mostly of women and usually a man as catcher. They played against men's teams, and the women wore bloomer-style pants—a marked improvement over skirts for running the bases and chasing after batted balls.

1911 At Wellesley College (Wellesley, Massachusetts), baseball was a club sport and became part of the physical education program, in which credit was given, from 1911 to 1935.

1920 Margaret Nabel, of Staten Island, New York, managed the New York Bloomer Girls. She was a good businesswoman, demanding payment before a game rather than after, and making sure fences were put around the fields so that spectators couldn't watch for free. The New York Bloomer Girls are reputed to never have lost a game against another Bloomer team in their 25-year history.

1920s Close to 25 colleges had established women's baseball teams.

1928 Elizabeth "Lizzie" Murphy was the first woman to play major-league baseball. She was invited to play with the American League All-Stars in an exhibition game against the Boston Red Sox in Fenway Park. From 1918 to 1935, she played with the New England All-Stars, a men's regional barnstorming team. Murphy was probably the first woman to get paid for playing baseball, demanding to be paid because the men received money. Initially, she earned $5 a game, but as her popularity grew, she got more, becoming known as the "Queen of Baseball."

1931 In April, 17-year-old Virne Beatrice "Jackie" Mitchell was hired as a pitcher by the Chattanooga Lookouts, a Class A team, and pitched an exhibition game against the New York Yankees. Mitchell became famous for striking out Babe Ruth, Lou Gehrig, and Tony Lazzeri in one game. Highlights of the game were carried in newspapers around the country and on newsreels that played over and over in movie theaters. Shortly after the game, baseball commissioner Kenesaw Landis voided Mitchell's contract, stating, "Life in baseball is too strenuous for women."

1931 Babe Didrikson Zaharias, the legendary track-and-field, golf, and multisport star, was the first woman to throw a baseball 296 feet, which she did on July 25 in Jersey City, New Jersey.

1934 Babe Didrikson Zaharias played about 200 games between April and October for the House of David barnstorming team. The same year, she became the first woman to play for a major-league team in an exhibition game, pitching for the Philadelphia Athletics against the Brooklyn Dodgers as well as for the Saint Louis Cardinals against the Boston Braves.

1943 The first and only women's league, the All-American Girls Baseball League (AAGBL), began play in cities in the Midwest. Founded and owned by Philip K. Wrigley, who also owned the Chicago Cubs, it represented the first professional opportunity for women in the sport, with weekly salaries ranging from $60 to more than $180. In the first league championship, the Racine Belles took the title by defeating the Fort Wayne Daisies. Until 1949, the standard ball size was 11 inches. The league then adopted a 10-inch ball, which resulted in higher batting averages. That led them to later adopt a 9-inch ball. The AAGBL lasted until 1954. At a convention years later, alumni added the word *Professional* to the league's name, making it the AAGPBL.

1946 Sophie Kurys, shortstop for the Racine Belles, stole a record 201 bases out of 203 attempts. Playing for the Belles for seven of her eight years, she set a career record with 1,114 steals, averaging 139 a year.

1946 Edith Houghton, a former star shortstop for the Philadelphia Bobbies, a professional Bloomer Girl team, became the first woman to be hired as a scout for a major-league baseball team when she was tapped by the Philadelphia Phillies. Within a week, she was a member of the National Baseball Congress, choosing the best major-league prospects in the country.

1947 The first African American woman to play professional baseball in a men's league was Marcenia Lyle Alberga, who played under the name Toni Stone. She joined the San Francisco Sea Lions, an African American barnstorming team, for the 1945–1947 seasons, traveling around the country. Stone was also the first woman to play in the Negro Leagues, playing second base from 1949 to 1954 on three teams, including the famous Indianapolis Clowns. She retired after nine years of playing professional ball but played recreational baseball until she was 60 years old.

1951 Jean Faut was the only pitcher in the AAGBL to throw two perfect games (no runs, hits, or errors), pitching overhand for the South Bend Blue Sox. The first was on July 21, 1951, and the other on September 3, 1953.

1972 The New York State Court of Appeals upheld the right of Bernice Gera to umpire a professional baseball game. Gera became the first woman to umpire in the modern era when she took the field in a minor-league game between the Auburn Phillies and the Geneva Rangers.

1974 Little League Baseball announced that teams would now be open to girls. Jeni Miller, of Millburn, New Jersey, became one of the first girls to play Little League when she was drafted by the Millburn Mustangs. In 1975, Miller chalked up another first for American girls when she hit a grand-slam home run.

1978 The first girl to play on a high school varsity team was Linda Williams, rightfielder for the Wheatley High School Wildcats in Houston, Texas. The University Interscholastic League attempted to prevent her from playing because of her sex, but a judge ordered her reinstated.

1980 At the national Pitch, Hit, and Run Championship, held at the Seattle Mariners' baseball stadium, 11-year-old Crystal Fields defeated boys in the 9- to 12-year-old age-group and became the first female winner in the history of the event.

1984 Darlene May, who coached at California Poly Pomona University and compiled a record of 519–119, became the first woman to officiate an Olympic baseball game.

1987 On July 27, Pam Postema became the first woman to work as a plate umpire in a major-league game, when the Atlanta Braves and New York Yankees played in exhibition.

1989 Julie Croteau became the first woman to play on an NCAA men's college baseball team when she took the field at first base for Saint Mary's College in Frederick, Maryland. Croteau was on the team for three years.

1989 On August 23, Victoria Brucker became the first girl from the United States to play in a Little League World Series game, as well as the first girl to be a starting pitcher, get a hit, and score a run.

1990 Jodi Haller became the first woman to pitch in a college baseball game as a member of St. Vincent's college team in Pennsylvania.

1990 Elaine Steward was hired by the Boston Red Sox as assistant general manager, which made her the first woman in major-league baseball history to hold this position. The second was Kim Ng, who was hired by the New York Yankees in 1998. In 2001, she joined the Los Angeles Dodgers as assistant general manager and was replaced in New York by the third woman to become assistant general manager, Jean Alterman.

1992 Sherry Davis became the first woman to serve as a public-address announcer in the majors, working games for the San Francisco Giants.

Kelly Sanders was number two, filling in for Rex Barney, the announcer for the Baltimore Orioles.

1994 On May 8, the Colorado Silver Bullets began their inaugural season as the first professional women's baseball team since 1954. The Silver Bullets were a barnstorming team organized to compete against professional men's minor-league teams at the double- and triple-A levels. The Silver Bullets were very popular but disbanded in 1997 due to lack of sponsorship.

1994 After completing their season with the Silver Bullets, Lee Anne Ketcham and Julie Croteau became the first women to be invited to play on a major league–sanctioned team. The invitation was issued by the Maui Stingrays of the Hawaiian Winter League.

1995 Julie Croteau became the first woman to join the coaching staff of an NCAA college baseball team when she was hired by the University of Massachusetts.

1996 Spaulding Sports introduced the first baseball glove designed for women.

1996 On June 4, Pam Davis became the first woman to pitch for an affiliated men's professional team in regular season play, notching one inning of scoreless relief for the Class AA Jacksonville Suns. In 1988, she was the first girl to pitch in the Junior League World Championships. Davis also pitched for the Silver Bullets.

1996 On November 15, Ila Borders became the first woman ever to pitch in a men's college baseball game. She tossed a complete game for Southern California College of Costa Mesa, a member of the National Association of Intercollegiate Athletes, against Claremont-Mudd, winning 12–1. Her second start was a 10–1 rout of Concordia University, and the run she yielded wasn't earned. Borders eventually went on to play minor-league ball.

1996 USA Baseball in conjunction with the American Amateur Baseball Congress (AABC) developed a pilot women's program. It began with a five-team league in the Midwest, the Great Lakes Women's Baseball League, representing Chicago; Lansing, Battle Creek, and Grand Rapids, Michigan; and South Bend, Indiana.

2001 At the World Series held in Toronto, the U.S. National team, sanctioned by U.S. Women's Baseball in Akron, Ohio, played and beat Japan (9–1) for the championship. Teams from Australia and Canada also competed. The 2002 championship will be held in the United States.

BASKETBALL

MODERN-DAY BASKETBALL is the product of evolution. Early baskets were actually wooden peach baskets that were affixed to the top of a long pole. By 1894, 18-inch iron hoops with braided cord netting attached to the rim started to be used. However, there was no open bottom; after the ball landed in the hoop, the referee pulled a hanging cord, which lifted the net, and the ball dropped out.

As a reflection of the extent to which things have changed, this chapter presents two time lines—the first covering the high points throughout the sport's history, followed by a separate review of the professional game.

1892 Senda Berenson, the first director of physical education at Smith College (Northampton, Massachusetts), created the original rules for women's basketball. The court was divided into three areas, with six players per team. Two players were assigned to each area, and they could not cross the line into other areas. A player could hold the ball for only three seconds. Berenson also organized the first women's collegiate basketball game, held on March 21, 1893, for her students at Smith.

1896 On April 4, the first women's intercollegiate basketball game on the West Coast took place between Stanford and the University of California at Berkeley, in Armory Hall in San Francisco. Stanford eked out a 2–1 victory. The University of Washington and Ellensburg State Normal School played another intercollege game on April 17 in Seattle. Washington won 6–3. Both games were played using the original "baskets"—peach baskets.

1899 The Women's Basket Ball Rules Committee was formed at the Conference of Physical Training, held at Springfield College, in Massachusetts. Bertha Alice Foster, of Oberlin College, was selected as chair. The committee's purpose was to make the rules consistent.

1899 The first official basket was made by Spalding. It had a bottom that held the ball. A chain was pulled to release the ball after a shot was made.

1901 The first official women's basketball rules, edited by Senda Berenson, were published by the Spalding Athletic Library.

1918 The bottom of the basket was removed to speed up the game.

1925 The National Section on Women's Athletics organized an Officials Committee.

1926 The first Amateur Athletic Union (AAU) national women's basketball championship was held in Los Angeles on April 8–9. Most of the teams were either athletic clubs' teams or company-sponsored teams. Games were played according to men's rules. In an announcement of the tournament, the *Los Angeles Times* headline read, "Amazons here from all over the country." The tournament was won by the Presidential Insurance Company of Newark, New Jersey.

1928 The Women's National Officiating Ruling Committee was formed, and the first pamphlet of instructions for women's basketball referees was published, under the title "Technique for the Woman Official as Referee or Umpire in Girls Basketball."

1932 Guarding, previously not allowed, became a part of the game.

1934 The United States joined the International Amateur Basketball Federation, also known as FIBA (Federale Internationale Basketball Association), which recognized the AAU as the organization responsible for selecting and overseeing U.S. teams.

1936 The All-American Red Heads were formed as a professional barnstorming team in Crossville, Missouri. They played by men's rules and competed against men's teams. The Red Heads remained on the scene for more than 50 years and were featured in popular magazines and on television.

1938 The three-section court was changed to two sections, but teams still fielded six players—three guards and three forwards.

1949 The double dribble was introduced.

1951 As a result of a rule change, players could, for the first time, receive coaching during intermission and time-outs.

1953 The first world championship for women's basketball was held in Santiago, Chile, during March 7–22. The U.S. team won the tournament with a 5–1 record. The team was composed mostly of the AAU national championship team, Nashville Business College.

1955 The United States sent a women's basketball team to the Pan American Games for the first time. The team won the gold medal with an 8–0 record. The games, which were established in 1951, are held every four years in the year preceding the Summer Olympics.

1958 Wayland Baptist College (Plainview, Texas) was a dominant force in AAU competition from 1954 to '58. The school's extraordinary program won 131 games in a row.

1959 Nera White, one of the early legends in women's basketball, played for Nashville Business College from 1954 to '69. At the time, AAU rules did not limit the number of years a player could participate. She was an AAU All-American for 15 consecutive years and was named AAU tournament MVP nine times. White was also one of the first women inducted into the Basketball Hall of Fame, in Springfield, Massachusetts.

1964 Fran Koening and Carol Walter were the first women to officiate at an AAU national tournament.

1966 The unlimited dribble was admitted to the official rule book.

1968 A U.S. women's team played in the Paralympics for the first time, at the games held in Tel Aviv, Israel. The team won the bronze medal. This event sparked interest in wheelchair basketball programs around the country.

1969 The first National Collegiate Invitational basketball championships were held at West Chester State College (Pennsylvania), under the direction of Carol Eckman, the school's women's basketball coach. Eckman organized selection of the country's best teams under the auspices of the Division of Girls and Women in Sport (DGWS). This was the first time women competed in a national tournament without AAU teams.

1971 Women played a full-court game for the first time, with five players, under AAU and DGWS rules.

1972 The Association for Intercollegiate Athletics for Women (AIAW) held its first women's national collegiate basketball championship at Illinois State University. Immaculata College (Pennsylvania), coached by Cathy Rush, won its first of three consecutive national championships. The AIAW governed women's sports until it was incorporated into the National Collegiate Athletic Association (NCAA) in 1982.

1973 The Amateur Basketball Association of the United States (ABAUSA) was formed, replacing the AAU as the national governing body.

1973 The AIAW first offered college scholarships to female athletes.

1974 Immaculata College won its third consecutive national championship under Cathy Rush. Delta State University (Cleveland, Mississippi), coached by Margaret Wade, also won three consecutive AIAW national championships, in 1975–'77.

1974 The ABAUSA was officially recognized by both FIBA and the United States Olympic Committee.

1974 Ann Meyers was the first high school student to play on the U.S. national team, as well as the first woman to receive a basketball scholarship from UCLA.

1975 The U.S. National Wheelchair Basketball Association held its first women's national tournament.

1975 February 22 marked the first time a women's college basketball game was played at Madison Square Garden. Eleven thousand fans watched Immaculata College defeat Queens College (Flushing, New York) by a score of 65–61.

1975 The first all-American college team was selected, sponsored by Kodak. Coaches nominated players from their respective regions, and the winners were selected from videotape. William H. Lowe was the force behind the team.

1976 Basketball became an Olympic event for women for the first time, in Montreal. Twelve teams competed. The U.S. team won the silver medal, and the Soviet Union took the gold. Lucy Harris, a star from Delta State University, scored the first basket.

1977 The United States participated in the World University Games for the first time. Playing in Bulgaria, the U.S. team won the silver medal, under Queens College coach Lucille Kyvallos.

1978 As a senior at New Jersey's Montclair State College, Carol Blazejowski scored 1,235 points—a single-season record. That same year, playing in a game at Madison Square Garden, she scored 52 points, a record at the time for both men and women.

1978 The first Wade Trophy, named after the legendary coach Margaret Wade of Delta State, was awarded to Carol Blazejowski, recognizing her as the nation's finest female collegiate player. The trophy was established by the National Association for Girls and Women in Sports (NAGWS).

1978 The first Final Four for women was held at UCLA's Pauley Pavilion. NBC televised the action as UCLA trounced Maryland, 90–74, and Montclair State captured third place in a 90–88 squeaker against Wayland Baptist. The tournament was held under AIAW auspices.

1980 Marianne Crawford Stanley was the first person to win the AIAW title both as a player (for Immaculata College—1973 and '74) and as a coach (at Old Dominion, Norfolk, Virginia—1979 and '80). In 1988, under Stanley, Old Dominion won the NCAA Championships.

1980 The United States boycotted the Moscow Olympics.

1982 Cheryl Miller, of Riverside Poly High (California), was the first and only athlete ever to be named a high school all-American four times. She achieved the honor in 1979 through '82. In a game on January 6, 1982, Miller scored 105 points, which still stands as the high school scoring record. Miller went on to become an all-American at the University of Southern California, a coach in the WNBA, and, currently, a television commentator for the NBA.

1982 The first NCAA-sponsored Division I women's basketball Final Four championship was held at Old Dominion University in Norfolk, Virginia. CBS carried the game nationally as Louisiana Tech defeated Cheyney State (Pennsylvania), 76–62. The championship was a 32-team bracket, with all first-round games at home sites of the top seeds, followed by four regional tournaments. Louisiana Tech also won the AIAW championship in 1981.

1982 In a regional final game against Maryland, Lorri Bauman of Drake University (Des Moines, Iowa) scored 50 points, the most points ever scored in a single tournament game.

1982 The Women's Basketball Coaches Association was formed. The association held its first convention at Virginia Beach in conjunction with the NCAA tournament; 100 coaches attended.

1982 In March, California Polytechnic University in Pomona beat Tuskegee University (Alabama), 93–74, in the first Division II national championship sponsored by the NCAA. Pomona repeated in 1985, beating Central Montana State, 80–69; in 1986, beating the University of North Dakota, 70–63; and in 2001, again defeating North Dakota, 87–80.

1982 In the first Division III national championship sponsored by the NCAA, Elizabethtown College (Pennsylvania) beat Greensboro College (North Carolina), 67–66.

1984 The first woman to dunk in a college game was 6-foot-7-inch junior Georgeann Wells, of West Virginia, in a game against the University of Charleston.

1984 At the Los Angeles Olympics, the U.S. women's basketball team, coached by Pat Head Summitt, of the University of Tennessee, won its first gold medal.

1985 Billie Moore was the first coach in women's basketball history to lead two schools to national titles and the eighth to register 400 wins. Having coached California State University at Fullerton to the championship in 1970, she did the same for UCLA in 1985. She also served as coach for the first U.S. women's Olympic team in Montreal in 1976, which took home the silver medal.

1985 Women were inducted into the Basketball Hall of Fame for the first time. The three inductees were Senda Berenson Abbott, the founder of women's basketball and the editor of A. G. Spalding's first women's basketball guide; Margaret Wade, coach at Delta State University; and Bertha F. Teague, who coached for 42 years at Bryn High School, in Ada, Oklahoma.

1985 The inaugural Women's Junior World Championships were held in Colorado Springs. The Soviet Union won the title, while the United States finished fifth with a 4–2 record.

1986 Jody Conradt, of the University of Texas, became the first NCAA Division I women's basketball coach to take a team undefeated (34–0) in regular-season and postseason play and win the national championship. The feat was matched in 1995 when the University of Connecticut team, under coach Gene Auremmio, went undefeated—winning 35 games en route to the NCAA title. In 1988, the University of Tennessee team, this time with Pat Summitt as coach, was 39–0 and won the championship.

1986 The inaugural Goodwill Games were held in Moscow. A team of outstanding collegiate players coached by North Carolina State's Kay Yow won the title, crushing Yugoslavia by a score of 72–53 and going 5–0.

1986 Cheryl Miller, who played for USC from 1983 to '86, set an NCAA career free-throw record with 91.

1988 The U.S. team, coached by Kay Yow of North Carolina State University, won the gold medal at the Olympics in Seoul.

1988 The three-point field goal was adopted.

1989 The NCAA Championship bracket expanded to 48 teams.

1989 ABAUSA changed its name to USA Basketball on October 12. After FIBA modified its rules to allow professional players to participate in international competitions, the National Basketball Association (NBA) and later the Women's National Basketball Association (WNBA) became active members in USA Basketball, which is based in Colorado Springs.

1990 Pat Head Summitt, coach of the University of Tennessee, received the John Bunn Award, the most prestigious honor given by the Basketball Hall of Fame. She was the first woman to receive this award in its 19-year history.

1990 Bernadette Mattox became the first woman to coach a Division I men's team, serving as assistant coach at the University of Kentucky under Rick Pitino. In 1999, Stephanie Ready became an assistant coach at Coppin State (Baltimore).

1991 USC star Lisa Leslie was named to the Pac-10 all-conference first team; she became the first player in history to receive the honor four times, 1991–'94.

1992 Dawn Staley, a four-year starter for the University of Virginia, set an NCAA career record with 454 steals.

1993 Sheryl Swoopes, of Texas Tech, scored 47 points in the national championship game, an NCAA record for men and women. Swoopes scored a total of 177 points during the tournament.

1993 Vermont beat Northeastern, 50–40, for its 50th straight victory, breaking the women's Division I college basketball record for consecutive regular-season wins.

1994 The NCAA Division I women's basketball field expanded to 64 teams, and Division III expanded to 40.

1994 Charlotte Smith, of the University of North Carolina, set a Final Four record with 23 rebounds—but her heroics went further: with seven seconds left in the game, she sank a three-point shot that yielded a 60–59 triumph over Texas Tech in what remains a classic finish.

1994 Anne Donovan, of Old Dominion University, set an NCAA record with 801 career blocks. She was also recognized as a two-time Academic All-American and was inducted into the Academic All-American Hall of Fame.

1995 All-American player Rebecca Lobo played in every game of the University of Connecticut's undefeated season and was named the Final Four tournament MVP.

1995 When C. Vivian Stringer took the reins as head coach of women's basketball at Rutgers University (New Brunswick, New Jersey), she became the first female coach to earn a base pay of $150,000.

1995 Kerri-Ann McTiernan became the first woman head coach of a men's team, taking over at Brooklyn's Kingsborough Community College.

1995 Jody Conradt, of the University of Texas, was the first women's basketball coach to win 600 games.

1995 The University of Alabama scored a record 121 points versus Duke in the second round of the NCAA Championships.

1995 Capital University (Columbus, Ohio) was the first team to win back-to-back Division II championships. The Crusaders pounded Washington University (Saint Louis), 82–63, in 1994, and then outlasted the University of Wisconsin at Oshkosh, 59–52, in 1995.

1996 At the Olympics in Atlanta, the U.S. team won the gold medal. Teresa Edwards set an Olympic record with 15 assists in the game against Australia. Edwards became the first basketball player, male or female, to play on five consecutive Olympic teams. She also holds a record four Olympic gold medals and one bronze, more than any other basketball player of either sex.

1996 Kasey Morlock, of North Dakota State, was the first player to win the Division II MVP Award back-to-back. Jenny Crouse, also of North Dakota, won back-to-back awards in '98 and '99.

1997 On December 18, Jody Conradt achieved another amazing first when her University of Texas Lady Longhorns beat Northwestern, giving her a total of 700 victories. Conradt is the eighth coach and first woman to reach this milestone. Pat Summitt also reached this milestone on December 5, 1999, when Tennessee beat the University of Wisconsin.

1997 The University of Tennessee was the first team to win a national championship and lose as many as 10 games during the regular season.

1997 Kristeena Alexander, playing for George Mason University (Fairfax, Virginia), set an NCAA all-division record by going 20 for 20 from the free-throw line, in a game against Central Florida.

1997 The U.S. women's junior national team won the gold medal at the FIBA women's junior world championships, becoming the first U.S. team to earn a medal in the event.

1998 Julie Kromenhoek, from the University of Utah, set an NCAA record for three-point field goals with eight, in a game against Louisville, but Louisville won, 69–61.

1998 For the first time in NCAA tournament history, a 16th-seeded team defeated a top-seeded team, when Harvard beat Stanford, 71–67, in the first round.

1998 Pat Summitt, of the University of Tennessee, became the first and only coach to win six national championships: 1987, '89, '91, '96, '97, and '98. Also in 1998, Summitt became the first female coach to appear on the cover of *Sports Illustrated* in the March 2 issue.

1998 Tennessee's Chamique Holdsclaw became the first player to be named MVP of the NCAA Division I tournament in two consecutive years. Holdsclaw led the Lady Volunteers to their third consecutive NCAA title in March. She also was the first women's basketball player to win the Sullivan Award, given annually to the nation's top amateur athlete.

1998 The ninth-seeded Arkansas Razorbacks were the lowest-seeded team in Division I NCAA tournament history to reach the Final Four.

1999 Chamique Holdsclaw, who played at Tennessee from 1996 to '99, holds the NCAA record for points scored with 479 and for career field goals with 195.

1999 Carolyn Peck, coach of Purdue (Lafayette, Indiana) became the first African American head coach to win the women's NCAA title, when her team defeated Duke, 62–45, in the finals.

1999 On June 3 in Knoxville, Tennessee, the Women's Basketball Hall of Fame opened as the world's first and only all-women's Hall of Fame sports museum.

1999 Jennifer Rizzotti, former star of the University of Connecticut, signed on as the coach of the University of Hartford women's basketball team, becoming the youngest NCAA Division I coach in the nation.

1999 The University of Tennessee set a record of 334 wins for the decade, more than any other women's team. Connecticut placed second with 313 wins.

2000 At the national tournament, Tennessee made its 12th Final Four appearance, the most ever by any team. Louisiana Tech ranks second, having won its 11th in 1999.

2000 Michelle Snow, a 6-foot-7-inch sophomore at the University of Tennessee, broke a Final Four record with seven blocked shots in Tennessee's 64–54 semifinal victory over Rutgers. Kara Walters, of the University of Connecticut, held the previous record—six blocked shots against Tennessee in 1996.

2000 C. Vivian Stringer became the only coach to take three schools to the Final Four: Cheyney State in 1982, the University of Iowa in 1993, and Rutgers in 2000.

2000 The University of Connecticut set a record for most points scored by a team during the national championship tournament, compiling 547 points in six games.

2001 On January 11, Kay Yow of North Carolina State won her 600th career game. She joins Jody Conradt of Texas, Pat Summitt of Tennessee (both now over 700), Sue Gunter of LSU, and Vivian Stringer of Rutgers.

2001 In March, Washington University (Saint Louis) defeated Messiah (Grantham, Pennsylvania), 67–42, to win its fourth consecutive Division III title. Washington's streak began in 1998, when it squeaked past South-

TEAM USA. (PHOTO © HARRY HOW/ALLSPORT.)

ern Maine, 72–69. It then went on to beat Saint Benedict (Saint Joseph, Minnesota), 74–65, in 1999 and, in 2000, crushed Southern Maine, 79–33.

2001 Attendance for NCAA women's basketball set a record for the 17th consecutive year. A total of 8,824,776 fans attended games in all divisions, including a record 6.5 million in Division I.

2001 On July 19, Duke University's Alana Beard scored a team-record 28 points in a 99–80 win over Russia at the Women's Junior World Championship in Bruno, Czech Republic. The team, coached by Geno Auriemma of the University of Connecticut, won the bronze medal. The Czechs defeated Russia for the gold. Beard's effort bested Maylana Martin's 24 points versus Japan in 1997.

2002 On January 5, the largest crowd ever for a women's college basketball game (24,611) watched the University of Connecticut beat the University of Tennessee, 86–72.

2002 On February 3, Rene Portland of Penn State became the seventh Division I coach to win 500 games at one school. She joins Jody Conradt, Pat Summitt, Sue Gunter, Kay Yow, Marion Washington (Kansas), and Debbie Ryan (Virginia).

2002 Coaches Jody Conradt of the University of Texas and Pat Summitt of the University of Tennessee finished the season tied, with 788 victories each —an all-time NCAA record.

2002 On March 29, at the NCAA Division I semi-finals, 29,619 fans packed the Alamodome in San Antonio, Texas—the largest crowd ever to watch a women's basketball game.

2002 The University of Connecticut won the NCAA Division I championship by defeating the University of Oklahoma, 82–70. UConn's victory gave the team a perfect record of 39–0, becoming the first school to have two undefeated women's seasons (35–0 in 1994–'95) in NCAA history. They set another NCAA record by winning their games by the largest average point margin—35.4.

Professional

1977 Luica Harris, of Delta State University, was the first woman drafted by a men's professional basketball team. Harris was selected by the New Orleans Jazz but chose instead to launch her professional career with the Houston Angels in the Women's Basketball League (WBL).

1978 The sport's first women's league, aptly called the Women's Basketball League, was launched, with eight teams playing a 34-game schedule. The first game took place between the Chicago Hustle and the Milwaukee Does. With expenses high, attendance low, and media support weak, the league folded in 1981 after three seasons.

1979 Ann Meyers became the first woman to sign a contract with the NBA—a one-year stint with the Indiana Pacers. Meyers participated in a three-day tryout but did not make the team. She subsequently joined the Pacers' broadcasting staff.

1987 Nancy Lieberman became the first woman to play in a men's pro basketball league. She played for the Long Island Knights in the United States Basketball League as well as for a professional team in Springfield, Massachusetts.

1988 Former University of Kansas star Lynette Woodard signed on as the first female player for the Harlem Globetrotters in October. She played for two years.

1991 On July 15, Sandra Ortiz-Del Valle became the first woman to officiate a men's professional basketball game, working the contest between the New Haven Skyhawks and the Philadelphia Spirit.

1996 The American Basketball League (ABL), a professional women's league, debuted on October 18, in Hartford, Connecticut, with a game between the New England Blizzard and the Richmond Rage. The league folded in 1998.

1996 The Columbus, Ohio, Quest won the ABL national championship in the league's inaugural 1996–'97 season. The Quest repeated in 1998, beating the Long Beach, California, Sting Rays.

1997 The WNBA was established by the NBA, with Val Ackerman as president. Ackerman, a lawyer for the NBA, was a four-year starter for the University of Virginia from 1977 to '81.

1997 Dena Head, a former University of Tennessee star who played on two U.S. national teams in 1994, was the first selection in the WNBA draft. The Utah Starzz selected Head on February 27.

1997 Dee Kantner, 37, and Violet Palmer, 33, became the first female officials in the NBA.

1997 The first WNBA game took place on June 21, at the Los Angeles Forum. The New York Liberty defeated the Los Angeles Sparks, 67–57, before 14,284 fans.

1997 The first championship game of the WNBA took place in Houston on August 30. The Houston Comets defeated the New York Liberty in the finals.

1997 The Liberty's Teresa Weatherspoon was the first WNBA Defensive Player of the Year, leading the league in assists and steals.

1997 The WNBA presented its first MVP Award to Cynthia Cooper, of the Houston Comets. Cooper was also the only unanimous selection to the first All-WNBA team. She finished the regular season as the league's leading scorer, averaging 22.4 points per game. Houston's coach, Van Chancellor, was named Coach of the Year. Cooper was MVP again in 1998 and '99.

1998 Nancy Lieberman, who had been a player for the Phoenix Mercury, became head coach of the Detroit Shock, making her the first WNBA player to become a coach. In 2000, Cynthia Cooper, MVP of the four-time-champion Houston Comets, was the next to make the transition, taking the helm at Phoenix.

1998 In an ABL game against the New England Blizzard on January 2, the Columbus Quest became the first team to hit 37 straight free throws; 11 of those were by Valerie Still.

1998 Dawn Staley, of the Philadelphia Rage (formerly the Richmond Rage), set an ABL record for three-pointers in a season, sinking her 100th in February.

1998 Teresa Edwards, player-coach of the ABL Atlanta Glory, was the first woman to score as many as 31 points in a half, which she did in the second half of a game against the Colorado Xplosion on February 3.

1998 Cynthia Cooper, playing for the WNBA Houston Comets, became the first player to score more than 1,000 career points.

1999 The first WNBA All-Star Game was held on July 14, in Madison Square Garden, before a sellout crowd of 18,649. The Western Conference All-Stars prevailed over their Eastern counterparts, 79–61. Lisa Leslie scored 13 points and was named the first MVP.

1999 Lisa Leslie, of the Los Angeles Sparks, was the first to receive three WNBA Player of the Week honors in one season.

2000 On August 27, Houston Comets guard Cynthia Cooper, 37, was named MVP of the championship series for the fourth consecutive year, having led the Comets to their fourth consecutive title with a 79–73 victory over the New York Liberty.

2000 The Houston Comets retired the jersey of Kim Perot, who died in 1999 of brain cancer. Perot's number 10 was the first WNBA jersey to be retired.

2001 Twin sisters Coco and Kelly Miller, of the University of Georgia, became the first sisters selected in the top 10 of the WNBA draft. Kelly was selected by the Charlotte Sting as the number two pick, and Coco went to the Washington Mystics as the number nine pick.

2001 On June 21, the Houston Comets ended the Los Angeles Sparks' season-opening winning streak—a WNBA-record nine straight wins—with a 69–65 victory, in Houston. Later in the season, the Sparks set another WNBA record with an 18-game winning streak that ended

August 23, when the Utah Starzz beat them in overtime, 80–78, with a 10th of a second left on the buzzer.

2001 On July 8, Katie Smith, of the Minnesota Lynx, broke the WNBA single-game scoring record with 46 points, in a 100–95 loss to the Los Angeles Sparks. Smith scored 36 of the points in the second half.

2001 On July 11, the Los Angeles Sparks set a WNBA record with 13 blocked shots, as the Sparks frustrated the Phoenix Mercury, 75–61.

2001 On August 16, Stephanie Ready was named coach of the Greenville, South Carolina, Groove—a member of the new eight-team NBA developmental league, considered a minor-league NBA. Ready thus became the first female coach of a men's professional basketball team.

2001 The Los Angeles Sparks were the first WNBA team to go undefeated at home, nailing 18 wins and no losses in the regular season.

2001 League MVP Lisa Leslie set a WNBA play-off record for rebounds in a half, with 14, which she scored in the first half for the Los Angeles Sparks in a game against the Sacramento Monarchs. L.A. went on to win, 93–62. The New York Liberty's Tari Phillips held the former record with 10. On August 8, Leslie also became the WNBA all-time scoring leader, with 2,614 points, surpassing Cynthia Cooper's 2,537.

2001 The Los Angeles Sparks defeated the Charlotte Sting 3–0 in the WNBA play-offs.

2001 Lisa Leslie was the first player to be MVP of the All-Star Game, regular season, and play-offs.

BEACH VOLLEYBALL

SOME ATHLETES define their sport—Gabrielle Reece is one of them. Her luminous stature first appeared on the professional beach volleyball tour in 1992. At 6 feet, 3 inches, and 170 pounds, Reece combined agile moves in the sand with glamorous looks, became an immediate media star, and brought the sport national (even worldwide) attention. Beach volleyball, first made popular in California, follows most of the same rules as indoor volleyball, but it's played outdoors on a sand court usually with two people per team.

> *When you are playing at the highest level you can play at, it doesn't matter if anyone else is better than you. I love watching other people play good volleyball because I know what I can do. My game may be different, but I can still appreciate their game.*

> —GABRIELLE REECE, from *Big Girl in the Middle*, by Gabrielle Reece and Karen Karbo

1986 The Women's Professional Volleyball Association (WPVA) was created by a group headed by Nina Grouwinkel Matthies, formerly a player at UCLA and then a coach at Pepperdine University (Malibu, California). This was the first effort to organize women's pro beach volleyball. While at UCLA, Matthies was captain of two AIAW championship teams and was a member of the U.S. team in 1974 and '75; she also competed in the 1971 Pan American Games.

1987 On May 16–17, the WPVA held its first professional event in Newport Beach, California. Winners Linda Chisholm and Jackie Silva split

$300 in prize money. Chisholm dominated the inaugural season, winning eight out of nine tournaments with two different partners: Silva (seven) and Nina Matthies (one). Chisholm repeated her record in 1988, winning seven tournaments with Silva and one with Janice Harrer.

1989 The WPVA increased its tournament series to 15 events. The team of Patty Dodd and Jackie Silva won 11 out of the 15. Silva, who is Brazilian, continued her domination in 1990, winning 5 of 7 tournaments with Janice Harrer and 7 of 9 with Karolyn Kirby.

1991 Karolyn Kirby and Angela Rock were the first team to win more than $50,000 in one season, earning $67,815, with victories in 12 of 17 tournaments.

1991 In September, the first Federation Internationale de Volleyball (FIVB) Beach Volleyball World Council met in Lausanne, Switzerland, to determine an international program for beach volleyball.

1992 On July 5, in Atlantic City, Gail Castro and Lori Forsythe ended the longest partnership in beach volleyball. They had been playing together since 1988 and competed in 70 tournaments, with three victories. Castro came out of retirement to join Forsythe for 4 events in 1995, bringing their record as a team to 74 tournaments.

1992 From August 5–12, the first FIVB beach volleyball tournament took place in Almeria, Spain, with a total purse of $50,000. Karolyn Kirby and Nancy Reno were the first world champions. Kirby repeated the following year with Liz Masakayan. Kirby, who had been an All-American in indoor volleyball at Utah State, followed her coach to the University of Kentucky, where she again was named an All-American. She was named MVP of the WPVA in 1991 and '92.

1993 With eight of the top players moving to the American Volleyball Professionals (AVP) Tour, Karolyn Kirby and Liz Masakayan began the most dominant era in the WPVA. They won 11 of 12 tournaments and split $74,550 in prize money. Masakayan, a two-time indoor volleyball All-American at UCLA, and Kirby, recipient of the 1985 Honda Award as the outstanding NCAA Division I female athlete, began a partnership that tied for the second longest at 51 tournaments. Kirby became the first woman to earn more than $200,000 in a career.

1993 The AVP held women's events at 16 of the men's tour stops. In a new four-team format, eight players exchanged partners weekly and played all season. Prize money was distributed at the end of the year, based on the number of wins. Holly McPeak won the tour championship with 11 victories and received $65,000 as first prize.

1993 On September 21, at the International Olympic Committee meeting in Monte Carlo, France, beach volleyball was granted medal status beginning in 1996 in Atlanta.

1994 Four more women's teams joined the AVP Tour to play at 14 men's events. The format no longer consisted of exchanging partners, and prize money was awarded after each tournament.

1994 At the Goodwill Games in Saint Petersburg, Russia, beach volleyball was an event for the first time. Karolyn Kirby and Liz Masakayan won the gold, and Barbra Fontana (Harris) and Lori Forsythe took the bronze. Kirby and Masakayan also won the FIVB World Series title.

1995 The AVP Women's Tour folded, and Holly McPeak and Nancy Reno transferred to the WPVA, where they won 8 of 14 events. McPeak set a single-season earnings record of $84,838. She won 8 of the 14 events, 7 with Nancy Reno and 7 with Lisa Arce.

1996 Gabrielle Reece was instrumental in the growing popularity of professional beach volleyball through her exposure in televised matches. In 1999, *Women's Sports and Fitness* magazine (no longer published) named

Gabby as one of only three athletes on its list of the "20 Most Influential Women in Sport."

1996 At the Olympics in Atlanta, beach volleyball became a medal sport for the first time, but the U.S. women did not take home a medal. Barbra Fontana Harris and Linda Hankey defeated Holly McPeak and Nancy Reno in the quarterfinals; they finished fourth after being defeated by the Australians.

1996 Holly McPeak was selected MVP of the WPVA tour for the second year in a row.

1997 In the final WPVA season, Holly McPeak and Lisa Arce won 7 of 12 events. They were defeated in the world championships by Brazilians Jackie Silva and Sanda Pires.

1997 Karolyn Kirby and Nancy Reno were the first team to win six Women's Pro Beach Volleyball Tour titles.

1997 Ericsson and Nike sponsored the Women's Beach Volleyball World Championships at the UCLA campus. Men and women received equal prize money of $600,000, and 120 countries broadcast the round-robin event. The United States teams placed first.

1998 For the first time, the FIVB World Tour awarded equal prize money of $170,000 to both men and women for each open event.

1998 From July 22 to August 2, the Goodwill Games were held at New York's Central Park. Holly McPeak and Lisa Arce were the only Americans to place, taking the bronze.

1999 The AVP again sanctioned women's events in conjunction with men's tournaments. At the season's end, Holly McPeak was crowned the first Queen of the Beach.

1999 Beach volleyball became an event at the Pan American Games for the first time in Canada, with no U.S. team garnering a medal.

2000 On January 12, Charlie Jackson helped establish Beach Volleyball of America (BVA), a tour created to guide and promote women's beach volleyball in the United States. In May, the first BVA event was held in Oceanside, California. Lisa Arce and Barbra Fontana split the $15,000 prize. Later that year, Fontana was named Queen of the Beach.

2000 The American women dominated the FIVB season as three teams finished in the top four and combined for 7 out of 13 events. Holly McPeak and Misty May finished second; Annett Buckner Davis and Jenny Johnson Jordan finished third; and Liz Masakayan and Elaine Youngs finished fourth.

2000 Annett Buckner Davis and partner Jenny Johnson Jordan were the U.S. team's top seed going into the Olympic Games in Sydney. Davis had quickly moved up the FIVB beach volleyball rankings, rising from No. 147 in '97, to No. 60 in '98, and to No. 3 in '99. Twenty-four teams of two women participated in the Sydney Olympics, but the U.S. team came up short of a medal once again.

2000 Holly McPeak became the richest woman in beach volleyball, passing Karolyn Kirby. McPeak topped the $700,000 mark in career earnings, with a total of 55 victories, 12 fewer than Kirby.

2001 On May 31, Management Plus acquired the AVP and united the world's best women and men professional beach volleyball players under one organization. The historic unification of women's and men's competition allowed the 2001 AVP Tour to maximize sponsor dollars.

2001 On June 17, fourth-seeded Barbra Fontana and Elaine Youngs won the gold medal in Cagliari, Italy, at the Women's FIVB Championships.

BOBSLED

Bobsled is one of the most exciting winter races. It is raced on a chute (track) made of ice. The chute's walls are typically one to two feet high, and the chute runs approximately 1,365 meters long with many sharp twists and turns. The pull of gravity powers the bobsled. Since the bobsled is gravity and human powered, racers in the early days of the sport would get in the sled and rock back and forth to get it moving. This was called bobbing, and thus the name bobsled evolved.

There are special heros in each sport, and bobsled is no different. In September 2001, Bonny Warner saw the images of the burning World Trade Center and Pentagon and had the same reactions as millions of other Americans. "I wanted to do something to help," she said. She has one advantage that most other Americans don't: she knows how to fly a jet. In addition to being a three-time Olympic athlete in luge, Warner is a pilot for United Airlines, which had two planes hijacked in the September attack.

Warner had taken a leave from flying in mid-August to train for the bobsled competition at the Salt Lake City Olympics in February 2002, but as she watched the September 11 tragedy unfold, she determined that it was time for her leave to end. She picked up the phone and volunteered to return to work whenever and wherever she was needed. Within a few days, she was flying again. The all-encompassing drive toward Olympic gold was pushed aside—at least temporarily.

—Karen Allen, September 2001, *USA Today*
—Bonny Warner, former champion luger, now a bobsleder and 2002
  Olympic commentator

1915 Bobsledding was a mixed sport that *required* women team members. A four-person bobsled team had to have at least one woman. In 1924 women began to be banned because the sport was thought to be too dangerous.

1932 The first bobsled run in America was built in Lake Placid, New York, for the Winter Olympics. Only men competed.

1940 Under the auspices of the Amateur Athletic Union, Katherine Dewey piloted a four-person team that won the U.S. four-man bobsled championship, becoming the first and only woman in the history of bobsledding or any other sport to win a national championship in open competition against men. Shortly thereafter, the AAU revised its policies—stating women could only compete against other women—because it would be "improper" for a woman to defeat a man.

1980s Julie Walzak would bobsled on the Mt. Hovenberg run in Lake Placid. She was one of the few women involved with the sport and was considered a pioneer.

1994 The first U.S. women's national team was formed with eight members. They competed in the first Women's National Push-Track Championship. Team members included Jill Bakken, Patty Driscoll, Nancy Lang, Laurie Millett, Liz Parr-Smestand, Alexandra Powell-Allred, Michelle Powe, and Sharon Slader. Powell-Allred won the gold, and Parr-Smestand took silver.

1994 The first-ever Women's Bobsled International Cup race held in the United States was in Park City, Utah.

1994 American women bobsledders participated in international competition for the first time, in Saint Moritz, Switzerland. The two American teams placed 8th and 10th.

1995 The first national bobsled championships for women were held in Lake Placid, New York. National champions from that competition were Michelle Powe (driver) and Sharon Denk-Slader (brake).

1997 The first time an American team won a silver medal in an international competition was at the FIBT Women's International Cup in Park City. Jill Bakken (driver) and Meg Henderson (brake) had cumulative times for the two races of 1:45.04.

1997 Elena Wise won the gold medal at the national championships.

1997 Top-ranked U.S. women's driver Jill Bakken became the first medalist in U.S. women's bobsled history—winning a gold and silver at the women's International World Cup race in Park City. At the international push competition in Gotha, Germany, she won the gold medal with Elena Primeroano. Bakken was the top-ranked driver from 1995 to '97.

1998 Jean Racine and Krista Ford, of the U.S. team, won two silver medals at the International Cup competition in Winterberg, Germany, in February. These were the first medals won by U.S. women on a foreign track.

1998 At the world push championships in Monaco, France, Jean Racine and Mary Henderson won the bronze.

1999 The International Olympic Committee announced on October 2 that women's bobsled would make its Olympic debut at the 2002 Games in Park City, Utah.

1999 In January, the teams of Jill Bakken–Meg Henderson and Jean Racine–Jen Davidson were the recipients of the United States Olympic Committee's first Team of the Month Award.

1999 Jean Racine finished the season ranked second in the international driver standings, the highest for a U.S. woman. She also was the first woman to earn a number one ranking in the U.S. driver standings. Racine placed first in three out of four World Cup races, taking second place in the fourth.

2000 Jean Racine and Jen Davidson won the gold medal at the World Cup in Igls, Austria, in February. As a team, they hold three track records in World Cup races. Bonny Warner placed sixth in World Cup rankings.

2001 Jen Davidson and Jean Racine won the silver medal at the World Championships.

2002 Bobsled debuted as a medal sport for the first time at the Winter Olympics in Park City, Utah.

2002 The U.S. team of Jill Bakken (driver) and Vonetta Flowers (pusher and brakeman) won the gold medal—beating heavy favorites. Flowers became the first African American ever to win a gold medal in the Winter Olympics. Bakken and Flowers were also the first Americans to medal in the sport in 46 years. Bakken has been on the U.S. team since its first camp in 1994. The other U.S. team of Jean Racine and Gea Johnson took fifth place.

BOWLING

W HAT IS considered the first published reference to bowling in the United States was in 1819 by author Washington Irving in his story "Rip van Winkle." The game was played throughout the world, but there was no uniformity to equipment or rules. In Europe, bowling was played with 9 pins, and in the United States, with 10. The game was popular in New York City and throughout the state, as well as in Chicago, Cincinnati, and other Midwest cities. The first effort to create a governing organization came in September 1895 in New York City, when the American Bowling Congress (ABC) was formed.

1901 At what was called the United States Championship, conducted along with the American Bowling Congress tournament in Chicago on January 8–11, women's events were held in Mussey's Alley. Elizabeth Jeschke emerged as the individual champion and received a silver cup valued at $100 for her five-game total of 701 points.

1903 One of the earliest leagues for women was organized in Chicago by Peter J. Howley. The league comprised six teams and was called the Daughters of Columbia. A league was also formed in New York City.

1907 Dennis J. Sweeny, who covered bowling for six Saint Louis newspapers, believed women had a place in bowling and organized a league. One of its better-known players was hometown bowler Birdie Kern (Humphrey), who won many tournaments and was given the title "National Champion."

1915 Sweeny and Ellen Kelly, also of Saint Louis, organized the Saint Louis Women's Bowling Association. It was the first organization of its type with a prize fund: $225. The all-men's National Bowling Association (a similar prize-fund club) had been established since 1875 in New York City.

1916 The Women's National Bowling Association (WNBA), the first bowling organization created for and run by women, was organized in Saint Louis after a tournament on November 27–28.

1923 Emma Jaeger, of Toledo, Ohio, won a record third consecutive WNBA championship.

1925 The WNBA changed its name to the Women's International Bowling Congress (WIBC). Jeannette Knepprath assumed the presidency of the organization, and remained president for 36 years. In 1971, the organization modified the title again, from "Woman's" to "Women's."

1927 In an exhibition that can be called an early "Battle of the Sexes," Floretta McCutcheon, legendary pioneer and champion, challenged world champion bowler Jimmy Smith to a three-game set at the Denver Bowling Company. A packed crowd watched McCutcheon beat Smith by a score of 704–697.

1929 The WIBC moved its tournament out of the Midwest for the first time, to Buffalo, New York.

1929 Rose Jacobs, of Schenectady, New York, was the first woman credited with bowling a perfect game of 300 points. In February of the next year, Jennie Hoverson (Kelleher) of Madison, Wisconsin, bowled another 300-point game, and she was matched only a few months later by Emma Fahning of Buffalo, New York.

1933 At age 54, Addie Ruschmeyer, of White Plains, New York, traveled to Frankfurt, Germany, for the International Championships. Ruschmeyer beat a bowler from Berlin to win the women's title and is credited with being the first international champion.

1934 Marie Clemensen of Chicago bowled 712 at the first WIBC 700 Tournament. This was the first 700 score in any women's bowling event and is a record that has stood for 42 years.

1936 The WIBC tournament moved west of Saint Louis for the first time—to Omaha, Nebraska—facilitating broader registration of participants from southwestern and western states.

1939 Floretta McCutcheon's average of 206 was the highest in the country.

1941 The WIBC events were held on the West Coast for the first time, as bowlers convened in Los Angeles. Trains for participants traveling to the tournament were organized in several cities. A record 452 participants attended.

1948 The first Woman Bowler of the Year Award was given by the National Bowling Writers Association, a men's group. Val Mikial, of Detroit, was the recipient.

1949 The first Bowling Properties Association of America (BPAA) tournament was held. Marion Ladewig won her first of five consecutive titles.

1951 The Federation Internationale de Quilleurs (FIQ), the international governing body for bowling, was founded. Its first world championship was held in 1954. The United States did not become a member of the federation until 1961.

1957 Automatic pin-setting equipment was used for the first time ever at a WIBC championship tournament in Dayton, Ohio.

1957 Marion Ladewig was the first woman named International Bowler of the Year.

1959 The Women's Pro Tour was established. Legendary bowler Marion Ladewig took top honors at the first event. Ladewig won the distinction of being named Bowler of the Year a record nine times: 1950–'55, '58, '59, and '63. During this run, she helped organize the Professional Women's Bowling Association (PWBA) and won its first event in 1960. Ladewig won the All Star Tournament 10 times: 1949–'54, '56, and '59, '63. A 1973 poll named her the greatest woman bowler of all time.

1960 WIBC membership grew to 1,543,362, reflecting the popularity of bowling among American women.

1961 In the first WIBC Queens tournament, held in Fort Wayne, Indiana, Janet Harmen placed first, and Eula Touchette took second out of 122 entries.

1963 The fifth Federation Internationale de Quilleurs World Championships were held in Mexico, and it was the first year in which a women's division was included. The WIBC sponsored an amateur team that won three of the four gold medals, two silvers, and a bronze.

1965 Emma Phaler retired as secretary of the WIBC after serving in the post for 38 years.

1966 The WIBC approved a resolution to establish a college division for the purpose of increasing interest in women's bowling at the intramural and intercollegiate levels and tournament competition.

1970 The last All Star Tournament was held. In 1971 the name was changed to the U.S. Open.

1971 Mildred Ignizco, of Rochester, New York, was the first person to win three Queens tournaments—1967, '70, and '71—and the first to win back-to-back. Dorothy Fothergill won back-to-back in '72 and '73, Donna Adamek in '79 and '80, and Japan's Katsuko Sugimoto in '81 and '82.

1971 At the first BPAA U.S. Open, Paula Sperber Carter won the title. Carter won again in 1975.

1975 Judy Soutar was the leading money winner and Bowler of the Year for the second consecutive year. She won the WIBC Queens tournament in 1974 and '75.

1976 Lucy Giovinco, of Hillsboro Community College (Tampa, Florida), was the first U.S. bowler to win the World Cup, which was held in Tehran, Iran.

1976 On June 2, Betty Morris became the only woman to bowl two perfect games in the same day, while also setting a six-game record of 1,546, in the BPAA U.S. Open. Morris won titles in four decades: the 1960s, '70s, '80s, and '90s. In 1974, she scored a first- or second-place finish in 11 of the 15 tournaments she entered.

1976 Patty Costello set a record by winning seven professional titles in a single season, three of which were back-to-back.

1979 Dorothy Fothergill defeated Donna Adamek at the first women's "Great and Greatest" tournament.

1979 Nikki Gianulias joined the professional tour and was the first member to roll four 800 series (an 800 series is a three-game session with 800 pins). She set a record in 1986 with an average of 213.89 pins.

1980 Donna Adamek became the first woman to win bowling's triple crown: the BPAA Open, WIBC Queens, and Sam's Town Invitational.

From 1978 to 1980, she essentially dominated women's bowling, winning several major tournaments and being selected Woman Bowler of the Year. In the 1981–'82 season, she rolled three perfect games. In 1988, she became the only woman to win the Australia Melbourne Cup.

1980 Patty Costello won her third BPAA U.S. Open—a record.

1980 The Women's Pro Tour was replaced by the Ladies Pro Bowlers Tour (LPBT).

1980 Lisa Wagner was named Rookie of the Year. In 1983, Wagner became the first woman bowler to earn more than $100,000 in a year, winning $105,000—nearly $25,000 more than the former record.

1980 The WIBC made the decision to link the Queens event to a commercial sponsor. Avon became the sponsor for five years. In 1984, Avon's final year of sponsorship, the Queens event offered $100,000 in prize money, $25,000 of which went to the winner.

1982 The first WIBC/ABC National Senior Championships were held in Baltimore; 43 women from 17 states qualified.

1982 Wendy Macpherson, 14, was the youngest woman ever to roll a perfect game. At age 18, she was named Rookie of the Year on the LPBT, and in 1987, she led the tour with a 211.11 average.

1983 The LPBT Player of the Year Award was established.

1983 Bowling was included in the Pan American Games for the first time as a demonstration sport. In 1991, it became eligible for medals, at the games in Havana, Cuba.

1983 Legislation was passed defining the WIBC as an amateur organization separate from the professional WIBC Championship tournament.

1984 The first Sam's Town Invitational tournament was held. Aleta Sill was the winner, and Cheryl Dains placed second. Sill won again in '86. Over the years, this tournament has become one of the major tour events.

1984 Aleta Sill was the leading money winner, with $81,452, and held the top average of $210.68, good enough for LPBT Bowler of the Year. She repeated as money winner in 1985 with $52,655 and was again selected Bowler of the Year. She won the WIBC Queens tournament in 1983 and '85; in 1994 and '98, she won the BPAA U.S. Open.

1984 The WIBC and the ABC opened a Hall of Fame and Museum in Saint Louis. Marion Ladewig was the first inductee.

1985 Team USA was created by the WIBC and ABC. Meeting with United States Olympic Committee (USOC) approval, the team selection started with eliminations at the local level, followed by state and then regional eliminations, culminating with a final national selection tournament.

1986 Bowling was accepted as an exhibition sport at the Olympics in Seoul, South Korea. A month earlier, the first Team USA national finals were held in Milwaukee.

1988 Bowling was included in the 1988 Olympics as a demonstration sport, and Debbie McMullen, of Denver, qualified to represent the United States. Bowling was later accepted as a medal sport by the USOC for participation in the U.S. Olympic Festival.

1988 The WIBC Championship tournament in Reno/Carson City, Nevada, was the first to encompass more than 75,000 competitors, as 77,735 bowlers took to the alleys.

1990 At age 22, Wendy Macpherson became the youngest player to have won all three triple-crown events in the course of her career: the 1986

U.S. Open, 1988 WIBC Queens, and 1990 Sam's Town Invitational. She began her charge with a record: winning the U.S. Open at age 18 (the youngest ever to win) and as an amateur.

1990 At the 30th annual Women's Intercollegiate Championships, Linda Woods won the title after being undefeated in match play—a first for a collegiate tournament.

1992 Leanne Barrette became the only player to win the PWBA High Average Award three consecutive years, 1990–'92. She also was the first player to win consecutive PWBA Player of the Year honors—which she did in 1990 and '91. At the close of the 2000 season, Barrette had 21 career titles.

1993 Lisa Wagner became the first woman in the sport to pass the $500,000 mark in career earnings.

1993 Patricia "Tish" Johnson set a record with seven perfect games in a season. In both 1990 and 1992, she was named LPBT Bowler of the Year and led the tour in earnings, with $94,420 in '90 and $96,872 in '92.

1995 Tish Johnson and Norm Duke faced off in a bowling "Battle of the Sexes" in Las Vegas. Both were ranked number one in the nation; Duke won.

1995 Linda Wallace was the first woman to compete in the ABC Masters tournament.

1995 Anne Marie Duggan bowled the highest PWBA eight-game block in history, averaging 262.12. She also holds the record for the most 800-series victories in a season, with three.

1996 Tish Johnson became the only woman to win a "Megabucks" tournament, raking in $100,000 in the Super Honkie Classic. At the end of the 2000 season, Johnson and Lisa Wagner were the only players to have won three consecutive PWBA titles; Johnson's collection includes 23 national titles.

1997 At the Southern Virginia Open, Michelle Feldman became the first woman to roll a perfect game in a televised final of the LPBT.

1997 Jackie Mitskavich set a new WIBC record with an 877 series.

1998 Lynda Norry became the first woman to earn a berth on Team USA seven times.

1998 On April 24, Kathy McNeil received the first WIBC/AMF Bev Ortner Award, presented to the WIBC member with the highest 800 series of the season. While eight months pregnant, McNeil bowled an 856 series, the eighth best three-game series (278, 299, 279) in WIBC history.

1999 Kelly Kwlick won the gold medal in the women's singles at the 14th FIQ World Championships, held in the United Arab Emirates. Her 1,405 six-game total was a women's record for the event and was the highest singles score bowled by any competitor in FIQ World Championship history.

1999 Aleta Sill became the first member in the history of the PWBA to achieve $1 million in career earnings, and Wendy Macpherson became the second. As of midyear 2001, Sill had won $1,580,872, Macpherson $1,310,985, and Tish Johnson $997,340. Sill also won the triple crown twice.

2000 Wendy Macpherson won the PWBA Player of the Year Award for the fourth time and was named Bowler of the Year by the BWAA for the fourth time. The Bowling Writers Association of America also named her Best Woman Bowler in the World in the same four years—

1996, '97, '99, and 2000. In 2000, she appeared in televised finals a record 15 times. Macpherson also was the first woman bowler to be nominated for the ESPN ESPY Awards.

2000 Robin (Romeo) Mossontte set the PWBA record for the most consecutive player appearances, with 77, and most consecutive cashes, 80.

2000 Kendra Gaines rolled games of 280, 265, and 267, for an 812 set, her first 800 and the first ever in a WIBC tournament.

2001 With a membership of more than 1.4 million, the WIBC ranked as the largest single-sport membership organization for women in the world.

2001 Carolyn Dorin Ballard won six tournaments in a row—her first, the Three Rivers Open in October 2000, and her sixth in July at the Southern Virginia Open. She led all PWBA players in victories, earnings, ranking points, and average. She also made a record 17 television final appearances, was unanimously named the PWBA Player of the Year, and was the Bowlers Journal International Magazine's Person of the Year.

BOXING

ONE OF the few sports expected to remain a male domain is rapidly drawing women to its ranks. With their fierce jabs and hooks, women are throwing punches before sell-out crowds. Sweden is considered the pioneering country in women's boxing, with the United States and Canada close behind in expanding women's programs. Sweden sanctioned women's boxing events as early as 1988, and today 34 countries recognize women in the ring.

1876 The first women's boxing "match" in the United States was held at Hills Theater. Nell Saunders defeated Rose Harland to win a silver butter dish.

1940 On May 2, Belle Martell, of Van Nuys, California, officiated eight matches in San Bernardino, California, becoming the first female prizefight referee.

1977 On September 29, Eva Shain became the first woman to officiate a heavyweight championship fight, a match between Muhammad Ali and Ernie Shavers.

1993 USA Boxing officially lifted its ban on women boxers in October after 16-year-old Dallas Malloy, of Bellingham, Washington, filed a lawsuit. The first women's bout took place later that month, with Malloy outscoring Heather Poyner in Lynnwood, Washington. As a result of the litigation, women were permitted to register with USA Boxing and compete in sanctioned amateur competitions. In 1994, 54 women registered.

1993 Frankie Globoshutz and Barbara Buttrick, a former boxer from England, who fought internationally from 1948 to 1960, founded the Women's International Boxing Federation. Rules established regarding women were similar to those for men, with principal differences being the length of the rounds, required use of breast protectors, and a required waiver attesting that the boxer is not pregnant.

1995 Women participated in the New York Daily News Golden Gloves amateur boxing tournament for the first time in its 69-year history thanks to an application by Dee Hamaguchi, who signed up as simply D. Hamaguchi. The event finals, held in Madison Square Garden, drew worldwide attention. Jill Matthews took the flyweight championship over Hamaguchi, and in the 165-pound division, Tanya Dean won the final over Sekka Scher.

1996 The first female professional fighter to appear in a bout on primetime TV was Christy Martin, who fought Deirdre Gogarty in a Pay-Per-View special that shared the bill with Mike Tyson in October. Martin was also the first woman boxer to be featured on the cover of *Sports Illustrated* (immediately following the match). The story about her in *SI* and newspapers helped draw attention to women's boxing. Martin's skill and record have established her as a renowned champion and women's boxing pioneer.

1997 USA Boxing held the first women's national championship in Augusta, Georgia. Sixty-seven women competed for twelve titles. In the 106-pound division, Patricia Martinez from Miami, Florida, won; in the 112-pound division, Elizabeth McGongial from Erie, Pennsylvania, took honors; in the 119-pound division the winner was Patricia Alcivar from Queens, New York; in the 121-pound division, Alicia Ashley from Westbury, New York, won; in the 132-pound division, Mellisa Salamone from

Miami, Florida, took honors; the 139-pound division winner was Denise Lutrick from Mt. Vernon, New York; in the 147-pound division, Sky Hosoya from New York, New York, won.

1997 The International Female Boxing Association was formed. Jackie Kallon, who had already worked in boxing for 19 years, was chosen as commissioner. Based in Los Angeles, the organization is vying for control of the sport over USA Boxing.

1997 The only all-women's boxing gym in the United States (to date) is the Academy of Boxing for Women, run by Frankie Globoshutz in Huntington, New York.

1998 The national championships were held in Anaheim, California, with a field of more than 100 boxers. A junior division was added for 15- and 16-year-olds, and two weight classes were added—95 and 100 pounds.

1998 The first international match was held in Scranton, Pennsylvania. The United States defeated Canada, 6–1.

1999 The Feenix Boxing Cup, the first international boxing tournament for women, was held in Finland, with American Jamie McGrath winning the gold medal.

1999 The first National Golden Gloves competition for women was held in Augusta, Georgia.

2000 Hiawatha G. Knight, a former Michigan boxing commissioner, became the first woman to head the International Boxing Federation, the sport's major sanctioning organization.

2000 Kathy Collins won the International Boxing Association Junior Welterweight Championship, making her the first fighter to win the

International Women's Boxing Federation (IWBF), International Female Boxing Association, and World Welterweight titles.

2001 The first women's world championship was held in Scranton, Pennsylvania. Over 140 women from more than 25 countries competed in 12 divisions for titles. Devonne Canady, age 30, was the only U.S. boxer to win a gold medal, taking the 198-pound title.

2001 In March in a highly media-hyped match that drew attention to women's boxing like never before, the daughters of famous champion boxers Muhammad Ali and Joe Frazier fought each other near Syracuse, New York. In a hard-fought, fast-paced bout, Laila Ali, 23, defeated Jacqui Frazier Lyde, 38, in a majority decision (one judge scored the match a draw). Prior critics later agreed that women's boxing had made a breakthrough.

2002 More than 70 women submitted entries for the New York Daily News Golden Gloves tournament.

CANOEING/KAYAKING

CANOEING AND kayaking for recreation as well as transportation can be traced back hundreds of years. A kayak is a type of canoe in which paddlers sit with their legs stretched out in front of them. Canoeists generally paddle from a sitting or kneeling position. All kayaks are canoes, but not all canoes are kayaks; while most canoes have covered hulls, kayaks also have covered decks. Four types of canoe competitions exist for women: 500-meter flat-water singles, pairs, and fours, in which canoes race in lanes; white-water; slalom, which is raced through a gated course; and 1,000 meters (only in National and World Cup competitions), which consists of a series of 25 gates that paddlers must negotiate downstream without touching the pole or missing a gate.

1880 The American Canoe Association was established. It set all rules and regulations for the sport.

1924 In Paris, canoe/kayak made its first Olympic appearance as a demonstration sport; only six nations participated.

1924 Delegates from all national associations met in Denmark to establish the International Represent antskapet for Kanotidrott (IRK) as the international governing body.

1946 The IRK became the Fédération Internationale de Canoe (FIC), which became the official name of the international governing body for canoe sports.

AUGUST
FIFTEEN C

1948 Kayak 500-meter singles became an Olympic event for the first time on the River Thames in London. It was not until 1964 in Tokyo that a U.S. woman medaled, when Marcia Jones won the bronze. The 500 meters is a sprint race that requires tremendous upper-body strength and precision paddling.

1948 The International Canoe Federation was established.

1949 The first world championship in canoe racing was held.

1959 National championships for women were established. Mary Ann Duchai became the first national women's champion in the kayak singles. She also teamed with Diane Jerome to win the doubles title.

1960 Kayak pairs became an Olympic event when the women's 500-meter race was added at the Rome games.

1962 A women's national championship was established in the four-woman kayak.

1964 Marcia Jones, Francine Fox, and Gloriane Perrier became the first American women to medal in Olympic canoe/kayak. At the Tokyo games, Jones won a bronze in the kayak 500-meter singles, and Fox and Perrier won a silver in the doubles with a time of 1:59.16. Fox became the youngest female Olympic medallist in canoe/kayak, at 15 years and 220 days. Jones later competed in the 1968 and '72 Olympics.

1972 Kayak slalom singles were added at the Olympics in Munich, Germany. Based on white-water canoeing, the paddles must contend with fast water, rapids, and falls while navigating specific gates.

1979 Cathy Hearn became the first American woman to win an individual world championship. One of the world's top-ranked female kayakers, she has won 11 world championship medals in white-water events.

1984 The 500-meter fours was added to women's kayak at the Olympics in Los Angeles. The U.S. team of Sheila Conover, Shirley Dery, Leslie Klein, and Ann Turner finished fourth.

1988 After several years of negotiations and several organizations' attempts to govern the sport in the United States, the American Canoe Association was chosen as the national governing body. It was further recognized by the IOC.

1988 The first canoe marathon world championships were held in Nottingham, England. No American has medaled to date.

1989 The USA Canoe/Kayak Team was formed, which is now called simply USA Canoe/Kayak.

1992 At the Barcelona Olympics, Dana Chladek won the bronze medal in the inaugural kayak slalom race. In 1994 she was ranked ninth in the world cup standings.

1996 Dana Chladek topped her bronze with a silver at the Atlanta games. Rebecca Giddens also made a good showing, making it to the finals of the women's slalom and placing sixth overall.

1997 The women's 1,000-meter event was added; previously, women raced only at the 500-meter distance.

1997 Dru Van Hengel, of Santa Barbara, California, was the first woman to win three national titles in one year. After acing the 1,000-meter singles, Van Hengel teamed with Lia Rousset, of Newport Beach, California, to win the 1,000-meter doubles and 500-meter doubles.

1997 At the world championships in Tres Coroas, Brazil, Cathy Hearn won the bronze medal.

1998 Cathy Hearn won her third consecutive slalom national singles championship in South Bend, Indiana, sweeping 1996–'98. In '97, she had finished ninth in the final World Cup point standings.

2000 In Bakersfield, California, Rebecca Bennet Giddens won her second consecutive slalom national singles championship. Every year since 1996, she placed in the top three at the national level. Giddens also finished the 2000 season at fourth on the World Cup points standings—the highest ever for an American. She later took sixth place in the Sydney Olympic Games.

2001 At the first wild-water national championships, at Pigeon River in Tennessee, Shannon Reeves took the gold, Jennie Goldberg the silver, and Trisha Chambers the bronze.

2001 At the national sprint championships, Kathy Colin and Ruth Nortje teamed to win the gold in the kayak 1,000-meter doubles. Nortje also earned the gold in the 1,000-meter singles, while Colin took the silver. Nortje and Colin took the gold in the 200, 500, and 1,000 meters. Ruth won gold in all K-1 races, while Colin won silver. The two also competed at the 2001 World Championships in Pozan, Poland, finishing fourth in the 1,000 meters and eighth in the 500 meters. The fourth-place finish was the highest K-2 finish (male or female) for the United States at the World Championships in the last 10 years.

CYCLING

T HE BICYCLE was invented in 1888 and soon became a popular mode of transportation. Female cyclists, in conformity with the social mores of the day, wore long skirts and petticoats, but the fabric kept getting caught in the spokes, impeding travel. To ride with freedom, women started to wear split skirts or knickers, which were considered unfeminine. As time passed, this new attire received less ridicule, and the bicycle is credited with bringing much-needed reform to women's status and broadening attitudes toward acceptable public dress.

1895 Frances Willard, who taught herself to ride in her early 50s, wrote *A Wheel Within a Wheel*, a book on the liberating effects of cycling.

1896 The first women's cycling marathon took place January 6–11, at Madison Square Garden in New York. Thirteen women competed, drawing 300 spectators on the first day; by the sixth day, more than 4,000 spectators had packed the stands. The cyclists rode in nine-hour shifts, taking six-hour breaks in between. Frankie Nelson won, traveling 418 miles.

1937 On September 4, the first sanctioned "girl's division" bicycle championship in the United States was held in Buffalo, New York, under the aegis of the United States National Amateur Bicycle Association. Doris Kopsky, of Belleville, New Jersey, won the one-mile race in 4 minutes and 22.4 seconds.

1942 The ABL suspended the nationals due to the lack of funding.

1945 The ABL national championships were revived by the Schwinn Bicycle Company, who sponsored the event. Mildred Dietz, of Saint Louis, won the women's titles.

1954 The ABL held the national championships in Minneapolis. After winning the title for the second year in a row, 21-year-old Nancy Neiman Baranet told ABL officials to change the designation *girls'* championship to *women's*, and they did. She won the race again in 1956 and '57.

1955 On the Paddington track in Leicester, England, Nancy Neiman Baranet tied the world record for the 200 meter, with a time of 14.4 seconds. Baranet was the first American to appear in a European stage race: in France, she competed in an eight-day stage, placing 14th out of 40 finishers; 87 riders started the race. Baranet, a pioneer in women's cycling, was the only woman officer of the ABL from 1956 to 1983.

1969 Audrey Phleger McElmury Levonas, of La Jolla, California, became the first American, male or female, to win a world road racing title, at the women's world road racing championship in Bruno, Czechoslovakia. Levonas won in spite of a mid-race crash in the rain. In 1966 and '70, she won the U.S. road racing and pursuit championships.

1970s The decade marked the expansion of interest in bicycling and growing demand for racing-style models. Average consumers were purchasing lighter, streamlined bikes, which facilitated speed and endurance.

1971 Sheila Young-Ochowicz, from a Detroit cycling family, won the national match sprints championships. She won again in 1973 and '76.

1972 Sheila Young-Ochowicz finished third in the women's match sprints at the world championships in Marseille, France.

1973 Sheila Young-Ochowicz won the women's world match sprint championships in San Sebastion, Spain. This was the first world track championship for a U.S. cyclist in 61 years.

1973 Sheila Young-Ochowicz became the first athlete in history to hold world championships in two sports at the same time. She held the world sprint titles in cycling and speed skating, a feat she repeated in 1976. Overall, she won five world cycling medals, including three championships, but the Olympics eluded her, since cycling was not an Olympic sport at the time.

1974 At the Montreal world championships, Sue Novara, of Flint, Michigan, placed second in a photo finish in the match sprints. Novara won three national match sprint titles—in 1972, '74, and '75—and placed second in '71, '73, and '76 in addition to 1974. Then she won the national championship four years in a row, 1977–'80.

1975 Sue Novara captured the gold medal in the match sprints at the world championships in Liege, Belgium. At 19, she became the youngest person to win the women's world sprint championship. Novara won again in 1980. In her career, she won seven consecutive world medals, including the gold in 1975 and 1980. She later became a road racer and coach for the U.S. women's team.

1976 In order to be uniform in name with other national sports organizations, the Amateur Bicycle Federation became the United States Cycling Federation.

1976 At the world match sprints championships in Medrisca, Italy, Sheila Young-Ochowicz won the gold, and Sue Novara won the silver.

1979 Beth Heiden, speed skater turned cyclist, became the first woman to finish a 25-mile time trial in less than an hour. In 1980, she won the world road race championships in Sallanches, France.

1982 In Leicester, England, Connie Paraskevin-Young won the world match sprints, beating her sister-in-law, Sheila Young-Ochowicz. Rebecca Twigg won the individual pursuit over Connie Carpenter (Phinney).

1983 At the worlds in Zurich, Connie Paraskevin-Young won the match sprints, and Rebecca Twigg finished second in the road race.

1983 The six-day International Women's Challenge was created. The rider with the lowest accumulated time over six days is the champion and earns $10,000 of the $100,000 purse.

1983 Connie Carpenter (Phinney) set a world record of 3:49.53 in winning the world individual pursuit championship in Zurich. In 1981 and '82, she was national points champion.

1984 With an enormous burst of speed at the end, Connie Carpenter (Phinney) won the first women's Olympic road race, in Los Angeles, taking the 79.2-kilometer race and the gold medal by half a wheel length over teammate Rebecca Twigg.

1984 The first Tour de France Femine was held. American cyclist Marianne Martin completed the 616-mile course with a winning time of 29 hours, 39 minutes, and 2 seconds.

1984 In Barcelona, Spain, Connie Paraskevin-Young won the match sprints, becoming the first woman to win three consecutive world championships. In addition to her 1982–'84 sweep, she won in 1990 and '91.

1984 At the world championships, Rebecca Twigg won the individual pursuit.

1985 At the world championships in Bassano del Grappa, Italy, Twigg won the track pursuit, and Peggy Maas placed third.

1986 The world championships were held in Colorado Springs—the first return to the United States since 1912. Rebecca Twigg won silver in the individual track pursuit, Janalle Parks won silver in the road race, and Connie Paraskevin-Young won bronze in match sprints.

1988 The first Olympic individual match sprint 1,000 meters was held, in Seoul, South Korea. Connie Paraskevin-Young won the bronze medal.

1989 Janie Eickoff, of Los Angeles, won the bronze medal at the women's track points race in Lyons, France.

1990 At the world championships in Maebashi, Japan, Ruthie Mathes took second in the individual, and the women's time-trial team took second overall.

1991 At the world championships in Stuttgart, Germany, Connie Paraskevin-Young took third place in match sprints, Inga Thompson took second in the road race, and Janie Eickoff took second in individual pursuit and third in the points race.

1992 The first Olympic 3,000-meter individual pursuit was held at the Barcelona games. Rebecca Twigg won the bronze medal.

1992 At the world championships in Valencia, Spain, Janie Eickoff took third in the women's point race, and Twigg took third in the individual pursuit. The road time-trial team of Jan Bolland, Bunki Bankaitis-Davis, Jeanne Golay, and Eve Stephenson won the gold.

1993 At the world championships in Hamar, Norway, the time-trial team of Jan Bolland, Dede Demet, Jeanne Golay, and Eve Stephenson won the road race. Jessica Greico took third in the women's point race, and Rebecca Twigg won her fourth individual pursuit championship.

1993 Inga Thompson became the first woman to be issued a professional bicycle-racing license.

1993 Janie Eickoff won the bronze in the individual pursuit at the world track and field championships in Norway. In 1994, she was third in the individual pursuit.

1995 Rebecca Twigg won her sixth world individual pursuit championship at the worlds in Bogotá, Colombia.

1995 On July 1, USA Cycling Inc. became the umbrella organization for the sport.

1996 The Olympics in Atlanta marked several milestones for the sport: professionals were permitted to compete in open road and track races for the first time, and the individual cross-country 32-kilometer race was introduced—Susan De Mattei won the bronze.

1996 Janie Eickoff was selected U.S. Cycling Federation Female Athlete of the Year for the third time. In her career, she was national champion 17 times, a 7-time medalist in the world championships, and a 9-time medalist in World Cup competition. Eickoff holds the Pan American Games record in the 3,000-meter pursuit and was a Pan American Games pursuit and point race champion.

2000 In the Sydney Olympics, Mari Holden was the only American woman to medal, winning the silver in the individual time trial with a 42:36 finish. Holden is a five-time national champion in the time trial.

2001 Kimberly Bruckner was the winner of the National Road Race and Time Trial as well as the Tour de Snowy in Australia and the Tour de Suisse Feminin in Switzerland.

2002 The U.S. road racing team was ranked number one in the world.

DIVING

IVING IS scored based on a particular dive's degree of difficulty (DOD). In the Olympics, each dive is first judged by a panel of seven judges, who award scores ranging from 0 to 10. The lowest and highest scores among all judges are eliminated, and the remaining five are then multiplied by the DOD, which ranges from 1.1 to 3.5.

There are many types of dives and dive variations. A reverse dive starts with the diver facing the front of the board and rotating toward the board. An inward dive begins with the diver standing with his or her back to the water and rotating toward the board. Saying that a diver "ripped it" means the dive was performed well, with the body so straight as it entered the water that there was hardly a ripple.

1912 Plain high diving was introduced in the Olympics in Stockholm, Sweden. The 3-meter springboard was added in 1920. U.S. women did not compete in any event until 1920.

1916 U.S. nationals in the indoor 3 meters and outdoor platform were held for the first time. Aileen Riggin and Evelyn Burrett were the winners.

1920 Aileen M. Riggin (Soule) was the first person ever to win Olympic medals in both swimming and diving. The 4-foot-8-inch, 70-pound athlete was nicknamed "Tiny." At age 14, she won the gold medal in the first women's Olympic springboard event; Riggin, Helen Wainwright, and

Thelma Payne placed first, second, and third in a U.S. sweep. In 1924, at the Olympics in Paris, Riggin won a silver in the springboard and a bronze in the backstroke. She also won four national springboard championships.

1921 The outdoor 3 meters was held at the U.S. nationals for the first time.

1924 In another U.S. sweep in springboard, Elizabeth Becker Pinkston, Aileen Riggin Soule, and Caroline Fletcher won the gold, silver, and bronze, respectively, at the Olympics in Paris.

1924 Platform diving was an Olympic medal event for the first time. Caroline Fletcher Smith, of Cairo, Illinois, became the first U.S. woman to win the gold medal. The United States won the gold and silver in the platform at the next seven Olympics.

1924 Elizabeth Becker Pinkston became the first woman Olympian to win medals in both springboard and platform diving. She took the gold in the springboard and the silver in the platform. In 1928, she won a second gold, this time in platform. Elizabeth Becker Pinkston and Clarence Pinkston were the first husband and wife to be inducted into the International Swimming Hall of Fame, in Fort Lauderdale, Florida; they were both honored in 1967.

1928 Helen Meany was the first American woman to compete in three consecutive Olympic games—1920, '24, and '28. In a U.S. sweep in Amsterdam, she won the gold in springboard, Dorothy Poynton (Hill) won the silver, and Georgia Coleman won the bronze.

1928 Dorothy Poynton (Hill) was 13 when she won the silver in the springboard at the Amsterdam games, making her the youngest American, to date, to win an Olympic medal. She won the gold in platform in

1932 in Los Angeles and repeated in 1936 (and also took the bronze in springboard) in Berlin, becoming the first American to win the event in consecutive Olympics. She also won seven national titles during her career.

1928 Georgia Coleman won two medals at the Olympics in Amsterdam—a bronze in the springboard and a silver in platform. Coleman, an unusually athletic diver for her time, was the first woman to perform a two-and-a-half forward somersault, which she did at the Los Angeles games in 1932.

1932 At the Los Angeles Olympics, the United States swept the medals in both platform, with Dorothy Poynton (Hill), Georgia Coleman, and Marion Roper, and springboard, with Coleman, Katherine Rawls, and Jane Fauntz.

1936 At the Olympic Games in Berlin, Marjorie Gestring, at age 13, won the gold medal in springboard. As of 2002, Gestring, an eight-time U.S. champion, remained the youngest Olympic gold medalist on record.

1938 Katherine Rawls won 28 national championships in springboard diving, as well as three swimming events, between 1932 and 1939. She also won the national outdoor championships at seven consecutive meets between 1931 and 1938. In 1937, Rawls became the first woman to win four national championships at one meet, a feat she repeated in '38.

1944 Ann Ross won seven national titles between 1941 and 1944. Ross garnered less fame than she deserves, since her career coincided with World War II, when many events were canceled.

1945 Helen Crienkovich Moyon won seven 3-meter springboard championships between 1939 and 1945. She also won two national platform championships, in 1941 and '45.

1948 The women's indoor 1 meter was held at the nationals for the first time. Zoe Ann Olsen (Jensen) won the event and repeated in 1949.

1948 At the Olympics in London, Vicki Draves was the first woman to win gold medals in both the 10-meter platform and 3-meter springboard events.

1951 Pat McCormick became the first woman to sweep all three Amateur Athletic Union (AAU) outdoor diving championships. That same year, McCormick became the first diver ever to win all five national championships.

1952 Zoe Ann Olsen (Jensen) medaled for the second time in her career in the Olympics in Helsinki, Finland, taking the bronze in springboard. In 1948, she won the silver in the event and was the only U.S. woman diver to medal at the London Olympics. Jensen also won 14 national titles in springboard between 1945 and 1949.

1956 Pat McCormick became the only person in Olympic history to score back-to-back golds in both platform and springboard diving, first in 1952 in Helsinki and then in Melbourne, Australia. McCormick also became the first diver to win four gold medals in successive Olympics. In her career, she won 26 national championships as well, including a record six outdoor 3 meters.

1956 The U.S. women made their second sweep in platform diving at the Olympics in Melbourne, with Pat McCormick winning the event, followed by Juno Stover Irwin and Paula Jean Meyers. In 1952, the order was Pat McCormick, Juno Stover Irwin, and Paula Jean Meyers.

1960 Paula Jean Meyers (Pope) won three medals in three Olympics: the silver in platform in 1952, the bronze in 1956, and the silver in 1960 at the Rome games. Meyers also won 11 AAU national championships and took gold medals in the 1959 Pan American Games in springboard and platform.

1960 Juno Stover Irwin, a 28-year-old mother of three, appeared in her fourth Olympics, winning the silver in platform. In 1952, she won the bronze while she was three-and-a-half months pregnant.

1964 The women's indoor platform was held at the nationals for the first time. Barbara Talmaze was the winner.

1964 At the Olympics in Tokyo, Japan, Lesley Bush won the gold medal in platform. Joanne Collier took silver and Mary Willard took the bronze.

1965 The International Swimming Hall of Fame was founded in Fort Lauderdale, Florida. Pat McCormick and Katherine Rawls were the first two women inducted.

1968 At the Olympics in Mexico City, Sue Gossick won the gold in springboard and Keala O'Sullivan took the bronze. Anne Peterson also took bronze in the platform.

1970 Micki King notched her fourth national outdoor 3-meter championship, having won previously in 1965, '67, and '69. She also won the 1-meter championships in 1967 and the platform championships in 1969.

1972 At age 28, Micki King, a captain and budget officer in the U.S. Air Force, won a gold medal in springboard diving at the Olympics in Munich, Germany. Four years earlier in Mexico City, she was in first place when she struck the board and broke her arm. In spite of the accident, she performed her next dive and finished in fourth place. King was the first military woman to medal in an Olympic event. Later, at the Air Force Academy, she became the first woman to coach an all-male team. King won 10 indoor and outdoor national titles between 1965 and 1971.

1973 The world diving championships were held for the first time. In 1975, Janet Ely won the world title in platform. In 1982, Megan Neyer won the title in the 3-meter springboard, and Wendy Wyland won the platform crown.

1976 Jennifer Chandler, a 17-year-old high school junior from Langdale, Alabama, won the gold medal in the 3-meter springboard at the Olympics in Montreal. Cynthia Potter won the bronze while Deborah Wilson took the bronze in platform. Potter holds the record for the most national diving championships, with 28, including a record 9 championships in the outdoor 1 meter between 1968 and 1976. She was selected for the Olympic team in 1972, '76, and '80.

1979 The diving World Cup began and is held every two years, bringing together the top competitors from all nations.

1981 U.S. Diving was formed, replacing the AAU as the governing body.

1982 The National Collegiate Athletic Association (NCAA) held its first diving championships in the 1-meter and 3-meter springboard. In Division I, Megan Meyer, of the University of Florida, won the first three championships, 1982–'84, in both events, and won the 3 meters again in 1986.

1982 The first Division II diving champions both hailed from California State University at Northridge: Dana Mar Burgess won the title in the 1-meter, and Karla Helder won in the 3-meter springboard. Doria Mamelo, of Clarion State College (Pennsylvania), won the 1 meter in 1986 and '87 and won the 3 meters in 1985 and '86. Mary Ahlin, of Saint Cloud State University (Minnesota), won both the 1 meter and 3 meters in 1998 and '99.

1982 The first Division III championships in the 1-meter and 3-meter springboard were won by Lynn Adams, of Lake Forest College (Illinois). Elizabeth Olson, of Colorado College, won both events in 1986 and '87.

1984 Kelly McCormick, Pat McCormick's daughter, won the silver medal in the springboard at the Olympics in Los Angeles. In the 1988 games in Seoul, South Korea, she won the bronze.

1988 Wendy Williams won bronze medals in platform and springboard at the Seoul games. Michelle Mitchell won her second consecutive silver in the springboard.

1989 Between 1981 and 1989, Wendy Wyland won seven national championships in platform, the most in U.S. diving history. She also won two world championships in 1982 and '86.

1990 NCAA Division I championships were held in platform for the first time. Courtney Nelson, of Brigham Young University (Provo, Utah), won the first two titles. Eileen Richetelli, of Stanford (California), won three titles between 1992 and 1995.

1991 Wendy Lucero won the silver medal at the world championships in Perth, Australia.

1992 When Mary Ellen Clark, at age 29, won the bronze medal in platform in Barcelona, she became the oldest U.S. woman to win an Olympic diving medal. In the Atlanta games in 1996, she won the bronze again, at 33 years, breaking her own age record.

1995 The women's outdoor synchronized 3 meters was held at the national championships for the first time. Jenny Klien and Reyna Boriy won the inaugural event. The indoor winners were Janae Lauter Schleger and Amy Sylvan.

1995 The first women's outdoor synchronized platform was held. Patty Armstrong and Laura Wilkinson won the event and repeated in 1996. The indoor winners were Kristin Link and Panji Weiskittel.

1996 The cliff diving championships were opened to women for the first time. Lucy Streeter, who owned the U.S. record for the longest dive by a woman, took third place at the contest, in Acapulco.

1997 Meghan Heaney-Grier, 19, broke her own American free-dive record, descending to 165 feet—eclipsing her previous record by 10 feet.

2000 On September 25 at the Sydney Olympics, Laura Wilkinson won the first women's gold medal on the high platform for the United States since 1964.

2000 In August, Lauryn McCalley, 19, of Moultrie, Georgia, won the 3-meter springboard title and repeated it in 2001. McCalley also teamed with Lane Bassham to win the 3-meter synchronized springboard; they too repeated in 2001.

2001 At age 18, Trisha Tumlinson won her first national title in platform, with a score of 484.77. Olympic gold medalist Laura Wilkinson took fifth place in her first competition since undergoing surgery for a broken foot.

2001 At the Goodwill Games in Brisbane, Australia, Kimiko Hirai Soldati won the bronze medal for the 3-meter springboard.

DOGSLED RACING

THE IDITAROD is the most famous event in dogsledding. It follows the Iditarod Trail—a grueling 1,158 miles (1,872 kilometers)—starting in Anchorage, Alaska, and finishing in Nome. It typically takes 9 to 11 days to complete. The weather conditions are usually grueling, ranging from below freezing to full-out blizzards with temperatures of minus 50 degrees. Men and women compete as equals.

In 1985, Libby Riddles, racing for the third time, became the first woman to win the race. The second was Susan Butcher, whose extraordinary career was instrumental in bringing attention to the sport. Of the 17 Iditarods in which she competed, she was a top 10 finisher 15 times and the winner 4 times in 1986, '87, '88, and '90.

1946 The Alaskan Sled Dog and Racing Association was established, and the first World Cup was held. In 1947, Leslie Storey was the first woman to place in the top three, finishing second behind Earl Norris.

1953 The first women's world championship was won by Joyce Wells.

1955 Kit MacInnes won her first of five world championships, repeating in 1956 and winning again in 1959–'61, when she also became the first woman to win three consecutive world titles. Barbara Parker then matched that streak, winning the world championship in 1962–'64.

1970 The first two-day world championship for men and women was held in Anchorage, Alaska, with winner Shirley Gavin registering 37.40

minutes the first day and 37.53 minutes the second day. The following year, Gavin finished second at the Eagle River Open.

1973 The first Iditarod was run and took 20 days to complete.

1977 Roxy Brooks won her fifth consecutive world championship, reigning from 1973 to '77.

1978 Susan Butcher, of Cambridge, Massachusetts, participated in her first Iditarod race. She finished 19th, making her the first woman to win prize money—$600.

1979 Butcher finished ninth in the Iditarod, making her the first woman to finish in the top 10.

1979 Butcher and Joe Redington, with a team of sled dogs, spent 44 days climbing to the top of Mount McKinley, becoming the first dogsled team to reach the summit.

1982 Butcher took second place in the Iditarod—the first woman to do so—and then repeated the feat in 1984.

1985 Libby Riddles, originally from Minnesota, then from Alaska, was the first woman to win the Iditarod Trail Sled Dog Race.

1986 Ann Bancroft became the first woman to reach the top of the world by dogsled, when she traveled overland to the North Pole.

1988 Susan Butcher won her third consecutive Iditarod, becoming the first person to do so. In 1990 she won her fourth.

1993 Linda Leonard won her fourth world championship. Her first three were consecutive, 1988–'90.

1999 Kathy Frost won her fifth consecutive world championship and her eighth overall, more than any other musher, taking the title in 1985, '87, '92, and '95–'99. Before Frost, the last woman to win five straight was Roxy Brooks, 1973–'77.

2002 In January at the Copperbasin 300 Alyeska Pipeline race in Glennallen, Alaska, Jessica Hendricks placed sixth overall and was the highest woman finisher. She also won the Copper Valley Electric Rookie Award.

EQUESTRIAN

THE EQUESTRIAN sports that we know today developed during the latter half of the 19th century. The traditional disciplines are dressage, jumping, and eventing. Dressage derives from the French word *dresser*, meaning "to train," and dates back to the Renaissance. It has come to denote both a training method and a competitive sport. As a training method, it prepares the horse for specific disciplines, such as show jumping. As a sport, competitive dressage challenges the horse and rider to perform a series of required movements at specific locations within a 20-by-60-meter arena.

Show jumping dates back to the early 1800s. Riders and horses jump 15 to 20 obstacles throughout a specially designed course. Penalty points ("faults") are assessed if the horse refuses or brings down the highest element of an obstacle—such as the rung of a fence—or if the jump exceeds the time allowed. The ultimate goal is a clean round in which no faults are assessed.

Cross-country is a long-distance obstacle run comprising four parts: two road and tracks, one steeplechase, and one cross-country. Penalty points are assessed for falls and failure to complete the run in the allowed time, with bonus points given if the run is completed within the time limit.

The three-day event is the triathlon of equestrian, combining dressage, cross-country, and show jumping. It remains the ultimate test of teamwork between the rider and horse.

Initially, women riders used a sidesaddle. As women progressed in the sport, they began to ride astride. Today, equestrian sport provides one of the few opportunities for men and women to compete on equal terms.

1866 Grand prix show jumping debuted in Paris.

1912 Individual equestrian sports were introduced at the Olympic Games in Stockholm, Sweden. The eventing competition was limited to military officers, but jumping and dressage were open to civilians. It wasn't until 40 years later that a woman equestrian competed in the Olympics.

1912 Eleanora Sears won a quarter horse race in San Diego, California. Known as one of the country's greatest women athletes at the turn of the century, Sears won national championships in squash and tennis, engaged in the less conventional pursuits of football and boxing, and was a yachtswoman and an aviator. She gained notoriety for riding astride and in trousers. She played polo, drove a four-in-hand, and maintained a Thoroughbred racing stable until her death in 1968. As an owner and rider, Sears achieved prominence in the show ring, competing for nearly 50 years at the National Horse Show and other events. Sears was inducted into the Show Jumping Hall of Fame in 1992.

1918 On January 29, the Association of American Horse Shows (AAHS) held its first annual meeting, which was attended by representatives of 26 well-known shows, including Bryn Mawr, Brooklyn, Devon, Tuxedo, and Wilmington.

1920s Polo leagues were organized, and women participated.

1921 At the New York National Horse Show in Madison Square Garden and at England's biggest international horse show, women rode astride.

1921 In May, delegates from 10 countries met in Lausanne, Switzerland, to form the Federation Equestre Internationale (FEI) as the regulatory body for Olympic and other international competitions.

1924 The AAHS extended its influence throughout the country, enrolling 67 new shows. In 1933, the AAHS changed its name to the American Horse Shows Association (AHSA).

1927 At the age of 14, Barbara Worth (Oakford) opened her own hunter-jumper training business. An elite competitor for 40 years, she developed several world-class jumpers, the most famous being Snowbound, ridden by Bill Steinkraus to an Olympic gold medal in 1986. In 1956, she was one of the founders of the Pacific Coast Horse Shows Association. During her career, she was named Horsewoman of the Year by three different associations: the American Horse Shows Association, in 1962; the California All Breeds Award Association, in 1971; and the California Professional Horsemen's Association, in 1977.

1928 Dressage team events were added to the Olympics in Amsterdam.

1930s Foxhound hunting continued as a popular activity, and events such as "ladies races" were frequently held in conjunction with the hunt.

1936 The FEI invited women to enter all events.

1936 Mary Hirsh received a horse trainer's license.

1940s Judy Johnson—a complete horsewoman who rode in steeplechase events, ran a stable, and was involved in many areas of competition—received a jockey's license.

1941 Margaret Cotter won the 1941 jumper championship at the New York National Horse Show.

1949 The U.S. equestrian team was formed, and open tryouts for the Olympics were held. Two women were selected (for jumping)—Carol Hagerman Durand, of Kansas City, and Norma Mathews, of California—but they did not compete in the Olympics because there were only dressage competitions.

1951 Carol Durand was the first woman rider to qualify for an Olympic team.

1952 In Helsinki, Finland, women competed directly with men for the first time in Olympic history in equestrian events. Four women competed in dressage, in which the rider puts the horse through a series of movements that show cooperation and communication between them. Marjorie Haines Gill was the first American horsewoman to compete in the Olympics; she placed 17th in individual competition, riding Flying Dutchman, and 6th in the team competition.

1953 At the New York National Horse Show, Carol Durand took part in eight team victories in jumping and was named Individual International Champion.

1959 Patricia Galvin was the first U.S. woman to win an individual medal at the Pan American Games, taking the gold in dressage, in Chicago. She was also a member of the all-women silver-medal dressage team, with Jessica Newberry and Karen McIntosh. Galvin won gold again at the 1963 Pan American Games in São Paolo, Brazil. In the 1960 Rome Olympics, she placed sixth in dressage, and in the 1964 Tokyo Olympics, she placed eighth.

1961 Kathy Kusner joined the U.S. equestrian team. In 1964, she and Mary Mairs (Chapot) were the first women to represent the United States in Olympic show jumping. At the Munich games in 1972, Kusner won the silver team medal in show jumping. She was a two-time winner of the Leading International Rider Award at the National Horse

Show and was the Ladies European Champion in 1967. In 1968, after mounting a successful legal challenge, she became the first licensed woman jockey in the United States. She later became the first licensed woman jockey in Mexico, Germany, Chile, Peru, Panama, South Africa, and Rhodesia. In 1971, Kusner became the first woman to ride in the Maryland Hunt Cup, the world's toughest timber race, where she finished fifth. Kusner was also a skilled pilot, scuba diver, and competitive runner, winning the Colorado Pikes Peak Ultramarathon three times. In 1989, she became the first woman inducted into the Show Jumping Hall of Fame.

1963 Mary Mairs (Chapot) was the first woman to win a gold medal in show jumping at the Pan American Games. She also won team gold along with Kathy Kusner and was named Horsewoman of the Year by both the AHSA and the *Los Angeles Times*. She and Kusner were the first women to ride on the U.S. Olympic show jumping team. Her career highlights include winning the first U.S. Grand Prix, in Cleveland, in 1965, and a team silver medal in 1967's Pan American Games, in addition to riding on 22 winning Nation's Cup squads. She was inducted into the Show Jumping Hall of Fame in 1992.

1964 In Tokyo, Lana du Pont became the first woman in the world to ride in an Olympic three-day event, as well as the first U.S. woman to receive an Olympic medal in equestrian competition, when her team won the silver. Kathy Kusner and Mary Mairs (Chapot) placed sixth in team show jumping.

1968 At the Olympics in Mexico City, the jumping team of Kathy Kusner, Mary Chapot, and Frank Chapot placed fourth.

1972 At the Munich Olympics, 21 of the 33 riders in individual dressage were women. Kathy Kusner won a silver medal as a member of the U.S. show jumping team.

MARGIE GOLDSTEIN ENGLE. (PHOTO © DOUG PENSINGER/ALLSPORT.)

1976 In Montreal, the first all-woman U.S. dressage team, comprising Hilda Gurney, Edith Master, and Dorothy Morkis, won the Olympic bronze medal. Mary Anne Tauskey won the gold as a member of the three-day eventing team. Gurney, Morkis, and Tauskey had previously won team gold at the 1975 Pan American Games in Mexico City, where Gurney also won an individual silver medal. Gurney won four more Pan American Games medals: individual and team gold in 1979 in San Juan, Puerto Rico, and team gold and individual silver in 1983 in Caracas, Venezuela.

1979 Leslie Burr (Howard), one of the top U.S. equestrian riders, won two grand prix events riding Chase the Clouds. The following year, she rode on two winning Nation's Cup teams. In 1983, she placed first and third in American Gold Cup competitions, also placed first and third at the Mercedes Grand Prix at the National Horse Show, and won an unprecedented three consecutive grand prix events.

1980 Joy Slater Carrie won the Hunt Club, Maryland steeplechase's toughest challenge.

1983 Anne Kursinski won the individual gold medal after five rounds of competition at the Pan American Games in Caracas and also led the U.S. team to its fifth team gold medal in show jumping. Kursinski, who began competing for the U.S. equestrian team in 1978, won silver medals in 1988 and 1996. She was also the first American rider to win the Grand Prix of Rome.

1984 Melanie Smith—a member of the 1980 Olympic team that didn't compete because of the boycott—and Leslie Burr-Howard won Olympic gold in Los Angeles as members of the jumping team. In three-day eventing, Karen Stives won gold in the team event and silver in the individual competition.

1987 Elizabeth McKnight won the Hunt Club.

1988 Lisa Jacquin and Anne Kursinski were members of the silver-medal show jumping team at the Seoul Olympics.

1989 Margie Goldstein Engle won her first American Grandprix Association (AGA) Rider of the Year Award.

1991 Jane Forbes Clark became the first female president of the AHSA.

1992 At the Olympics in Barcelona, Spain, Charlotte Bredahl and Carol Lavell medaled in bronze as members of the dressage team. Lavell had previously won a team silver in dressage at the 1987 Pan American Games.

1994 FEI general assembly met in the United States for the first time, in Tampa, Florida.

1995 Anne Kursinski won the American Gold Cup for a record fourth time.

1996 At the Atlanta Olympics, Kerry Millikin won the individual bronze medal in the three-day event, and Karen O'Connor competed on the silver-medal jumping team, which also included her husband, David O'Connor, as well as Bruce Davidson and Jill Henneberg. Michelle Gibson won bronze in team dressage.

1997 Leslie Burr-Howard, who represented the United States in international competition for 18 years, won the $725,000 du Maurier Classic in Calgary, Canada, the richest jumping competition in the world.

1997 Dorothy Alexander Matz, a bronze medalist in team show jumping at the 1995 Pan American Games, was the first woman elected president of the U.S. equestrian team.

1997 Margie Goldstein Engle won the Budweiser AGA Show Jumping Championship and clinched her record fifth AGA Rider of the Year Award.

1998 The Women's Sports Foundation and the American Quarter Horse Association joined together to present the first annual National Female Equestrian Award, designed to help female equestrians realize their athletic dreams and to promote America's horse sports. The first recipient was Winona Anhaiser-Smitherman.

2000 Margie Goldstein Engle, one of the most accomplished riders in the history of the sport, qualified for her first Olympic team, which placed sixth in the team show-jumping competition in Sydney. At the 1999 Pan American Games in Winnipeg, she finished fifth individually and earned a team silver medal. Her legion of U.S. records includes 11 grand prix victories in a season and the most AGA wins in a season—five of which were with the same horse. In addition, she was the first rider to earn six ribbons with six different horses in one grand prix class, the leading money-winner in U.S. show-jumping history, and a six-time AGA Rider of the Year.

2000 The U.S. dressage team of Susan Blinks, Robert Dover, Guenter Seidel, and Christine Traurig won a bronze medal at the Sydney Olympics.

2000 Karen O'Connor represented the United States in the 1988, 1996, and 2000 Olympic Games. Despite the team's losing some of its best horses, she turned in key performances as the anchor rider on the 2000 team and won the Olympic bronze medal.

2000 At the Olympics in Sydney, Nora Garson, Margie Goldstein, Lauren Hough, and Laura Kraut made up the first all-female show jumping team in Olympic history.

2001 Molly Ashe, on her horse Kroon Gavin, qualified for the FEI Show Jumping World Cup after winning four out of five starts, rarely accomplished in show jumping. One of her four wins came in Berlin at the Eternit Grand Prix of Germany, where Ashe was the first American to win, defeating members of Germany's two-time gold-medal Olympic team.

FENCING

THE PAGEANTRY of fencing is one of the reasons women were first drawn to the sport. By the middle of the 19th century, women's participation had become socially acceptable, and many formerly all-men's fencing clubs included programs for women. Women's fencing today encompasses three events: foil, épée, and saber. Essential qualities for all three sports include quick reactions: advancing, retreating, and evasion. Speed and power are also major aspects, used especially in attacking motions. The foil is the lightest of the three swords and has a flexible blade with a blunt tip; fencers must only touch between the shoulders and hips in competition. The épée is heavier than the foil and the blade is rigid. The point is covered with a cone, and touches are scored on any part of the body. The saber is similar to the foil, but points are awarded by touching any part of the body above the waist, with the tip or sides of the blade. In a bout, a point is awarded each time a fencer touches an opponent. The first fencer to score 15 points or the leader after nine minutes is the winner.

1888 The Amateur Athletic Union held its first fencing championships in New York City. No women competed.

1888 Professor J. Hartl, of Vienna, Austria, toured the United States with a women's fencing team and gave demonstrations. This sparked an interest in fencing, and classes for women increased at private clubs.

1896 Fencing was included in the first modern Olympic Games, in Athens, Greece; Olympic competitions were limited to men. Fencing is one of only four sports to have been included in every single Olympics since 1896.

1912 The first women's national fencing championship was won by Dr. Adelaide Baylis and was sponsored by the Amateur Fencers League of America.

1913 The Federation Internationale d'Escrime (FIE), the international federation for fencing, was founded in Paris.

1919 Hits received, called "indicators," first had an impact on final placement at the national championships, eliminating ties and fence-offs.

1924 Women fencers first competed at the Olympics in Paris. The individual foil, with bouts of five touches, was the only event. The épée competition was not added until 1996.

1928 Marion Lloyd (Vince) was national women's foil champion, winning the title again in 1931.

1929 The Intercollegiate Women's Fencing Association was founded by Bryn Mawr College (Pennsylvania), Cornell University (Ithaca, New York), New York University, and the University of Pennsylvania.

1929 Women's foil competitions were held for the first time at the European championships in Naples, Italy.

1932 At the Olympics in Los Angeles, Marion Lloyd (Vince) placed eighth, becoming the first U.S. woman to make it to the finals of an international competition.

1936 The World's Professional Championships were held in London. American Olympian Joanna de Tuscan won the title.

1936 The FIE announced that Olympic bouts would change from five touches to four touches, where they remained until 1976.

1948 At the Olympics in London, Maria Cerra (Tishman) finished two touches away from the gold medal, placing fourth after being in a three-way tie for second. If she had scored one more touch to win a close bout that she lost, she would have won the gold. Tishman reigned as the national champion and was the first U.S. fencer to place as high as fourth in the Olympics.

1955 The FIE held the first World Under-20 Championships in women's foil. The épée event was added in 1989.

1957 Electric foil was used for the first time at the national championships.

1960s Nikki Franke became a role model for African American women. Franke fenced internationally, winning a U.S. championship, and later coached at Temple University (Philadelphia).

1963 Legendary fencer Maria Cerra Tishman was the first woman inducted into the FIE Hall of Fame. Janice York-Romary joined her in 1978.

1968 At the Olympics in Mexico City, champion fencer Janice York-Romary became the first woman to carry the American flag in the opening ceremonies. She was a member of all six Olympic teams from 1948 to 1968 and won the national women's championship 10 times, from 1959 to 1968. At both the 1952 and 1956 Olympics, she placed fourth.

1969 Ruth White became the first African American U.S. fencing champion. In 1972, she won the bronze in foil at the World Under-20 Championships.

1970s At clubs and other organizations throughout the country, efforts were made to increase épée and saber competition for women.

1982 The United States Fencing Association sanctioned an official women's individual épée event. The first winner was Susan Badders, who had been on the Olympic team; Marlene Adrian took second place, and Anne Klinger took third. All three women were more than 35 years old.

1982 The National Collegiate Athletic Association (NCAA) held its first fencing championships. Wayne State University (Detroit) won the team competition by a score of 2–0. San Jose State was second. San Jose's Joy Ellingson was the individual winner.

1987 Caitlin Bilodeaux, of Barnard College of Columbia University in New York City, won her second NCAA individual championship. Her first was in 1985.

1988 Caitlin Bilodeaux placed ninth in the foil at the Olympics in Seoul, South Korea, and the U.S. foil team placed sixth—the first breakthrough into the top 10 in 60 years.

1988 Molly Sullivan, of Notre Dame, won her second NCAA title. Her first was in 1986.

1989 At the World Championships in Denver, Colorado, women's épée was held for the first time. Donna Stone, of the U.S. team, made it to the finals.

1990 The NCAA discontinued fencing championships for women and added a combined men's and women's championship. At that time, Wayne State women had won three team championships, Yale had won two, and Notre Dame and Pennsylvania State University had each won one.

1990 Notre Dame hosted the first national collegiate men's and women's fencing championships, which combined men's and women's teams.

1991 Felicia Zimmerman became the first female fencer in history to win three gold medals in one Junior Olympics. She won the Under-20 and Under-17 foil and Under-17 épée competitions.

1992 At the World Championships, the U.S. épée team placed seventh, the highest U.S. finish at the Worlds.

1993 Iris Zimmerman, at the age of 12, won the Under-19 National Championship and was a silver medalist in 1995.

1995 NCAA fencing championships were changed to a straight individual format, with team totals based solely on the individual events. Women's épée was added, and Tina Loveny, of Saint John's University (Jamaica, New York), won the title.

1995 At the world championships, saber was included as a demonstration event. Kelly Williams won the gold.

1995 At the FIE World Under-17 championships, Iris Zimmerman became the first American to win the title in the foil. Felicia Zimmerman, Iris's older sister, who also competed in foil, became the first American to earn the title of Junior World Cup champion; she held the number one ranking in the Under-20 age group.

1996 Olga Kalinouskaya, of Penn State, won her fourth consecutive NCAA foil title.

1996 The épée was added at the Olympic Games in Atlanta, and women's saber was added to the national championships.

1996 At the Olympics in Atlanta, Ann Marsh placed seventh in foil, the highest U.S. women's result in 40 years. Marsh is a three-time Olympian, participating in the 1992, '96, and 2000 games. She is also the first U.S. fencer to be ranked in the top eight in the world.

1996 Elaine Cleris, at the age of 50, was the oldest member of any U.S. Olympic team in any sport. She was a three-time Olympian, participating in the 1980 and '88 games in foil and the 1996 games in épée. Elaine was also a seven-time member of the U.S. World Championship team in épée and a three-timer in foil.

1996 The first international competition for women over 50 was held in Germany. Cynthia Carter placed second in foil, and Veronica Mousin took second in épée.

1997 Jessie Burke, at age 16, became the youngest U.S. women's fencing champion at the U.S. Senior Championships in Colorado Springs. In 1998, Burke won a silver medal at the Junior épée competition in Palermo, Italy, and two bronze medals at the Junior épée in Tauberbischofsheim, Germany.

1997 Iris Zimmerman repeated as the World Under-17 champion and took the silver at the World Under-20 Championships. She also won the World Cup Championship, making Iris and her sister Felicia, who won in 1995, the only siblings to have earned this title. Iris also won the Division I National Championship for Stanford University. She was only 16 years old at the time.

1998 Team USA members Jessica Burke, Katie Cavan, Kate Rudkin, and Arlene Stevens won the bronze in épée at the World Under-20 Championships.

1998 Women's saber became an NCAA Division I national championship event. It was also accepted as a demonstration event at the World Championships for the first time—Kelly Williams won the gold medal.

1999 Andrea Ament, at the Under-17 World Championships, was the first ever double bronze medalist in foil and épée.

1999 The first world championships in women's saber were held in Seoul, Korea.

1999 Felicia Zimmerman won her second NCAA championship while at Stanford. In 1999 she won in épée and in 1998 in foil. She is the only woman to win an NCAA title in both.

2000 Iris Zimmerman was the first American to win the Under-20 World Championship and in 1999 she was the first American to medal at the Senior World Championships, earning a bronze. Iris was the first U.S. fencer in any weapon and any age category to win a medal at the World Championship.

2000 The first U.S. team ever to win a gold medal at the World Championships was in saber. Team members included Sada Jacobson, Christine Becker, Nicole Mustilli, and Mariel Zagunis.

2000 The Penn State fencing team won its sixth straight NCAA fencing national championship, an NCAA record. The Penn State team held a total of eight titles, having appeared in 11 championships. Notre Dame appeared in 6 championships, winning in 1994.

2000 The U.S. Under-20 team in Saber won the silver medal at the World Championships.

2000 Ann Marsh competed in her third Olympics, a record for women's fencing.

FIELD HOCKEY

IN THE late 1880s, socially acceptable sports for women were mainly limited to croquet, archery, and lawn tennis. Field hockey, which was played in England, was originally considered too dangerous. Gradually, as more and more women became active in sports, attitudes changed and field hockey became a popular team sport. In 1920, the United States sent a touring team to England—the first U.S. sports team ever to participate in international competition.

1901 Constance Applebee, at age 28, brought the sport of field hockey from her native England to the United States and demonstrated the game while attending a seminar at Harvard. The next year, she demonstrated and taught the sport at Vassar (Poughkeepsie, New York) and other women's colleges in the East. Applebee, affectionately called "the Apple" by the hockey community, coached at Bryn Mawr College (Pennsylvania) and remained one of field hockey's main promoters until she was 95 years old. She also published the first women's sports magazine, *The Sportswoman*, a bimonthly that circulated for 10 years. In addition to coverage of hockey, the magazine contained articles and news about many other sports. Applebee lived to be 107.

1901 The first field hockey club was formed in Poughkeepsie. Many other cities on the East Coast established clubs and adopted the rules of the All England Ladies Hockey Association. With more women taking up the sport, field hockey gained acceptance as the only "proper" team sport for women of the day.

1902 The first prep school game in the United States was held between Rosemary Hall, in Greenwich, Connecticut, and the Staten Island (New York) Ladies.

1904 Constance Applebee was appointed director of outdoor sports at Bryn Mawr College; in 1906, she became director of physical education. She retired in 1927 at age 56 and went back to England but returned each season until 1965. She was associated with Bryn Mawr for more than 65 years.

1917 The Committee on Women's Athletics, a division of the National Amateur Athletic Federation, established a subcommittee to set, revise, and interpret the rules for women's field hockey.

1920 In line with the growth of field hockey in high schools and colleges over the previous decade, the popularity of club teams continued.

1920 The first women's team in any sport to represent the United States in international competition was coached by Constance Applebee. Composed of players from Philadelphia, the field hockey team played its first game in Great Britain and finished with a record of two wins and eight losses.

1922 The United States Field Hockey Association (USFHA) was founded and held its first meeting in January at the Philadelphia Cricket Club, with Constance Applebee presiding. One hundred colleges representing 15 states attended. The purpose of the organization was to promote and generate enthusiasm for the sport. Helen Krumbhaar was the first USFHA president, serving from 1922 to '25, and became the first American officer of the International Federation of Women's Hockey Associations (IFWHA).

1922 The first U.S. tournament was held in Philadelphia from November 30 to December 2. Teams from Boston, Chicago, New York, Philadelphia, and Richmond, Virginia, competed, with Philadelphia emerging victorious.

1923 Constance Applebee set up the first hockey camp, Tegaurtha Hockey Camp, in Mount Pocono, Pennsylvania. At this first residential athletic camp devoted solely to girl's athletics, an outstanding staff of British coaches trained U.S. players and coaches.

1924 Anne Townsend captained the first official U.S. team to play in England against European clubs at the First Women's International Hockey Conference. Townsend led the U.S. teams until 1938. She was selected to the first 15 all-American teams—from 1924 to 1938. In 1947, at age 47, Townsend was again named an all-American.

1924 The USFHA created an umpiring committee to train and rate officials. Twelve officials became rated.

1925 Spalding published the *Field Hockey Guide Rules for America*. It was the first women's rule book written by women coaches. The rules were drawn mostly from the English game.

1926 U.S. teams competed in regional sections under the USFHA, with competitions held between sections. In 1927, the Northeast section was organized.

1927 The IFWHA was formed. The first conference was held in 1930 in Geneva, Switzerland, with eight countries participating.

1927 The first West Coast hockey camp, Camp Sirano, was established at Mills College (Oakland, California) under the direction of Hazel J. Cubberley. Hilda Barr and Mae Fogg later coached at the camp.

1932 The USFHA organized an equipment committee to receive and distribute sticks, shin guards, and goalkeeping equipment.

1933 The second IFWHA conference was held in Copenhagen, Denmark, with eight teams represented. After the tournament, the U.S. team, captained by Anne Townsend, toured Europe and the British Isles.

1933 Gertrude Hooper became president of the USFHA.

1936 Helen Krumbhaar became the first American president of the IFWHA.

1937 The USFHA sent Constance Applebee on a coaching tour of Cleveland, Detroit, and Ann Arbor, Michigan, to help spread the game nationwide.

1947 For the 25th anniversary of the USFHA, the English touring team came to the United States to join the national tournament at Adelphi University in Garden City, New York. The game between England and the United States was televised.

1950 At the IFWHA conference in Johannesburg, South Africa, the U.S. team beat Ireland and Scotland. The corner rule, the technique of placing six players behind the goal line, used by U.S. teams since 1937, was adopted for future international tournaments.

1951 The 50th anniversary of American field hockey.

1955 Betty Shellenberger was elected executive secretary of the USFHA and served for 15 years. Shellenberger was on either the U.S. team or the U.S. reserve team from 1939 to 1960.

1957 Anne McConaghie Volp was a member of the U.S. national team for 13 years from 1940 to 1957 and coached for Temple University (Philadelphia) for 15 years.

1959 The national tournament was held in Washington, D.C. Vice President Richard Nixon opened the tournament. Colorful flags designed for the different sections of the country were introduced.

1959 In one of the most exciting international matches in history, the visiting U.S. team played England in Wembley Stadium. Fifty thousand fans watched the teams play to a 3–3 tie. The English team had not lost at Wembley in the prior 10 years, and this was its first tie.

1967 The USFHA implemented the squad program to increase the level of performance of top players. A 44-player squad was selected and trained to compete internationally.

1968 Kilts became the official uniform. Early players wore ankle-length skirts, blouses, and hats, which later developed into tunics with blouses and long black stockings or tights—and eventually kneesocks.

1970 Eleanor Snell was a legendary coach at Ursinus College (Collegeville, Pennsylvania). In her 38-year coaching career, she compiled a record of 196 wins, 61 losses, and 29 ties. In the 1960s, her teams had six unbeaten seasons; her 1970 team went 35–1. Many of her students went on to be successful coaches or remained active in various aspects of the sport, including Beth Anders, Vonnie Gros, and Jen Shillingford. She died in 1993 at age 92.

1970 In November, the U.S. team beat England for the first time, 2–1, in Lancaster, Pennsylvania. Vonnie Gros was the U.S. captain.

1971 Dominant players included Frances Elliot, Vonnie Gros, and Mary Ann Harris, who had played on 14 U.S. teams, as well as Alison Hersey, Pat Nichols, Eleanore Pepper, Barbara Strebeigh, Anne McConaghie Volp, Harriet Walton, and Alice Willets, who had been on 10 teams.

1975 The United States appeared in the first IFWHA World Cup Championships in Edinburgh, Scotland, placing 10th.

1975 The first national championship took place. Regional tournaments were held, and the top 16 teams advanced to the nationals.

1976 The International Olympic Committee announced that women's field hockey would be added to the Olympics in Moscow, in 1980.

1976 The IFWHA voted to make artificial turf the official playing surface.

1978 On March 11 at Empire Stadium in London, 65,165 people—the highest attendance ever for an international match—watched England and the United States play. England won.

1979 California State University at Long Beach, coached by veteran national team member Anita Miller, became the first non-Eastern team to win the Division I national title. The championship was held under the auspices of the Association for Intercollegiate Athletics for Women (AIAW).

1979 The U.S. national team entered the World Cup championships in Vancouver, Canada, with an 11th-place world ranking and finished third in the tournament. The U.S. team beat England for the first time ever and qualified for the Olympics. Vonnie Gros, a 14-year veteran of the national team and a player in four world championships, was the U.S. coach.

1980 The U.S. team was scheduled to participate in the Olympics in Moscow, but the United States boycotted the games in protest of the Russian invasion of Afghanistan.

1980 The national indoor tournament was held for the first time.

1981 Beverly Johnson was named president of the USFHA.

1981 The first NCAA Division I field hockey championships were held at the University of Connecticut, which won the title. The first Division II championships were held at Pfeiffer College (Misenheimer, North Carolina) and won by Pfeiffer. The first Division III championships were held at Westfield State College (Massachusetts) and won by the College of New Jersey.

1983 The IFWHA came under the auspices of the Federation of International Hockey.

1984 The United States competed in the Olympics for the first time in Los Angeles, winning the bronze medal after a dramatic penalty shoot-out. Beth Anders set an Olympic record by scoring eight goals in five games. The team competed in Seoul, South Korea, in 1988 and in Atlanta in 1996 but did not qualify for the 2000 Olympics in Sydney, Australia.

1984 Beth Anders became the first American woman to compete in 100 international field hockey matches and was named USA Field Hockey's Athlete of the Year. In her 14 years on the U.S. team, Anders was named captain five times and scored more than 100 international goals.

1984 The Futures program, geared to young women, was developed by the USFHA for the purpose of teaching the skills of the game to up-and-coming players.

1985 Judith Davidson was elected president of the USFHA.

1987 Suzanne Tyler coached the University of Maryland to the NCAA championship. Tyler earned the distinction of being the only Division I coach to win an NCAA championship in two different sports, having coached the Maryland lacrosse team to the NCAA championship in 1986.

1987 The. U.S. team won the silver at the Pan American Games.

1988 The USFHA Hall of Fame was established at Ursinus College, with 23 original inductees. Selection criteria, based on a point system, include achievement as a player or coach and a minimum of five years on a U.S. team.

1988 In Seoul, Sheryl Johnson and Beth Beglin competed as members of the U.S. Olympic team for the third time. The team placed eighth.

1989 The Junior World Cup was played for the first time and helped develop players for the senior tour. The United States fielded an under-21 team at the inaugural event, which was won by Germany.

1991 At the Olympic qualifying tournament, an all-encompassing tournament sponsored by the International Hockey Federation was held for the first time, with the selection of eight teams.

1991 The United States won the bronze medal at the Pan American Games.

1993 Jenepher Shillingford was elected president of the USFHA.

1993 From October 1990 to September 1993, Old Dominion University (Norfolk, Virginia) had an unprecedented 66-game winning streak.

1993 The Field Hockey Association, the men's governing body, and the USFHA merged to form one national governing body for men's and women's field hockey, the United States Field Hockey Association.

1994 The U.S. team won the bronze medal in the World Cup tournament in Dublin, Ireland. The team had placed fifth in the 1993 International Continental Cup.

1995 The U.S. team won the silver medal at the Pan American Games.

1996 On November 2, Beth Anders, in her 15th season as field hockey coach at Old Dominion, became the first NCAA Division I field hockey coach to reach 300 career victories as the Lady Monarchs blanked Virginia Commonwealth, 16–0.

1996 Barbara Marois, who had played in 152 sanctioned matches, retired. Marois was a three-time Olympian, a member of the national team for 10 years, captain of the 1996 Olympic team, and a four-time USFHA Athlete of the Year.

1997 U.S. Field Hockey established an under-16 squad for the purpose of introducing young players to the team system while preparing them to become good enough to move up and eventually be considered for the national team.

1998 The first IFH International Player of the Year Award was presented to Alyson Annar, of Australia.

1999 Legendary Australian player Beth Beglin was named head coach of the U.S. national team in January. The team won a silver medal at the Pan American Games. Beglin was a national team player for 11 years and a three-time Olympian. She finished her career at the University of Iowa, compiling a lifetime record of seven Big Ten championships, 10 NCAA tournament berths, three Elite Eight finishes, and seven Final Four appearances.

1999 Under coach Jan Hutchinson, Bloomsburg University of Pennsylvania became the first team to win four straight NCAA Division II championships, 1996–'99, and only the ninth NCAA team overall to take four straight division titles. Hutchinson led Bloomsburg to 23 winning seasons and 16 championship game appearances. She also served as head softball coach, and her teams appeared in three national championship games, winning the AIAW national championship in 1982.

1999 The College of New Jersey won its record ninth NCAA Division III championship, with titles in 1981, '83, '85, '88, '90, '91, '95, '96, and '99. Since 1981, the team played in 13 title games and appeared in all 20 NCAA Division III field hockey tournaments.

2000 Sharon Taylor was elected president of the USFHA, succeeding Jen Shillingford, who held the office for eight years. Jane Betts retired as executive director of the organization after a four-year term.

2000 The U.S. women's under-21 team, coached by Tracey Greisbaum, won a silver medal at the Pan American Junior Championships. Greisbaum became head coach of the University of Iowa.

2000 Linda Arena, after 27 years of coaching at State University College of New York at Brockport and Wittenberg University (Springfield, Ohio), retired. She was NCAA Coach of the Year three times and was named Regional Coach of the Year four times by the National Field Hockey Coaches Association (NFHCA).

2000 The Futures Elite program was introduced to provide supplemental training and development opportunities to the top 125 athletes in the Futures program.

2000 Barb Liles was named U.S. Field Hockey Developmental Coach of the Year by Active in the Midwest. For 22 years Liles led Oak Park River Forest High School, in Illinois, to seven state championships, five second-place finishes, and seven third-place finishes.

2000 A record 181 teams participated in the Hockey Festival, held in Palm Beach County, Florida.

2001 Field hockey celebrated its 100th anniversary in the United States.

2001 The first Women's Americas Cup, created by the Pan American Hockey Federation, was held in Jamaica. Ten countries qualified for the event, established as the inaugural continental World Cup qualifier for teams from North America, Central America, and South America, with winners receiving an automatic berth.

2001 NCAA field hockey comprised a total of 244 teams: Division I—75 teams, Division II—25, and Division III—144.

2001 Old Dominion University won its record ninth NCAA Division I championship under coach Beth Anders, defeating the University of North Carolina, coached by Karen Shelton, 3–1. This was Old Dominion's 20th NCAA tournament, making the Lady Monarchs the only team to appear in every NCAA tourney. It was also the fifth time the two schools met in the final game.

2001 Beth Anders, coach of Old Dominion, recorded her 390th career win and was inducted into the NFHCA Hall of Fame.

2001 The NFHCA established a High School Coach of the Year Award. Bob Derr, of Warwick High, in Pennsylvania, received the inaugural award after Warwick won the girls AAA state championship.

2001 Marina Di Giacomo, an outstanding player for Old Dominion, finished her college career as the NCAA's all-time leading scorer for goals, with 167, and points, with 414. Di Giacomo, a native of Argentina, was third in assists, with 80, and was the Honda Award winner.

2001 Tracy Fuchs, a two-time Olympian and the most capped woman in U.S. history—having played in more international games than any other player as a member of the U.S. team—marked her 14th year on the national team.

2001 Eight members of the 2000 national team returned to the 2001 team: Kate Barber, Tracy Fuchs, Tara Jelley, Katie Kauffman, Tracey Larson, Kristen McCann, Jill Reeve, and goalkeeper Peggy Storrarand, with alternate Jessica Coleman. Fuchs, Kauffman, and Reeve played on the 1996 Olympic team in Atlanta.

2001 The World Cup qualifier was held in September, in Abbeville and Amiens, France.

2001 A full-time residency program for the U.S. national team was established in Virginia Beach, to better prepare the team for qualification for the 2004 Olympics in Athens.

2002 The 10th IFH World Cup will be held in Perth, Australia, from November 26 to December 8.

FIGURE SKATING

Figure skating represents the ideal mix of art and athleticism, combining technique, creativity, strength, charm, skill, composure, and confidence. Figure skating derives its name from the figures etched on the ice by skaters doing variations of a figure eight. Early competitions required skaters to perform several of these school figures. Each figure had to be traced three times on the ice, with marks awarded based on the exactness of the tracings. In contrast, the free program requires skaters to move across the ice to music while performing a variety of jumps, spins, and steps that last four minutes and count for two-thirds of the final score.

Over time, figure skating attire has evolved into short skirts and flexible tights, allowing women to incorporate complicated and highly athletic movements into their programs. Figure skaters today combine power and grace as they launch into triple jumps while maintaining a dancer's posture and fluidity. School figures have been dropped from competition, allowing skaters to focus on the long and short free programs. The short program includes eight required elements, counts for one-third of the final score, and is scored by a panel of judges awarding separate marks for technical merit and presentation. Figure skating performances have become some of the most widely watched competitions in sports.

1892 The International Skating Union (ISU) was founded in Holland as the world governing body for figure and speed skating.

1906 The ISU sponsored the first world championships, featuring a separate ladies competition.

1908 Female skaters were among the first athletes to compete in the Olympics when winter sports were added. Competitions were held in singles and pairs skating, but the events were exhibitions, not official medal sports.

1912 The Olympics were not held due to World War I.

1914 The first U.S. ice skating championships were held in New Haven, Connecticut. The competition was open to outstanding skaters from all countries. Theresa Weld (Blanchard), representing the Skating Club of Boston, won the women's singles title. She later won five consecutive titles from 1920 to 1924. There were no championships from 1915 to 1918. Tenley Albright also won five straight, 1952–'56, as did Carol Heiss (Jenkins), 1956–'60.

1916 The Olympics were not held due to World War I.

1920 Theresa Weld Blanchard won a bronze medal at the Olympics in Antwerp, Belgium, becoming the first American of either sex to win a medal of any kind at a Winter Olympics. In Antwerp, figure skating was still considered an event—not an official sport.

1924 Figure skating was an official medal sport in singles and pairs for the first time at the Olympics in Chamonix, France; 13 women competed. Beatrix S. Loughran became the first American woman to win a medal, taking the silver. In 1928, she won the bronze in singles, and in 1932, she took a silver with partner Sherwin Badger in the pairs competition. She holds the distinction of being the only American skater to win medals at three different Olympic Games.

1924 At age 30, Theresa Weld Blanchard won her fifth straight U.S. title.

1932 Maribel Vinson Owen, a bronze medalist in singles at the Olympics in Lake Placid, New York, became the first female sportswriter for the *New York Times*.

1933 Maribel Vinson Owen became the first skater to win six consecutive national championships, spanning the years 1928–'33. She won three more in 1935–'37 and holds the record for the most U.S. titles, with nine. She also won five pairs titles.

1940 The Olympics were not held due to World War II.

1944 The Olympics were not held due to World War II.

1948 Gretchen Merrill won her sixth consecutive U.S. title. Prior to that, in 1941 and '42, she was the silver medalist. In 1947, she won the bronze at the world championships.

1952 Tenley Albright won the silver at the Olympics in Oslo, Norway.

1953 Albright became the first U.S. woman to win the world championship, a title she won again in 1955. She also became the first American to win the world championship, the North American crown, and the national title.

1956 At the Olympics in Cortina d'Ampezzo, Italy, Tenley Albright became the first U.S. woman to win the gold medal in figure skating, receiving first-place votes from 10 out of 11 judges. In her career, she won five U.S. titles; four world championship medals—the gold in both 1953 and 1955, and the silver in 1954 and 1956; and two Olympic medals—the 1956 gold and a silver in 1952. After graduating from Radcliffe College

(Cambridge, Massachusetts) at age 21, Albright became one of six women out of 130 students at Harvard Medical School.

1960 In January, Carol Heiss (Jenkins), of Queens, New York, performed the first double jump in women's competition at the Olympics, winning the gold medal in Squaw Valley, California.

1960 Carol Heiss (Jenkins) was the first skater to win the gold medal in both the Olympics and the world championships in the same year. Dorothy Hamill repeated the feat in 1976. In her career, Heiss won six world championship medals—five gold in a row from 1956 to 1960, and the silver in 1955; two Olympic medals—one gold and one silver; and four U.S. titles, 1957–'60. Heiss was one of the first skaters to become famous through exposure on television.

1960 Barbara Roles won the bronze medal at the Olympics in Squaw Valley.

1961 The U.S. championships were broadcast on television for the first time, by CBS.

1961 An entire generation of U.S. figure skaters and coaches was lost when the plane carrying the U.S. team to the world championships in Belgium crashed, killing the team. Among those on board were coach and former champion Maribel Vinson Owen and her daughters: Laurence, who was the U.S. singles champion, and Maribel, who was the U.S. pairs champion (with Dudley Richards).

1968 From the time she won the gold medal at the Olympics in Grenoble, France, Peggy Fleming was an internationally famous athlete much adored by the public. In her career, she won five consecutive U.S. championships, 1964–'68, and three consecutive world championships, 1966–'68, as well as the bronze in 1965. She was named the Associated Press Female Athlete of the Year and went on to have a professional skating career and do television commentary.

1969 Janet Lynn won her first national championship. Prior to that, Lynn, at the age of 12, won the national junior championships and took fourth in the national senior championships when she was 13.

1972 Competitions were changed to include a "short" program composed of certain required jumps and spins. Until 1972, the school figures and the long program each counted for 50 percent of a skater's score in competition. The short program, which decreased the importance of school figures, is generally thought to have been added to competitive figure skating because of Janet Lynn. One of the most extraordinary free skaters of all time, Lynn did not score well in the school figures and was therefore never able to win an Olympic or world title.

1973 Lynn won her fifth consecutive U.S. title, spanning the years 1969 to 1973. In 1972, she won a bronze medal at the Olympics, and in 1973 she placed second at the world championships. When Lynn chose to become a professional skater and signed a $1.4 million contract with the Ice Follies, she became the highest paid female athlete of her time.

1976 Dorothy Hamill finished her performances at the Olympics in Innsbruck, Austria, with her signature spinning "Hamill camel" to win the gold medal. She kept the gold coming by winning the 1976 world championship. In both of the prior two years, Hamill had won the silver at the worlds. From 1974 to 1976, Hamill won three consecutive national championships. After the Olympics, contracts with the ABC network and the Ice Capades made her the first athlete to earn more than $2 million in each of her first two years as a professional. Hamill's hairstyle, a short wedge cut, became a popular new look copied by many girls and women.

1979 Tenley Albright became the first woman officer of the United States Olympic Committee.

1980 Linda Fratianne won the silver medal at the Winter Olympics in Lake Placid and won another silver at the world championships. Fratianne, the first female skater to consistently hit triple jumps in competition, won the world championships in 1977 and '79 and took the silver in '78. She was a four-time U.S. champion, holding the title from 1977 to 1980.

1982 Elaine Zayak, the first skater to perform seven triple jumps in one program, won the world championships. In 1981, she won the silver at both the world and U.S. championships, and in 1984, she won the bronze at both.

1983 Janet Lynn won the first world professional championship.

1984 Rosalyn Summers won her third consecutive U.S. singles championship and took the silver medal at the Olympics in Sarajevo, Yugoslavia.

1985 Tiffany Chin won the U.S. title and won her second consecutive bronze medal in the world championships. In 1986, she took the U.S. bronze.

1986 Three days before her 19th birthday, Debi Thomas became the first African American to win the world championship in figure skating. Not only was this a major victory for Thomas, but also it was the first time Katarina Witt, the champion German skater, had lost in world competition. In 1987, Thomas won the silver at the world championships, and in 1988, she won the bronze. At the same time that she was training and competing, Thomas was a premed student at Stanford University (California).

1987 Caryn Kadavvy won the bronze at both the world championships and the nationals; she repeated in the nationals in 1988.

1988 Debi Thomas was the first African American to win an Olympic medal, taking the bronze in Calgary, Alberta. Jill Trenary placed fourth.

1990 The compulsory figures were skated in the world championships for the last time. Future events included only the free skating section of the short and long programs.

1990 At the world championships in Halifax, Nova Scotia, Jill Trenary took the gold. She took the gold as well at the U.S. championships for the third time, having won in 1987 and '89. Also in '89, Trenary won the bronze at the world championships. She turned professional, and in 1992, she won the U.S. Open championships.

1991 At the world championships, the United States completed its first and only medal sweep in women's figure skating: Kristi Yamaguchi won the gold, Tonya Harding took the silver, and Nancy Kerrigan took the bronze.

1991 At the U.S. nationals, Tonya Harding was the first U.S. woman to land a triple axel.

1992 In any sport, it doesn't get much better than the year had by Kristi Yamaguchi, of Fremont, California. After winning the national championships, she won the gold medal at the Olympics in Albertville, France—the first Asian American to do so. Then she went on to win the world championships, completing a rare triple in figure skating. Prior accomplishments included winning the world title in 1991, the national championships in 1989 and '90, and the pairs championships (with Rudy Galindo) in 1989 and '90. After her extraordinary year in '92, Yamaguchi turned professional and went on to collect a number of professional titles.

1993 The original program was renamed the "technical program."

1994 After Nancy Kerrigan was attacked at the nationals and could not compete, the nation learned that her rival Tonya Harding and Harding's then husband were associated with the assault. The media covered every angle of the incident, which brought new public interest to the sport. Kerrigan recovered from the knee-bashing and competed in the Olympics in Lillehammer, Norway, winning the silver medal. Prior to that, in 1993, she won the gold at the U.S. championships; in 1992, she won the silver; and in 1991, she won the bronze. Also in 1992, she won bronze at both the Albertville Olympics and the world championships. After the 1994 Olympics, Kerrigan turned professional.

1994 The technical program was renamed the "short program," and artistic impression was changed to "artistic presentation."

1995 Nicole Bobek won the U.S. championship and took the bronze at the world championships. In 1997 and '98, she won the bronze at the U.S. championships. After sustaining injuries from professional appearances, she could not compete at the 1996 nationals due to a sore ankle.

1996 At the world championships in Edmonton, Alberta, Tara Lipinski of Houston, Texas, became the first female skater to land a triple salchow–triple loop combination.

1996 Michelle Kwan, of Torrance, California, won the first of four world championships.

1997 Tara Lipinski's rise to fame came quickly. She became the youngest women's figure skating champion in history, winning both the U.S. championship and, one month later, the world championship in Lausanne, Switzerland. In winning the worlds on March 26 at the age of 14 years, 9 months, and 12 days, she was a month younger than the legendary Norwegian Sonja Henie was when she won the first of 10 consecutive world titles in 1927.

1997 On February 13, Andrea Gardiner, 16, of Houston, Texas, became the first African American to win the U.S. junior ladies' national championship. Gardiner's performance included four triple jumps.

GOLF

Good health, good poise, good muscles, balanced physical development, a reserve fund of bodily energy—all these advantages are derived by women from their contact with sport.

The real charm of golf is its permanence. It is a hobby for a lifetime. The rudiments of golf are easily mastered, and one can play long hours alone and need not be skilled to enjoy the full recreational and health-giving value to the game.

—GLENNA COLLETT (VARE), the first great U.S. women's champion, 1930

1892 The first golf course designated for women only was built at Shinacock Hills, in New York.

1893 The first all-women's club was established at the Morris County Golf Club, in New Jersey.

1895 The first United States Golf Association (USGA) women's amateur championship was held in New York on November 9 at the Meadowbrook Club, in Hempstead, Long Island. Thirteen women competed. Mrs. Charles B. Brown won the tournament, finishing with a score of 132 for 18 holes.

1896 Beatrix Hoyt won the U.S. women's amateur championship at age 16. She held the record as the youngest champion until Laura Baugh won in 1971. Hoyt won three consecutive national championships, 1896–1898.

1897 The Women's Golf Association of Philadelphia was founded. It remained the only women's golf association in the country until 1900, when New York's Women's Metropolitan Golf Association was formed. Years later, in 1950, the Ladies Professional Golf Association (LPGA) became the first official sports organization for women.

1900 The first Olympic gold medal won by a woman was in golf, won by Margaret Abbott. Golf was one of the three original Olympic sports for women—the others were tennis and yachting—but was later dropped from the games.

1922 The first national championship was held. Glenna Collette Vare, at age 19, won her first of six national championships, taking the title again in 1925, 1928–'30, and 1935. She was the first great American golfer. The Vare Trophy, given each year by the LPGA, is named after her.

1926 Freida Carter invented miniature golf. Carter was part owner of a resort, and her invention quickly became popular. In the next four years, 25,000 courses were built.

1932 In May, the first international women's golf match took place between the United States and Great Britain. The tournament was named the Curtis Cup, after Margaret and Harriet Curtis, two accomplished Boston golfers. The match is held every two years, alternating sites between the United States and Great Britain/Ireland. Today, the European team is composed of players from England, Ireland, Scotland, and Wales.

1938 Patty Berg became the first woman to sweep the major U.S. amateur women's tournaments. On August 16, 1998, Grace Pak, of South Korea, became the first player to match Berg's accomplishment.

1941 The first women's national collegiate golf tournament was organized by an all-women group of physical educators from Ohio State

BABE DIDRIKSON. (PHOTO © BETTMAN/CORBIS.)

University under the guidance of Gladys Palmer. It was the first inter-collegiate championship for women in any sport. The winner was Eleanor Dudley.

1944 Betty Hicks, a crusader for women's golf, became the first president of the Women's Professional Golf Association, which she founded and incorporated with Hope Seignious and Ellen Griffin. The organization later merged with the LPGA.

1946 Patty Berg defeated Betty Jameson in the final round to win the first U.S. Women's Open.

1947 Mildred "Babe" Didrikson Zaharias became the first American woman to win the British women's golf championship. From 1940 to 1944, she won 22 amateur tournaments; in one stretch, she won 14 in a row. Her other extraordinary winning streak occurred in one 12-month period during 1946–'47, when she won 17 straight tournaments. She was the Associated Press Female Athlete of the Year six times.

1948 Betty Jameson shot a 295 to win the U.S. Women's Open, becoming the first woman golfer to score lower than 300 in a 72-hole tournament. The tournament was hosted by the Atlantic City Country Club, in Northfield, New Jersey, the only club to have hosted the Women's Open three times—1948, '65, and '75.

1949 The LPGA was established on January 1. Wilson Sporting Goods agreed to sponsor the formation of the association. Patty Berg was one of the founders and the first president. The group became official in 1950.

1949 Louise Suggs became the first woman to win a major tournament by 14 strokes. At the U.S. Women's Open, she shot a 291, then a women's scoring record.

1950 During the 1950s, Patty Berg, one of the great pioneers of the game, became the first female golfer to have career earnings of $100,000. In her playing days, she was the Associated Press Female Athlete of the Year three times and had 57 professional wins.

1950 Founded by 12 women golfers including Babe Didrikson Zaharias, Louise Suggs, and Patty Berg, the LPGA started with a 14-event schedule and $50,000 in prize money. It was the first women's professional sports organization run entirely by players.

1950 At age 16, Marlene Bauer (Hague), a teenage prodigy, was the youngest member of the newly formed LPGA tour. Forty years later, she was the oldest active member.

1950 During the LPGA's first season, Babe Didrickson Zaharias won $14,800—more than any other player.

1953 The LPGA created the Vare Trophy, in honor of Glenna Collett Vare, a pioneer and champion in the sport. The trophy is awarded each year to the woman with the lowest score on the tour.

1956 On September 17, Ann Gregory became the first African American woman to compete in a national championship conducted by the USGA, at the U.S. women's amateur tournament held at Meridan Hills Country Club, in Indianapolis.

1959 Mickey Wright became the first woman to win back-to-back U.S. Open championships.

1960 The LPGA National Golf School was formed under the guidance of Shirley Spark and Barbara Rotrig.

1961 Mickey Wright became the first woman to win three consecutive majors, considered the grand slam of women's golf: the Titleholders (Masters), the U.S. Women's Open, and the LPGA Championship. Wright was also the first woman to win the Open and the LPGA Championship in the same year; she repeated this feat in 1963.

1962 The LPGA Rookie of the Year Award was created. Mary Mills was the first recipient.

1962 Patty Berg was the first woman to record a hole in one in a USGA competition. She was also the first American woman golfer to give an exhibition in Japan.

1962 Mickey Wright became the first female golfer to win four consecutive tour events two years in a row.

1963 Women's golf was televised for the first time during the final rounds of the U.S. Women's Open.

1963 Mickey Wright won 13 tournaments out of 32 tour events, a record that still stands.

1964 Althea Gibson earned her LPGA player's card by finishing in the top 80 percent in three tournaments. Gibson, a tennis champion, took up golf at age 32. In 1963, she became the first African American woman to play on the LPGA professional tour.

1966 Kathy Whitworth won the inaugural LPGA Player of the Year Award. Whitworth won the award every year through 1973.

1967 Catherine LaCoste became the first amateur to win the U.S. Open.

1967 Patty Berg, Betty Jameson, Betsy Rawls, Louise Suggs, Mickey Wright, and Babe Didrikson Zaharias were inducted into the LPGA Hall of Fame as the first members.

1969 JoAnne Carner, playing as an amateur, won a tournament on the professional tour. No amateur has done this since. A multiple winner of the LPGA Player of the Year Award as well as a multiple recipient of the Vare Trophy, Carner set an earnings record in the 1980s, winning more than $200,000 in three consecutive years.

1969 Mickey Wright's 68-win total was the most by any player in a single decade in LPGA history.

1970 Betsy Rawls, a Phi Beta Kappa graduate of the University of Texas, winner of 55 tournaments, and the fourth-ranked player on the all-time list, became the first woman to serve on the rules committee for the men's U.S. Open. Rawls led the LPGA tour in victories in 1952, '57, and '59 and also won the Vare Trophy in '59.

1971 Marlene Bauer Hague became the first woman to shoot nine holes in 29 strokes, a performance unsurpassed for 13 years.

1975 Amy Alcott was a 19-year-old rookie on the LPGA tour when she won the Orange Blossom Classic, only her third tournament. Alcott set a record for the fastest career win and was Rookie of the Year.

1975 The LPGA went from a player-run organization to a business. Betsy Rawls became the LPGA's first paid tournament director and for many years was head of the McDonald's Championship.

1976 The LPGA established a qualifying system for all entrants.

1976 Judy Rankin became the first female golfer to win more than $100,000 in a single season, with a take of $150,734. She had set an earlier record in 1959 when, at age 14, she won the Missouri Amateur and became the youngest player to win a tournament. Rankin collected $122,890 in prize money in 1977, winning the Vare Trophy and Player of the Year Award. Her 25 top-10 finishes set a record that still stands.

1978 Nancy Lopez is credited with putting women's golf in the limelight. She was the first female golfer to be named Rookie of the Year and Player of the Year in the same year. Lopez won five consecutive tournaments and a total of nine titles, winning the Vare Trophy and thus becoming the only player in LPGA history to win all three awards in the same season. She was also named the Associated Press Female Athlete of the Year.

1978 On July 10, Nancy Lopez appeared on the cover of *Sports Illustrated*. Her rookie earnings of $153,010 set a record for both women and men. In 1979, she won eight tournaments and received the Vare Trophy again.

1979 In the Women's Kemper Open at Mesa Verde Country Club, Jo Ann Washam had two holes in one, the most in one tournament.

1980 The first time the Professional Golfers' Association (PGA) allowed female caddies in the U.S. Open was at the Baltusrol Golf Club, in Springfield, New Jersey. Pamela Shuttleworth, of Santa Monica, California, caddied for Jim Dent.

1980 Jane Blalock became the first woman to earn more than $100,000 four years in a row, 1977–'80. During her career, she won 29 official LPGA events.

1980 Beth Daniel, in only her second year on the LPGA tour, became the first woman to exceed $200,000 in earnings in a single year, with $231,000. She finished her career with 32 LPGA titles.

1981 With a third-place finish in the U.S. Women's Open, Kathy Whitworth became the first female golfer to surpass $1 million in total career earnings.

1981 Carol Mann retired after 21 seasons on the LPGA tour. She had 38 career victories and won more than $500,000. In 1978, she set a record for playing 23 rounds under 70, which was broken by Amy Alcott in 1981. In 1965, Mann won the U.S. Open, and in 1968, she won 10 titles and the Vare Trophy.

1982 The Nabisco Dinah Shore tournament was the first LPGA event to have national television coverage for all four rounds.

1982 The first NCAA national collegiate golf championships were held at Stanford University (California). Kathy Baker, of Tulsa, Oklahoma, won with a score of 295.

1983 Juli Inkster became the only golfer to win two LPGA tournaments as a rookie. In her first year on the professional circuit, she won the Nabisco Dinah Shore and the du Maurier Classic. Prior to 1983, the Titleholders and the Western Open were majors.

1984 Kathy Whitworth broke Sam Snead's record of 84 lifetime wins. Whitworth became the winningest professional golfer in history, with a total of 88 wins.

1985 Patty Sheehan set an LPGA record when she won more than $200,000 for 11 consecutive years. She also earned $1 million faster than any other player, after playing in only 115 tour events.

1986 Pat Bradley set a single-season earnings record when she became the first woman golfer to earn $492,000.

1987 At age 30, Nancy Lopez was the youngest player to be inducted into the LPGA Hall of Fame. In 1985 she was the first woman to reach 20 under par (at the Henderson Classic) with a score of 20 under 265. In her career, she won 48 titles, was a four-time player of the year, and was a three-time Vare trophy winner.

1990 The Solheim Cup, featuring biennial matches between top female professionals from the United States and Europe, was established. The event consists of three days of competition similar to the men's Ryder Cup. The first Solheim Cup was held at Lake Nova Golf Club, in Orlando, Florida.

1990 Juli Inkster became the first woman to win the only professional golf tournament in the world in which men and women compete head-to-head. She parred the 18th hole at Pebble Beach to defeat PGA tour member Mark Brooks.

1990 Beth Daniel became the first woman to win more than $800,000 in a single season. She was also the United Press International Female Athlete of the Year.

1991 Financial rewards for women continued to grow. In 1989, Pat Bradley became the first woman to top the $2 million mark in career earnings; she reached the $3 million mark in 1990 and passed $4 million in 1991.

1994 In recognition of her contributions to women's golf, Dinah Shore was inducted into the LPGA Hall of Fame as its only honorary member.

1994 Amy Alcott marked her 29th career win on the LPGA tour. In 1988, she became the third golfer to pass $2 million in career earnings. Her first major victory was the Peter Jackson (later du Maurier) Classic in 1979. In 1980, she won the U.S. Open and averaged 71.51 to claim the Vare Trophy. Alcott won the Nabisco Dinah Shore in 1983, '88, and '91.

1996 Former golfer Judy Bell was elected the first woman president of the USGA.

1996 The NCAA national collegiate women's golf championship was split into two championships, Division I and a combined Division II and III. The University of Arizona won the first Division I championship, and Methodist College (Fayetteville, North Carolina) won the Division II and III championship. Methodist won four championships since 1996, the last in 2001.

1998 A record eight official events had $1 million-plus purses, including all four major championships.

1998 After completing the Standard Register PING tournament in Arizona, Betsy King became the first LPGA player to exceed $6 million in career earnings.

1998 The U.S. Women's Open lasted 92 holes, making it the longest tournament in the history of women's golf. It also marked the first sudden death in play-off history, as Jenny Chuasiriporn, of Duke University (Durham, North Carolina), and Se Ri Pak, of South Korea, vied for the title. Pak won, marking her second straight victory.

1998 In May, the World Golf Hall of Fame, which includes the LPGA Hall of Fame, opened in Saint Augustine, Florida.

1998 Arizona State won its sixth national collegiate golf championship, more than any other school, with titles in 1990, '93, '94, '95, '97, and '98.

1999 In winning the Nabisco Dinah Shore, Dottie Pepper became the first woman to shoot a 19-under-par 269, setting the LPGA record for lowest 72-hole score to win a major.

1999 After years of being known as the toughest Hall of Fame in sports, the LPGA Hall of Fame revamped its requirements. The old requirement of 30 wins was changed to a point system under which players must earn 27 Hall of Fame points.

1999 Juli Inkster won five tournaments, including two major championships—the U.S. Women's Open and the McDonald's LPGA Championship—becoming just the fourth LPGA player to achieve a grand slam. Pat Bradley—1986, Louise Suggs—1957, and Mickey Wright—1962 also won all four major championships. Wright and Suggs did so under a slightly different format that changed in 1983.

2000 The inaugural Nancy Lopez Award, named in honor of the world's best-known female golfer, was presented to Kellee Booth, an LPGA tour rookie. Booth was named to the all-American first team three times at Arizona State. She won five amateur championships in 1999.

2000 Hall of Famer Juli Inkster won the LPGA Championship at the Dupont Country Club, becoming the first back-to-back winner of the event since Patty Sheehan in 1983 and '84.

2000 Judy Rankin, the first woman to break the $100,000 barrier and the winner of 26 tour events, was voted into the LPGA Tour Hall of Fame. She was the first player elected from the tour's veteran category, which was established in 1999. Rankin set an LPGA record in 1977 with 25 finishes in the top 10.

2000 Dorthy Delsin became the youngest LPGA winner in 25 years when she won the Giant Eagle Classic, in Howland, Ohio, by defeating Pat Hunter in a play-off. Delsin was 19 years, 11 months, and 4 days old, and clinched the Rookie of the Year Award. On February 23, 1975, Amy Alcott won the Orange Blossom Classic the day after her 19th birthday. On March 2, 1952, Marlene Hagge won the Sarasota Florida Open at the age of 18 years and 14 days.

2000 Lisa Cave, of Florida Southern University, won her second consecutive Division II and III title, becoming the first back-to-back winner of the championship, shooting 313 in 1999 and 310 in 2000.

2000 The LPGA celebrated its 50th anniversary. Eighteen women have been inducted into its Hall of Fame.

2001 On May 14, Morgan Pressel, of Boca Raton, Florida, nine days away from her 13th birthday, became the youngest player to qualify for an LPGA event. At the U.S. Women's Open, Pressel posted back-to-back 77s, missing the cut. In 1994, Rae Anne Staples qualified at age 14, and in 2000, Naree Wongluekiet also qualified at age 14.

2001 On August 12, Wendy Ward set an LPGA scoring record for a 54-hole tournament. Her 21-under-par 195 at the Wendy's Championship for Children, in New Albany, Ohio, was a tour record in both par and scoring.

2001 In September, the LPGA named the Weetabix Women's British Open as its newest major championship, replacing the du Maurier Classic.

2001 At the second round of qualifying for the U.S. junior girls golf championship, 17-year-old Christina Kim, of San Jose, California, set a USGA record with an 8-under-par 62. Kim's score bettered the 63s shot by Jack Nicklaus, Tom Weiskopf, and Johnny Miller at the U.S. Open and by Helen Alfredsson at the Women's Open in 1994.

2002 In February, Michelle Wie, 12 years old, became the youngest golfer to qualify for an LPGA tour event. She shot an 83 at Waikoloa Beach Resort to earn a spot in the season opening Takefuji Classic. Natalie Gulbis was previously the youngest qualifier, at age 14 in 1997.

GYMNASTICS

IN ORDER to compete at the highest level, a gymnast must have absolute precision, tremendous courage, unwavering confidence, and the highest degree of stamina, along with a flair for the dramatic.

Women's artistic gymnastics is composed of four events: vault, uneven bars, balance beam, and floor exercise. The winner of the all-around competition is the person with the highest total score from each of the four events. The highest score a gymnast can have on any apparatus is a 10. Unlike most sports, the elite gymnasts do not generally compete at the collegiate level. Because of this, collegiate gymnastics has a separate chronology within this chapter. In addition, rhythmic gymnastics and tumbling and trampoline also have separate chronologies within gymnastics.

Artistic Gymnastics

1862 The first women's gymnastics class was held at Mount Holyoke College (South Hadley, Massachusetts).

1897 The Amateur Athletic Union (AAU) became the governing body for the sport.

1923 The AAU began sponsoring women's competitions.

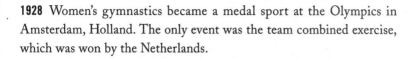

1928 Women's gymnastics became a medal sport at the Olympics in Amsterdam, Holland. The only event was the team combined exercise, which was won by the Netherlands.

1931 The first AAU championships for women were held. Roberta Ranck Bonniwell, of Philadelphia, won the side horse and parallel bars. Bonniwell also won the side horse in 1933 and was the team leader in the 1948 Olympics in London. She was the first and only American woman to coach Olympians in both gymnastics and track and field.

1934 International competition for women began with the world championships in the all-around. Medals for individual apparatus were added in 1950.

1936 A U.S. team appeared in the Olympics for the first time, in Berlin, but did not medal.

1945 During her era, Mariane Barone was one of very few athletes to have won national titles in more than one event. Barone won national gymnastics championships in the uneven parallel bars in 1945 and 1951, and she won the vault at the nationals in 1950. She competed in the Olympics as part of the U.S. women's team that won a bronze medal in 1948.

1948 At the Olympics in London, the U.S. women's team won the bronze in the combined exercise—the first Olympic medal ever in the sport for a U.S. team.

1948 The all-around event and side horse vault were held at the Olympics for the first time.

1950 Medals for individual apparatus were added at the world championship.

1951 Clara Schroth Lomady won a record 39 AAU national titles from 1941 to 1951. Lomady won 11 consecutive balance beam titles and was an Olympian in 1948 and 1952.

1952 Individual gymnastics events were introduced as medal sports at the Olympics in Helsinki, Finland. Athletes competed in the uneven bars, side horse vault, and all-around competition.

1962 Herb Vogel became the gymnastics coach at Southern Illinois University and over the next 20 years was instrumental in the growth and development of the sport. He organized and directed the first national collegiate championships and was director of the first United States Gymnastics Federation national women's championship.

1963 The United States Gymnastics Federation, now called USA Gymnastics, took over from the AAU as the national governing body. It sets the rules and policies and trains and selects the U.S. gymnastic team for the Olympics and world competitions.

1964 Doris Fuchs Brause and Muriel Davis Grossfield were the first women to make three Olympic teams—1956, 1960, and 1964. Grossfield was the winner of 17 national titles.

1968 At the Olympics in Mexico City, 15-year-old Cathy Rigby finished 17th in the balance beam and 16th in the all-around, setting a record for the highest Olympic finish ever for a U.S. gymnast.

1970 On November 27, at the world championships in Yugoslavia, Cathy Rigby became the first American ever to medal in international competition, winning the silver in the balance beam. In 1972, at the Olympics in Munich, she finished 10th in the all-around, the highest a U.S. woman had ever placed in this event.

a team silver, another silver in the individual vault, and bronze in both the uneven bars and the floor exercise. Retton was named the Associated Press Female Athlete of the Year as well as Sportswoman of the Year by *Sports Illustrated*.

1984 Julianne McNamara became the first American woman gymnast to win an individual Olympic gold medal, with a daring performance on the uneven bars. She was also the first American to win a silver medal in the floor exercise, with her teammate Mary Lou Retton taking the bronze. Retton and McNamara were the first U.S. women to medal in the event.

1984 The U.S. women's team won the silver medal in Los Angeles, the highest finish ever for a U.S. Olympic team.

1984 Kathy Johnson became the first U.S. woman to medal on the balance beam, winning the bronze.

1985 Mary Lou Retton was the first gymnast and youngest athlete inducted into the U.S. Olympic Hall of Fame.

1988 At the Olympics in Seoul, South Korea, Phoebe Mills won the bronze medal in the balance beam.

1991 Fifteen-year-old Kim Zmeskal, at 4 feet, 7 inches, and weighing 80 pounds, did something no American woman had done before when she won the gold medal in the all-around competition at the world championships in Indianapolis. In the 1992 world championships, she won gold in the balance beam and the floor exercise. She was the U.S. all-around champion three consecutive times—in 1990, '91, and '92.

1992 Sandy Knapp was the first woman selected to chair the board of USA Gymnastics. She was reelected for another four-year term in 1996, serving until 2000.

1992 At the age of 10, Dominique Moceanu was the youngest gymnast ever to make the U.S. junior national team.

1992 At the Olympics in Barcelona, Spain, Shannon Miller won five medals, taking the silver in the all-around and the balance beam, and taking the bronze in the uneven bars, floor exercise, and team competition.

1992 The U.S. team won the bronze medal at the Olympics in Barcelona, becoming the first U.S. team to medal in a nonboycotted Olympics.

1992 The first individual world championships were held in Paris. Kim Zmeskal won the gold in the balance beam and floor exercise, and Betty Okino won the silver in the uneven bars.

1993 At the world championships, Shannon Miller won the gold in the all-around, uneven bars, and floor exercise. Dominique Dawes won the silver in the uneven bars and balance beam.

1994 Miller, one of the most popular and successful gymnasts of all time, became the only American woman to win consecutive world championship all-around titles, duplicating her 1993 performance. The U.S. team also won in 1994, with Miller winning the gold in the balance beam.

1994 Dominique Dawes won the U.S. national championship. She is also the only person in the world who has performed five skills in a row on the balance beam.

1995 Thirteen-year-old Dominique Moceanu became the youngest U.S. champion. Also in 1995, at the world championships, she won the silver in the balance beam in a tie with Lilia Podkopayeva, of the Ukraine, and helped earn a team bronze. In 1996, as a member of the U.S. gold-medal team at the Atlanta Olympics, she became the youngest athlete ever to be pictured on a Wheaties box, when the gymnastics team was featured.

1996 Shannon Miller, the most accomplished U.S. gymnast in history, added two gold medals at the Atlanta Olympics to her five from Barcelona. She won a team gold and an individual gold on the balance beam, giving her a record seven Olympic medals.

1996 Kerri Strug's second vault at the Olympics ranks near the top of the all-time greatest sports moments. The U.S. team was in close competition for the team gold medal. Strug injured her ankle on her first vault and landed in great pain. She had to perform her second vault immediately because there are no time-outs in gymnastics. The world was watching as she attempted a Yurchenka one-and-a-half—a back handspring onto the horse and then a one-and-a-half-twist back flip into the air. She stuck her landing and then fell to the mat. Moments later, her score was posted. The score was good, and the U.S. team won its first ever all-around Olympic gold medal. After that, the team became known as The Magnificent Seven for its stars: Amanda Borden, Amy Chow, Dominique Dawes, Shannon Miller, Dominique Moceanu, Jaycei Phelphr, and Kerri Strug.

1996 At the Atlanta Olympics, Amy Chow won the silver medal in the uneven bars, and Dominique Dawes won the bronze in the floor exercise.

1996 Dominique Dawes won her third national championship in the vault (1993 and 1994), her third consecutive championship in the uneven bars, the balance beam, and the all-around title.

1998 To help prevent injury, the International Gymnastics Federation mandated that women use a thicker mat for floor exercises. A 20-centimeter mat, which male gymnasts had been using for 15 years, was adopted for better absorption.

1999 At the world team trials in Kansas City, Stephanie Carter became the first American to complete a double-twisting double-back in competition.

1999 Kristine Maloney became the first woman to win back-to-back U.S. national all-around titles—1998 and 1999—since Kim Zmeskal in 1990 and '92.

2000 A new Olympic rule was adopted, requiring a girl to be at least 16 years old in order to compete.

2001 Tasha Schweikert won the all-around title at the U.S. gymnastics championships in Philadelphia. Schweikert, a member of the 2000 Olympic team, finished with 74.912 points. Tabitha Yim took second, and Mohini Bhardwaj, an 11-time all-American at UCLA, finished third.

2001 Kristal Uzelac, at age 15, became the first woman to win the national junior all-around championship three times. Her total score was 74.00. Hollie Vise took second, with 72.525.

2001 The world championships were held October 28–November 4 in Ghent, Belgium.

Collegiate Gymnastics

1982 The first National Collegiate Athletic Association (NCAA) championships were held. The University of Utah won its first of five consecutive team championships.

1982 In the first individual championships, Sue Stednitz, of the University of Utah, won the all-around and the balance beam. Elaine Alfano, also of Utah, won the vault; Lisa Shirk, of the University of Pittsburgh, won the uneven bars; and Mary Ayotte-Law, of Oregon State University, won the floor exercise.

1985 Utah's Elaine Alfano won her third vault title—1982, '83, and '85—a record. Heather Steep, of the University of Georgia, won back-to-back

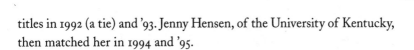

titles in 1992 (a tie) and '93. Jenny Hensen, of the University of Kentucky, then matched her in 1994 and '95.

1987 Lucy Wener, of the University of Georgia, won her third national title in the uneven bars, 1985–'87. In 1995, Beth Wymer, of the University of Michigan, won her third title in the balance beam, with ties in both 1993 and '94.

1989 Kim Hamilton, of UCLA, won a record third consecutive title in the floor exercise.

1992 Missy Marlowe, of Utah, and Jenny Hensen, of Kentucky, share the record for the most individual titles in a tournament, with four. In 1992, Marlowe captured the all-around, uneven bars, balance beam, and floor exercise. In 1995, Hensen secured the all-around, vault, balance beam, and floor exercise. Hensen holds eight individual career titles.

1992 The University of Utah set the record for most individual championships in a year, with five. Winners were Missy Marlowe in the all-around, uneven bars, balance beam, and floor exercise, and Kristen Kenoyu in the vault.

1995 Coach Greg Marsden and the University of Utah won a record ninth team championship.

1995 Kentucky's Jenny Hensen won a record third consecutive all-around championship. Kelly Garrison-Steves, of the University of Oklahoma, won back-to-back all-around titles in 1987 and '88, and Kim Arnold, of the University of Georgia, did the same in 1997 and '98.

1997 Repeating her 1996 performance, Summer Reis, of Utah State, won her second national title on the balance beam, in a tie. Two other gymnasts hold back-to-back national titles on the balance beam: Joy Selig, of Oregon State, 1989 (tie) and '90; and Jenny Hensen, of Kentucky, 1994 and '95.

1999 On April 24, the University of Georgia edged the University of Michigan by a score of 196.85 to 195.55 to win the NCAA women's gymnastic title. Georgia, with a record of 67–0, over the prior two years, became the only team in the country to have an undefeated record for two consecutive years.

2000 At the NCAA championships in Boise, Idaho, Mohini Bhardwaj, of UCLA, won three individual titles: balance beam, uneven bars, and vault.

2001 On July 21, in Athens, Georgia, UCLA won its second consecutive NCAA championship. The Bruins' Yvonne Touser and Mohini Bhardwaj captured individual titles in the uneven bars and the floor exercise, respectively.

Rhythmic Gymnastics

Rhythmic gymnastics is an exclusively feminine sport that is a choreographed blend of the mastery of body expression with the technical handling of apparatus such as hoops, ribbons, balls, clubs, and ropes. These come together in an imaginative dance routine that exhibits flexibility and coordination. Rhythmic gymnastics is popular around the world, with more than 40 countries participating in the annual rhythmic gymnastic world championships.

1928 The first women's gymnastics events appeared in the Olympics in 1928 in Amsterdam. The U.S. women first competed in 1936 in Berlin.

1962 The International Gymnastics Federation officially recognized rhythmic gymnastics as a sport.

1963 The first rhythmic world championships took place in Budapest, Hungary. Twenty-eight athletes from 10 European countries competed.

1970 The United States Gymnastics Federation, now known as USA Gymnastics, became the national governing body of the sport.

1973 The United States sent its first delegation to the rhythmic world championships.

1984 The individual all-around competition was added to the Olympics in Los Angeles.

1988 Wendy Hillard, a nine-time senior national team member (still a record) and one of the true U.S. legends and pioneers in the sport, competed from 1978 to '88. In 1978, she became the first African American to make the U.S. rhythmic gymnastics national team, and in both 1981 and '83, she was elected captain. In 1980, Hillard won the dual meet between the United States and Canada. In 1978, she won the bronze, and in 1980, she won the silver, in the Four Continents Championships in Canada. In 1986, she placed third in every event. Hillard's innovative routine, using two ribbons at the same time, became her trademark.

1996 The rhythmic group event was added as a medal sport at the Atlanta Olympics.

2001 In March, a new code of points was first used at the 2001 Rhythmic Challenge in Colorado Springs. A new scoring system was also introduced and is based on a 30-point scale, with 10 points each for technical evaluation, artistic evaluation, and execution.

2001 At the national championships in Philadelphia, Jessica Howard, of Jacksonville, Florida, won her third consecutive national senior all-around, with a score of 103.225. Olga Karmansky, of Brooklyn, New York, placed second, with 100.55 points. Lisa Wang, of Buffalo Grove, Illinois, won the juniors, with 85.850 points.

Tumbling and Trampoline

1999 Trampoline and tumbling became recognized sports within USA Gymnastics. At the world championships in Sun City, South Africa, Erin Maguire won the bronze medal.

1999 The U.S. women's team won the world championship.

2000 In Saint Louis, Jennifer Parilla won her second national trampoline championship, having taken the title in 1998. Amanda Lentz repeated as the national tumbling champion, following her 1999 victory.

2000 Trampoline made its debut as an Olympic sport in Sydney, Australia.

2001 The trampoline and tumbling national championships were held in San Antonio, Texas. Alaina Herbert scored 103.10 points, earning the gold in trampoline, and Alisha Robinson took first in tumbling, with 35.30 points.

2001 At the trampoline and tumbling world championships in Odense, Denmark, Lajean Davis, of Roscoe, Illinois, won the tumbling silver medal—the only medal for the United States.

HORSE RACING

As the first woman to win a Triple Crown race—the Belmont Stakes in 1993—and with 3,545 trips to the winner's circle, Julie Krone brought a whole new level of credibility to women jockeys. She won more than $81 million in her career and was the first woman inducted into the National Museum of Racing Hall of Fame.

1907 The first known woman jockey, Dorothy Tyler, won her first race, a quarter miler, at the age of 14, competing against several experienced jockeys, one of whom was a professional.

1911 Nan Jane Aspinwall became the first woman to ride coast to coast across North America, traveling 3,000 miles from San Francisco to New York in 301 days.

1968 Kathy Kusner, a world-class dressage rider, was the first woman to earn her jockey's license. The Maryland Racing Commission awarded her a license after a year-long legal battle. Unfortunately, she suffered a riding accident that resulted in a broken leg, preventing her from becoming the first woman to race on a pari-mutuel track.

1969 Three women were entered to ride in a race sanctioned by the National Steeplechase Association—the Spring Race, in Middleburg, Virginia. Ready Snodgrass, Katherine Chatfield Taylor (Kingsley), and Mary Ryan all competed, helping the cause of recruiting more women licensees, but didn't place.

1969 Diane Crump became the first American woman jockey to ride at a pari-mutuel track, in Hialeah, Florida. She rode a 48-to-1 long shot to a 10th-place finish in a field of 12.

1969 On February 22, Barbara Jo Rubin rode Cohesion to victory at Charles Town, West Virginia, to become the first woman jockey to win a race on a Thoroughbred track. In spite of harassments and fouls from male jockeys, Rubin won 9 out of her first 11 races. She was the first woman jockey to ride in New York and New Jersey.

1970 On May 2, Diane Crump became the first woman to ride in the Kentucky Derby. Astride Fathom, she finished 15th in a field of 17.

1971 On June 30, Mary Bacon became the first woman to ride 100 winners, nailing her 100th at the Thistletown Race Track in Cleveland, Ohio, aboard California Lassie.

1973 Robyn Smith became the first woman jockey to win a stakes race, riding North Sea to victory in the $27,450 Paumanauk Handicap at Aqueduct Raceway, in Queens, New York.

1982 Julieanne "Julie" Krone became the first female jockey ever to win a racing title at a major Thoroughbred track, in Atlantic City, New Jersey.

1987 Julie Krone became the first woman to win four races in one day, in New York. The same year, Krone was the first woman to win a riding title—most races won in a year—at a major track, for her 130 wins at Monmouth Park. She also became the first woman to compete in the Breeders' Cup. In 1988, she passed Patricia Cooksey's career record of 1,203 wins, to become the all-time winningest female jockey. In 1999, she earned her 3,500th career victory at the Fair Grounds, in New Orleans, making her the first female jockey to reach this number and pushing her earnings to nearly $80 million.

1989 Molly Blise was the first American ever selected to compete in the European Young Rider Championship, winning a silver in the three-day event.

1991 On June 8, Julie Krone became the first female jockey to ride in New York's Belmont Stakes, the third leg of the Triple Crown. At Belmont in May 1993, astride Colonial Affair, she became the first woman to win a Triple Crown race.

1995 Blythe Miller won the overall jockey's championship for the second consecutive year, having narrowly missed the title in 1993.

1996 Jenine Sahadi became the first female trainer to win $1 million, when Lit De Justice captured the Breeders' Cup Sprint.

1997 Tami Purcell became the first female jockey to win the American Quarter Horse, racing's richest race. She was also the leading female jockey, with seven victories. She tied for seventh as the leading jockey of either sex in American Quarter Horse Stakes races wins for the period August 1997 to July 1998. Purcell is the all-time leading female jockey in American Quarter Horse racing history.

1997 In September, 22-year-old jockey Chelsea Zupan entered the record books with a seven-race winning streak at Emerald Downs, in Auburn, Washington.

2000 On April 20, Jenine Sahadi became the first female trainer to win the Santa Anita Derby in its 63-year history.

2000 On August 7, Julie Krone, Thoroughbred racing's winningest female jockey, became the first woman inducted into the National Museum of Racing Hall of Fame. Krone won 3,545 races, earned more than $81 million, and won 119 graded stakes races. She retired on April 8, 1999.

2001 On August 26, at the 100-mile Pan American Endurance Championship, at South Woodstock, Vermont, Heather Bergantz, of San Jose, California, won the individual gold in 10 hours, 39 minutes, 42 seconds. She finished ahead of U.S. equestrian team veteran Melissa Crain, of Franklin, Tennessee, by 21 minutes. Rita Swift, of Worthington, West Virginia, was third. The U.S. team of Brenda Baird, Stagg Newman, Dina Rojek, and Meg Sleeper took first in the team competition.

ICE HOCKEY

WOMEN'S ICE hockey is one of the fastest-growing sports in the United States. The number of girls' and women's teams registered with USA Hockey rose from 149 in 1990–'91 to 1,406 at the end of 2000, a growth rate of more than 900 percent. In 1990–'91, the total number of players registered was 6,336, and at the end of 2000, the number was 39,693. Similar to the men's version, each team has six players on the ice at one time. The challenge is to hit the puck (which is small and can travel up to 100 miles per hour) into the opposing team's net. The rules are the same for women as for men, except checking is not allowed (unless two opposing players are attempting to play the puck): each goal counts as one point and there are three 20-minute periods in a game.

1916 The first international women's ice hockey tournament was played in Cleveland, Ohio, featuring teams from the United States and Canada.

1917 The first ice hockey game between two American women's teams was played in New York City. The hometown Saint Nicholas Rink team shut out a team from Boston in a 1–0 battle.

1920s College teams began to form in the United States and Canada.

1930s The sport developed more in Canada than the United States, with a proliferation of Canadian women's leagues. The game was slow to catch on outside of universities.

1964 Brown University (Providence, Rhode Island) was the first college to have a women's team club team.

1975 The Assabet Valley Girls Club, of Concord, Massachusetts, won the U.S. national ice hockey title. When the club won again in 1976, it became the first and only team to win in consecutive years.

1975 Brown University sanctioned the first varsity women's team. By the end of the '70s, Cornell University (Ithaca, New York), Hamilton College (Clinton, New York), Ithaca College (New York), the University of Minnesota, Providence College (Rhode Island), and the University of New Hampshire had programs. Club teams were also forming in the Midwest and Northeast.

1977 The Ivy League colleges established the first women's hockey tournament.

1979 Laura Stamm became the first woman to coach a professional team, the San Diego Mariners.

1987 The first Women's World Invitational Tournament was held in North York and Mississauga, Ontario, with teams from Canada, Holland, Japan, Sweden, Switzerland, and the United States. The U.S. team defeated Sweden, 5–0, for the silver medal.

1990s The growth of the sport continued, doubling each year.

1990 The U.S. women's ice hockey team was established to compete in the first International Ice Hockey Federation (IIHF) world championships, held in March in Ottawa, Ontario. Canada took the gold and went on to take future championships as well—including 1992 in Tampere, Finland, and 1994 in Lake Placid, New York. The United States won the silver in each of the three tournaments, losing to Canada each time, while Finland took the bronze.

1990 Kelly Dyer was MVP for the first U.S. women's ice hockey team when it competed for the first time in a world championship. Dyer was from the Assabet Valley women's hockey program in Concord.

1990 Body checking was allowed in the world championships but later was ruled illegal.

1990 The IIHF held its first women's world championships.

1992 The sport was gaining a whole new public profile, with more than 100 club and varsity teams in U.S. colleges.

1992 On November 17, the International Olympic Committee announced that it would include women's hockey as a full medal sport in Nagano, Japan, in 1998.

1992 Sherry Ross was the first woman to be a National Hockey League analyst. Ross worked for the New Jersey Devils from 1992 to '95.

1993 Erin Whitten became the first female goalie credited with a win in a minor-league men's professional game, when the Toledo Storm won over the Dayton Bombers, 6–5, in the East Coast Hockey League.

1994 The USA Hockey Women's Hockey Player of the Year Award was established. Goaltender Erin Whitten was the first recipient.

1994 Minnesota became the first state to declare women's hockey a varsity sport on the high school level. On November 14, the first officially sanctioned game took place between South Saint Paul and Holy Angels at Richfield Ice Arena. Kelly Kegley, an eighth-grade center for South Saint Paul, scored the first official goal.

1995 The first IIHF Pacific women's hockey championships were held in San Jose, California. Canada, China, Japan, and the United States competed. Canada beat the United States in an overtime shoot-out to win the gold. In 1996, Canada beat the U.S. team again.

1995 Karen Bye, a five-time national team member, was named USA Hockey Women's Player of the Year.

1995 More than 20,000 girls and women were registered in U.S. hockey programs.

1996 On June 3, USA Hockey named Ben Smith, of Gloucester, Massachusetts, as the first full-time head coach of the U.S. women's national and Olympic teams. In 1998, he was named Coach of the Year by the United States Olympic Committee (USOC).

1996 In the longest collegiate ice hockey game ever played—men's or women's—the University of New Hampshire defeated Providence College, 3–2, in five overtimes to win the Eastern College Athletic Conference championships.

1997 Katie King, a forward at Brown University, was named the Ivy League Player of the Year for the third consecutive season. She was also named the Eastern College Athletic Conference Player of the Year.

1997 The fourth world championships were held in Kitchener, Ontario. Canada again won the gold, defeating the United States in a 4–3 game, and Finland won its fourth bronze.

1997 In December, the U.S. team won its first gold medal in international play by defeating Canada, 3–0, at the Three Nations Cup, in Lake Placid. It was the first time Canada had been held scoreless in international play.

1997 On April 1, the USA Hockey Foundation launched its first annual award to honor the outstanding women's intercollegiate ice hockey player. The Patty Kazmaier Memorial Award is comparable to the Hobey Baker

Memorial Award for male players. Kazmaier, a former Princeton star, died in 1990 from a rare blood disorder. Brandy Fisher, of the University of New Hampshire, received the first award in 1998. Fisher scored the first goal ever in a national finals. She had a season total of 36 goals and 39 assists.

1998 The first American Women's College Hockey Alliance (AWCHA) Division I national championships were held at Boston's Fleet Center on March 20–22. Playing for the national title were the University of New Hampshire (first), Brown (second), Northeastern (third), and the University of Minnesota (fourth). New Hampshire defeated Brown, 4–1, for the title.

1998 New Hampshire's Winny Brodt was MVP of the national championship in March. The other finalists were Yale goalie Laurie Bellireau and Dartmouth forward Sara Hod.

1998 In Nagano, ice hockey made its Olympic debut. Six teams competed: Canada, China, Finland, Japan, Sweden, and the United States. The U.S. captain was Cammi Granato. On February 17, the U.S. team, in a thrilling game, won the first gold medal ever by defeating Canada, 3–1. This historic victory was significant in bringing increased attention to the sport.

1998 Vicki Kale, Deb Parece, and Evonne Young made ice hockey history in Nagano by being the first officials for an Olympic game.

1998 The U.S. national team was selected the USOC Team of the Year.

1999 At the IIHF women's world championships in March, the U.S. women's national team lost to Canada in the title game for the fifth time, 3–1.

1999 A. J. Mleczko, of Harvard, had the highest-scoring season in the history of women's intercollegiate ice hockey, with 114 points—37 points,

77 assists—in 34 games. She broke Harvard's all-time single-season and career scoring record for men and women. Mleczko also led Harvard to the 1999 AWCHA Division I national championship and won the Patty Kazmaier Award.

1999 Kristine Pierce, of Rochester (New York) Tech, received the Hockey Humanitarian Award. She was the first woman and first Division III player to earn the award, which is given to college hockey's "finest citizen." Pierce served as a volunteer for 24 organizations, including Big Brothers Big Sisters, Habitat for Humanity, Camp Good Days, and Special Times.

2000 USA Hockey, the sport's national governing body, established a standing women's national team. It is the first national women's hockey team established for any country.

2000 Cammi Granato was the only player to be a member of all six U.S. women's national teams that competed in the IIHF world championships. She ranked as the all-time leading scorer in the history of the IIHF women's world championships, as well as in the history of the women's program.

2000 In April, the U.S. national team lost to Canada in the gold-medal game of the IIHF world championships for the sixth time, earning its sixth silver medal. Canada won by a score of 3–2 in overtime.

2000 On April 23, Julie Sasner was named assistant coach for the U.S. national and Olympic teams, becoming the first female assistant coach for the women's U.S. national team.

2000 The University of Minnesota won the AWCHA Division I national championship by defeating Brown, 4–2. Minnesota was the first Western Collegiate Hockey Association team to win a national title.

2000 Ali Brewer, a senior goaltender at Brown University, won the Patti Kazmaier Memorial Award. She finished her career as Brown's all-time leader in saves and shutouts.

2001 The first NCAA women's ice hockey championships were held in Minneapolis.

2001 For the first time, Russia placed in the medal standings at a World Championship tournament, beating Finland for the bronze. The United States took the silver, losing to Canada.

2001 At the IIHF world championships in Minnesota, the United States lost to Canada for the seventh time, going down 3–2. Cammi Granato was the leading scorer of the championships, with 13 points—7 goals, 6 assists.

2002 At the Olympics in Salt Lake City, six of the eight competing teams had competed in the Nagano games.

2002 The U.S. Olympic team was defeated by Canada in the gold medal game (3–2). The U.S. team had a 35–0 record and was 10–0 in Olympic competition.

2002 In March, Elmira (New York) won the first NCAA Division III women's championship by defeating Manhattanville (New York), 2–1. Freshman Laura Hurd of Elmira set a single-season scoring record and scored the winning goal.

JUDO

ONE OF the first documentations of women practicing judo in the United States was at the White House. President Theodore Roosevelt had a small dojo (training hall) in the basement, and his wife and sister-in-law joined him. President Roosevelt achieved the rank of brown belt, while the women were white belts. The belt ranks, in order, are white, yellow, green, brown (which has 3 degrees), and black (which has 10 degrees). Judo also has seven weight classes, ranging from under 48 kilograms, to previously over 72 kilograms, later changed to over 78 kilograms.

1940 Ruth Gardner Oshita, of Chicago, practiced judo at the city's judo club. She was a member of the Women's Army Corps in World War II and traveled to several countries in Europe, where she taught the sport to women. At the time, she was a brown belt, but when she returned to the United States, she was awarded *shodan*, which is a first-degree black belt, becoming the first U.S. woman to receive that rank.

1955 Rusty Stewart (Kanokogi) learned judo in New York and began teaching at a YMCA. She was the only woman training with 40 men.

1956 Rusty Stewart's team was invited to the YMCA state championships in Utica, New York. Women were not allowed to compete, but she wasn't going to be stopped. Stewart, who wore her hair short, bound her breasts and competed anyway. The team made it to the finals, and Stewart won her final match for the championship. When an official discovered that she was a woman, he threatened to disqualify the team if she didn't give back her medal.

1957 Rusty Stewart competed on her club team and won more than half of the interclub competitions against men.

1962 After getting her first-degree black belt, Rusty Stewart went to Japan to train. She continued her training at the Kodokan, considered the best training for judo at the time. Stewart worked her way up to the main dojo, the first time in Kodokan history that a woman was invited to practice in the main dojo. She received *nidan*, second-degree black belt, in 1962.

1963 Rusty Stewart petitioned the Amateur Athletic Union (AAU) to include women's judo for competition. At a judo club in New York, she hosted the first interstate judo competition for women, with 55 women competing. The *Daily News* covered the event with a four-page color spread in its magazine section.

1964 Phyllis Harper, also a Chicagoan, had learned judo at the Jujitsu Institute and made *shodan* in 1955. She received her third-degree black belt—*sandan*—in 1964, the same year her daughter Stephanie received her first-degree black belt. She also attempted to get the AAU to allow women to compete.

1965 More and more women in the United States were practicing judo, accounting for 30 percent of all participants. Rusty Stewart formed two teams from the New York and New Jersey constituent area and competed in team and individual competitions in Washington, Pennsylvania.

1970 Maureen Braziel, like Rusty Stewart, practiced with men and went to Japan to get her black belt and train at the Kodokan. She had begun to play in every regional U.S. tournament available. From 1967 to 1977, she was the undisputed heavyweight champion of the East Coast.

1971 England had its own national championship for women and began hosting the British Open, which for many years was the largest international tournament in the world. Maureen Braziel went to England to participate and fought 10 matches in two divisions. She took the silver medal in the heavyweight division and a bronze medal in the open division. Up until then, only men had ever placed in international competition.

1974 Women were allowed to do *randori*—freedom fighting—in competition for the first time.

1974 The first national championships for women were held in conjunction with the men's championships in Phoenix, Arizona. There were six weight divisions and a grand champion. The first grand champion was Maureen Braziel, who defeated Diane Pierce. Braziel won again in 1976 and '77.

1975 Maureen Braziel went to Lausanne, Switzerland, for the fourth international judo championships. She won the gold medal in the heavyweight division, and the AAU named her the most outstanding player in judo among both men and women.

1976 The first women's national USA/AAU team was formed and traveled, with Rusty Stewart Kanokogi as coach, to the British Open, in which 14 countries competed. Maureen Braziel won the open division crown, marking not only the first time the event was won by an American but also the first time the title was taken out of Great Britain. Including Braziel's, the U.S. team won five medals.

1977 In conjunction with the national championships, the first Women's Pan American Judo Union championships were held, and seven countries competed. The United States won all the events.

1977 Efforts were launched to include judo in the Olympics. For the sport to be considered, more than 25 countries, representing three unions, had to compete in the world championships.

1980 The first women's judo world championship trials were held at New York's Madison Square Garden in November. Twenty-seven countries participated. The U.S. team, coached by James Takemori, won three bronze medals. Participants had to pay all of their own expenses. Rusty Kanokogi organized the event and raised more than $180,000 to help defray costs, with limited involvement by USA Judo.

1981 Rusty Kanokogi initiated a human rights complaint against the United States Olympic Committee (USOC), protesting the fact that women were not allowed at the U.S. Olympic Sport Festival or at the USOC training camp, and won. She then began a lawsuit against the International Olympic Committee to get women's judo accepted as an Olympic sport.

1981 The world championships were held in Paris. Margaret Castro (Gomez) won the silver in the over-72 weight class, and Eve Arnoff won the bronze in the under-56 division.

1983 The United States participated in the Fukuoka Cup, a prominent women's judo tournament in Kyushu, Japan. Margaret Castro won gold in the 72-plus and open divisions, Eve Arnoff won silver in the under-56 division, and Christine Penich took the bronze in the under-66.

1984 At the world championships in Vienna, Austria, Anne Marie Burno won the gold in the under-56 kilograms, and Darlene Anaya won the bronze in the under-48 kilograms.

1987 At the world championships in Essen, West Germany, a combined women's and men's championship was held for the first time. Lynne Roethke won the silver in the under-61 kilograms, and Margaret Castro won the bronze in the 72-plus division.

1988 Judo was included in the Olympics as a demonstration sport in Seoul, South Korea. Lynne Roethke won the silver in the under-61 kilograms, and Margaret Castro-Gomez won the bronze in the 72-plus. Rusty Kanokogi was the coach—the first woman to coach judo and the highest-ranked American woman, a sixth-degree black belt.

1992 Judo became a full medal sport at the Olympics in Barcelona, Spain. The U.S. team did not medal.

1995 Hillary Wolf became the first American ever to capture a gold medal in the world junior judo championships in the 48 kilograms (106 pounds). Wolf won the junior national championships four times.

1996 At the Olympics in Atlanta, more than 193 countries participated in judo. The U.S. team did not medal.

2000 Sayaka Matsumoto, of California, won the silver at the junior world championships in Tunisia.

2000 At the Olympic games in Sydney, Australia, the highest ranking for a U.S. woman was a fifth-place finish by Celita Schutz, a Yale graduate from New Jersey.

2000 Sandra Bacher, in the 154-pound class, appeared in her third Olympics (1992 and 1996). She won the national championship the last three years. In 1999 she won the bronze medal at the Pan American Games and also won the Women's World Freestyle Championship. Sandra is a fourth-degree black belt.

2000 Colleen Rosensteel, in the 172-pound class, appeared in her third Olympics (1992–'96). She won the national title every year from 1993–96, '98, and '99. She was also a silver medalist at the Pan American Games in 1999. Colleen is a third-degree black belt.

2001 Ellen Wilson, of Colorado, won first place at the British Open.

LACROSSE

L ACROSSE, AN open-field game that is played with sticks, or crosses, that have nets used to throw and catch the ball, traces its origins to Native Americans. The object of the game is to score by getting the ball into a six-by-six-foot goal. The women's game continues to be played much as it was under the earliest written rules developed in 1867: 12 players to a side, using the natural boundaries of the designated playing field.

The All England Ladies Lacrosse Association was instrumental in introducing the sport to American women. During the early 1900s, English coaches taught lacrosse in a few colleges. By 1920, there was a steady development of the game, initially in the eastern part of the country and then through the Midwest.

1890 The first women's game was played at Saint Leonard's School, in Saint Andrews, Scotland. Subsequently, in the early 1900s, several British players taught the game in the United States.

1914 The first collegiate game was played at Sweet Briar College (Virginia). Caroline Gascoigne, of Saint Leonard's, tried to establish a full-fledged lacrosse program at the Virginia women's school but was not successful.

1925 Joyce Cran Barry arrived in the United States from Dartford College, in England, to teach at Miss Applebee's camp, in the Pocono Mountains of Pennsylvania. The day she was to set sail for her return to England, she was offered a job at Wellesley College (Massachusetts), where she taught and coached field hockey. Considered one of the founding matriarchs of U.S. women's lacrosse, she was instrumental in developing the sport through field hockey camps, beginning with Miss Applebee's. She went on to found the CranBarry Equipment Company in Marblehead, Massachusetts, a sports equipment supplier that was the first to specialize in women's lacrosse equipment.

1926 After convincing parents that lacrosse was safe for their daughters to play, Rosabelle Sinclair, of Saint Leonard's, established the first organized women's lacrosse team, at the Bryn Mawr School, in Baltimore. The school has continued to field a team, which holds the distinction of being the oldest established team in the country.

1931 The United States Women's Lacrosse Association (USWLA) was formed by a group of physical education instructors meeting in the Poconos. Joyce Cran Barry served as the first president until 1935.

1933 With clubs already playing in Baltimore, Boston, New York, and Philadelphia, the first USWLA national tournament was held in Greenwich, Connecticut. Baltimore defeated Philadelphia, 5–1, in the final. The USWLA also selected a national team for the first time.

1933 Betty Richey was named to the inaugural U.S. national team, the first of 22 consecutive U.S. teams of which Richey was a member. She was also a member of the national field hockey team during those same years. She served as USWLA president from 1946 to 1949, and again from 1955 to 1958. A graduate of Radcliffe College (Massachusetts) with a master's degree from Columbia University (New York City), Richey taught physical education and coached at Vassar College (Poughkeepsie, New York) for 30 years. She was later the first woman inducted into the Harvard University Hall of Fame and was also inducted into the Lacrosse and Field Hockey Halls of Fame. The Betty Richey Award for outstanding sportsmanship and leadership in women's intercollegiate squash was named for her.

1933 The first touring team from England came to the United States.

1935 The first U.S. team went overseas to play England. Suzanne R. Crosse, of Philadelphia, who learned the game at Miss Applebee's camp, played on the team after having been a U.S. team member in 1933 and 1934. She subsequently played on the national team in 1937 and 1939–'42 and was a reserve team player in 1943 and '44. Crosse also designed the logo for, wrote, and assembled *Crosse-Checks*, the first magazine for women's lacrosse.

1939 Helena Wheeler was named to the national team after having been a member of the 1935 team that toured England. From 1939 until 1953, Wheeler was a member of either the national or reserve teams. Wheeler, who taught physical education for 40 years in Westchester, New York, was also the author of *Lacrosse for Girls*.

1939 Betty Shellenberger was selected for the first time to the national team. Until 1961, she was selected for the national team 11 times and the reserve team 5 times. In 1941, Shellenberger began a 40-year career as an umpire in the sport. In 1987, she was named a Distinguished Daughter of Pennsylvania for her contributions to various sports.

1949 The international tours with England resumed after having been suspended during World War II.

1954 Gretchen Schuyler was a member of the U.S. national team from 1935 to 1954. She played while attending Boston University, where she also played 10 other sports, and was inducted into the U.S. Lacrosse Hall of Fame.

1956 Marge Watson became head coach at Ursinus College (Collegeville, Pennsylvania), where she started the lacrosse program and coached for the next 25 years. For many years, Watson volunteered her time. Although she received a salary in later years, it never exceeded $500. She coached and taught several of the most significant players and coaches in the game, including Vonnie Gros, West Chester University (Pennsylvania) coach, and Sue Day Stahl, coach of four U.S. World Cup champion teams. In December 2000, Watson, who had been involved with the sport for more than 50 years, received the inaugural Lifetime Achievement Award from the Intercollegiate Women's Lacrosse Coaches Association (IWLCA).

1956 Barbara Longstreth, a sophomore at Beaver College (Glenside, Pennsylvania), was named to the national team and remained a member until 1964. She was renamed to the team in 1967. She went on to coach at the club and high school levels for 17 years and was an umpire for more than 20 years. In the 1970s, she pioneered women's lacrosse on the West Coast and founded Longstreth Sporting Goods.

1957 For the first time, the U.S. team was not defeated by England, when the teams played to a 7–7 tie.

1957 Marjorie Garinger began her 45-year career as an umpire. A member of the 1956 World Cup field hockey team, Garinger also managed the 1979 and 1984 Olympic field hockey teams.

1960 Elizabeth "Libby" Williams began her coaching career at Plymouth Whitemarsh High School, where seven of her teams were undefeated. Williams has the distinction of having coached the largest number of high school lacrosse players who have been selected for the national team. She went on to coach 25 undefeated teams in lacrosse, field hockey, basketball, and softball at the University of Pennsylvania.

1962 Enid Clinchard Russell, known for her exceptional speed and grace, and considered by many the player against whom all others are measured, was named to the national team. She remained a member until 1968 and played on the 1964 and 1969 touring teams.

L

1962 Judith Wolstenholme participated in her first USWLA national tournament. She went on to participate in every subsequent national tournament, either as a player or as an umpire, until she umpired her last game in 2001. A two-time all-American at Ursinus College, Wolstenholme was also a member of the national team nine times. During her career, she officiated at all but one National Collegiate Athletic Association (NCAA) final championship game.

1964 Vonnie Gros began a 12-year coaching career at West Chester University, where she coached lacrosse and field hockey. A graduate of Ursinus College and a nine-time member of the national team beginning in 1960, Gros studied new and innovative movement of the ball in space in both field hockey and lacrosse. She is best known for producing many top-level coaches, including University of Maryland coach Cindy Timchal.

1969 Tina Sloan Green was the first African American woman named to the U.S. national team, and in 1997 she became the first African American woman inducted into the Lacrosse Hall of Fame. From 1974 until 1992, she coached at Temple University (Philadelphia), taking the team to the NCAA Division I championships three times. She was also the founder of the Black Women's Sports Foundation and the Inner City Field Hockey and Lacrosse program at Temple.

1972 Margaret Boyd, who came to the United States from England following World War II and coached at camps and clinics along the East Coast, founded the International Federation of Women's Lacrosse Associations (IFWLA) and served as its first president.

1973 Kathy Heinze, originally from England, was named the national team coach, and the U.S. team defeated the visiting English team for the first time. In her two years at the helm, the U.S. team remained undefeated.

1975 The U.S. team, led by Meryl Werley and Connie Burgess Lanzel, played England and 12 other challengers during the five-week overseas tour. The U.S. team returned home undefeated, earning the distinction of "world's best" for the first time.

1978 The USWLA sponsored the first national collegiate tournament. Penn State won the first of three consecutive championships with a 9–3 defeat of the University of Maryland.

1979 Jacquelin "Jackie" Pitts, considered one of the trailblazers in the development of women's lacrosse, was named head coach of the U.S. squad. Pitts was a seven-time national team member between 1964 and 1973. She coached the U.S. team until 1987, leading the team to its first World Cup championship in 1982. She served as president of the USWLA from 1974 through 1978 and as president of the IFWLA from 1986 through 1990.

1980 Heather Dow was named to the national team for the first time. She was goalkeeper on the 1989 World Cup champion team and served as assistant coach of the World Cup champion teams in 1993, 1997, and 2001.

1981 The Association for Intercollegiate Athletics for Women sanctioned a three-division national collegiate championship. In Division I, the University of Maryland defeated Ursinus College; in Division II, the University of Delaware defeated Lehigh University, and in Division III, Millersville State College defeated Lynchburg College. Also, the International Raquetball Federation was established.

1982 Maggie Faulkner, of Towson State (Baltimore); Carole Kleinfelder, of Harvard University; and Anne McCoskley, of Loyola College (Baltimore) spearheaded the formation of the Intercollegiate Women's Lacrosse Coaches Association (IWLCA). Representatives of 47 schools met in Cherry Hill, New Jersey, in December in response to a letter from Kleinfelder regarding formation of an intercollegiate association for coaches.

1982 The first NCAA women's championship was played at Trenton State University (later renamed the College of New Jersey). The University of Massachusetts defeated Trenton State, 9–6, in the finals.

1982 The IFWLA held the first World Cup tournament in Nottingham, England, with six countries participating: Australia, Canada, England, Scotland, the United States, and Wales. The U.S. team, coached by Jackie Pitts, defeated Australia, 10–7, in overtime, to win the championship.

1984 Betsy Williams Dougherty was named to the national team. She played on the team until 1993 and was a member of three World Cup and four touring teams. She captained the championship 1993 World Cup team.

1984 Temple University won the NCAA championship, making Tina Sloan Green the first African American woman to coach a Division I team to a national title.

1986 Sue Delaney-Scheetz began her coaching career at Penn State, where she was the first college coach to lead her team to four consecutive championship games—1986–'89. In her four years at Penn State, she compiled a 67–9 record, including two NCAA championships—1987 and '89—and was named national Coach of the Year twice.

1986 Suzanne Tyler coached the University of Maryland to the NCAA championship. When she coached the field hockey team to the NCAA championship in 1987, Tyler earned the distinction of being the only Division I coach to win an NCAA championship in two different sports.

1986 The second World Cup championship, played every four years, was held in Swarthmore, Pennsylvania. Australia defeated the United States, 10–7, to win the title.

1988 Sue Day Stahl, a graduate of Ursinus College, was named head coach of the national team. She coached the team to four consecutive World Cup championships and coached two touring teams to undefeated records.

1989 Australia was unable to defend its World Cup title on its home fields in Perth as the U.S. team reclaimed the championship by edging England, 5–4.

1990 Caroline Hausserman was named the first executive director of the USWLA.

1992 Rosebelle Sinclair became the first woman inducted into the Lacrosse Hall of Fame.

1993 In Edinburgh, Scotland, the United States won its third World Cup.

1997 The University of Maryland became the first team to win 43 consecutive games, setting the record on April 3. The Terrapins broke the intercollegiate record set by the Cornell (Ithaca, New York) men during their 1976–'78 seasons. The Maryland streak stretched to 50 games, ending in an 8–7 loss to Loyola College. The Terrapins avenged the Loyola loss in the final game of the NCAA championships and became the first Division I team to win four consecutive championships. The team also set a single-season record of 21 victories.

1997 The United States claimed its fourth World Cup title in Edogowa, Japan.

1997 Pat Genovese, of William Smith College (New York), became the first collegiate women's lacrosse coach to record 200 victories, with a 12–7 win over Rensselaer Polytechnic Institute (Troy, New York).

1997 The College of New Jersey won its 102nd game.

1997 The Maryland Terrapins, with a 21–0 record, won their fifth consecutive NCAA title on May 16 by defeating the Virginia Cavaliers, 16–6. In that game, Maryland also set records for most goals in a half, with 11, most goals in a game, and largest margin of victory.

1999 The USWLA was merged into U.S. Lacrosse, which became the national governing body for both the men's and women's game.

2000 Ursinus College won its 400th game when it defeated Dickinson College (Carlisle, Pennsylvania).

2000 On May 21, the University of Maryland won a record sixth consecutive NCAA championship.

2000 The College of New Jersey won its 10th NCAA Division III title, all but one under coach Sharon Pfluger.

2000 U.S. Lacrosse named its All-Century Team: Heather Dow (goalkeeper), Kathleen Geiger, Cherie Greer, Vonnie Gros, Mandee Moore O'Leary, Elizabeth Richey, Candy Finn Rocha, Enid Clinchard Russell, Mary Fetter Semanik, Betty Shellenberger, Julie Ann Staver, Judith Smiley Wolstenholme, and coach Sue Stahl.

2001 Amherst College (Massachusetts) ended the 121-game regular-season victory streak of the College of New Jersey.

2001 On May 10, the University of Maryland's Jen Adams, who is Australian, scored 11 points in the second half of the Terrapins' first game in the NCAA tournament, against Monmouth College, to become the leading scorer in women's college lacrosse history, with 430 career points. She surpassed the record of 420 points set in 1984 by Karen Emas, of the University of Delaware.

2001 The University of Maryland won its seventh consecutive NCAA Division I title, defeating Georgetown in double overtime, and keeping alive the longest active streak among men's and women's Division I teams in any sport. The Terrapins hold the record for most final-game appearances, with 14—including 9 wins—followed by Penn State, Princeton, and Temple, each of whom appeared in 4. It was the 11th championship appearance for Maryland head coach Cindy Timchal.

2001 The Tewaaraton Trophy, recognizing a male and female Player of the Year in lacrosse, was awarded for the first time. The University of Maryland's Jen Adams, the all-time leading scorer in Division I, with 430 career points, won the inaugural trophy, and the University of Maryland received $10,000 for scholarships.

2001 In July, the World Cup was held in High Wycombe, England, with 12 countries competing. The United States won the championship for the fifth time, by beating Australia, 14–7. It was the fourth World Cup victory for coach Sue Day Stahl and for manager Kathleen Geiger, a player on the 1989, 1993, and 1997 World Cup champion teams.

2001 Lynetta Ware, of Virginia, stepped down after 15 years of service with the IFWLA, during which she served two terms as president.

LUGE

LUGE IS one of the fastest and most exciting of the winter sports. Competitors slide down a twisting ice-covered course while lying on their backs (feet in front) on a small sled. Each woman uses shoulder, leg, and body movements to apply pressure to the sled's runners, thus maneuvering the turns. Each run is a race against the clock, which is timed up to one-thousandth of a second (short track speed skating is the only other winter sport timed so closely). In 1987, Cammy Myler became the first American, male or female, to win a medal in World Cup competition, taking the bronze in Sarajevo, Yugoslavia. In 1994, at the Olympics in Lillehammer, Norway, Myler was given the honor of carrying the American flag in the opening ceremonies. In Nagano, Japan, she competed in her fourth Olympics.

1955 The world championships began, with only a singles event for women.

1968 Luge was an Olympic event for the first time in Grenoble, France. Three U.S. women competed—Karen Roberts placed 14th, Ileen Williams placed 16th, and Sheila Johansen placed 17th.

1979 The first luge track in the United States was built in Lake Placid, New York.

1979 The United States Luge Association was established to oversee the development of the sport.

1983 Bonny Warner won her first of five U.S. championships, repeating in 1984, '87, '88, and '90.

1985 Cammy Myler became the youngest person, at the age of 16, to win a senior national luge championship and was named to the national team.

1987 In Sarajevo, Cammy Myler became the first American luger of either sex to medal in World Cup competition, winning the bronze.

1992 Bonny Warner appeared in her third Olympics, in Albertville, France, finishing 18th. In 1988, she finished 6th, the best finish to that point in time for the United States, following a 15th-place finish in 1984. Warner was on the national team for 11 years and was a five-time national champion.

1992 In Albertville, France, Cammy Myler became the first American woman to place as high as fifth in Olympic competition.

1992 Erica Terwilliger began sliding when she was 14, in 1977. In 1992, she competed in the Olympics for the second time, finishing 9th. She finished 11th in 1988 in Calgary, Alberta, and was an alternate on the Olympic team in 1980 and '84.

1994 Cammy Myler, appearing in her third Olympics, was honored by being the U.S. flag bearer.

1995 In Lake Placid, Maryann Baribault became the first American woman to win the world junior championship. She repeated the feat the following year in Calgary. In 1994 and '95 she was first overall in the National Cup standings.

1998 In Nagano, Japan, Cammy Myler became the first woman to be a four-time Winter Olympian. At the women's national championships in Park City, Utah, she became the first woman to win seven national

L

titles. The most decorated woman luger in history, she was named U.S. Luge Female Athlete of the Year eight times. Myler graduated cum laude from Dartmouth College (Hanover, New Hampshire).

1998 The Olympic women's luge team of Erin Warren, Cammy Myler, and Bethany Calcaterra-McMahon finished sixth, seventh, and eighth in women's singles—the highest combined finish up to that time for the United States.

1998 At the World Cup championships, Ashley Hayden won the overall in the girls 13–16 age-group. She came in first in four out of six events and finished second twice en route to becoming the first American girl to win that title.

2001 Becky Wilczak won the national championship in the women's singles and the bronze in the team competition at the world championships.

2001 At the world championships in Lillehammer, Norway, Nicole Orlivera won the junior women's title. Courtney Zablocki won the silver and Brenna Margol took the bronze.

2002 At the Olympics in Salt Lake City, Becky Wilczak placed 5th in single luge, passing Cammy Myler (1992) for the highest Olympic finish. Ashley Hayden finished 8th and Courtney Zablocki placed 13th.

MOTORCYCLING

Tough, tenacious women riding their two-wheelers is a rapidly growing trend. The boom in interest for motorcycle riding is in both recreational and competitive arenas. Motorcyclists compete in classes based on the size of the motorcycle's engine cylinders. The races are held on many surfaces, including roads, dirt, hills, speedways, sand, and grass.

1907 Clara Wagner, the 15-year-old daughter of the manufacturer of Wagner motorcycles, was issued a membership card by the Federation of American Motorcyclists, the predecessor to the American Motorcyclist Association (AMA). In 1910, she rode a four-horsepower cycle in a 365-mile endurance race from Chicago to Indianapolis. Despite bad weather and poor road conditions, Wagner won the race, becoming the first woman to win a competitive motorcycle event. However, because she was a female, the organizer declared her win unofficial and refused to give her the trophy.

1915 Effie Hotchkiss and her mother, Avis, completed the first transcontinental motorcycle trip by women. They rode from New York City to the San Francisco Exposition aboard their Harley-Davidson V-twin with sidecar. Leaving New York on May 3, they traveled 9,000 miles, arriving in San Francisco in mid-August and then returning to New York.

1916 Adeline Van Buren and her sister Augusta rode coast to coast across the United States on motorcycles. They left Sheepshead Bay, in Brooklyn, New York, on July 4 riding their Power Plus Indians. They covered the 3,300 miles and arrived in San Francisco 58 days later, on September 2. They wanted to prove that women as well as men could serve in the Motorcycle Corps in World War I. While they were in Colorado, they became the only people to complete the 10-mile climb up Pikes Peak (and then return to complete the round trip) on a motorized vehicle.

1924 The American Motorcyclist Association (AMA) is formed.

1924 A daredevil rider who used the stage name Lilly La France performed throughout the United States on her custom-built Indian motorcycle.

1927 Bessie Stringfield was the first black woman to tour all 48 states on a motorcycle. During 66 years of riding, she owned 27 Harley-Davidsons—all of which were blue. She made eight solo cross-country tours.

1935 Dorothy Goulding-Robinson and her husband, Earl, made a coast-to-coast endurance run in 89 hours and 58 minutes. To mark the occasion, she painted her Harley-Davidson pink and wore only pink throughout the trip. In 1938, she competed in the two-day Jack Pine Enduro 500, traveling on a side hack weighing more than 1,000 pounds. Out of 88 entries, 41 finished; Goulding-Robinson finished second in her class. In 1940, she won the event.

1941 The Motor Maids was formed as a result of an intense letter writing campaign led by Linda Allen Dugeau, a motorcyclist hoping to establish a national organization of women riders. Dorothy Goulding-Robinson was the first president, a position she held for 25 years.

1950 Louise Scherbyn, an accomplished rider in several disciplines, founded the Women's International Motorcycle Association (WIMA)—the first group to recognize all women participants in the sport.

1969 Katharin Budris, known as Kitty, was the first woman to get an AMA mechanics license and be admitted to the pits.

1970s Motocross grew in popularity, replacing other traditional competitions. Local AMA organizations developed amateur programs that held wide appeal for both men and women.

1971 No woman had ever been granted a professional license from the AMA until Kerry Kleid, of Rye, New York, applied for and received one. AMA officials did not know that Kleid was a woman, and when she showed up on July 5 to ride in a race in Unadilla, New York, the AMA confiscated her license. Kleid filed a suit and won the case, which made the front page of the *New York Daily News*.

1974 Kasey Rogers established the Powder Puffs Unlimited Riders and Racers association—known as PURR. The first Powder Puff National was held at Indiana Dunes on July 6 and 7. Sue Fish won the event.

1975 Kasey Rogers and Mike Goodwin organized 10 women to compete during the Super Bowl of Motocross, in the Women's Invitational Trophy Dash, at the Los Angeles Coliseum in front of 80,000 spectators.

1980s Two national champions continued to elevate the interest in women's competitions: Lisa Akin-Wagner, who won the title in 1982, '85, and '88, and Mercedes Gonzalez, who won in 1986, '87, and '89–'91. They were the only women to win five AMA titles each at Loretta Lynn's, an annual competition. Gonzalez also won nine other championships affiliated with various organizations.

1983 Tammy Kirk, riding a 75 DCC V-twin bike, became the first woman to qualify for a starting position in the AMA Grand National finals.

1986 Fran Crane, who in her career competed in approximately 30 endurance runs, became the first woman to finish in the top ranks of the Iron Butt Rally—a long-distance endurance rally covering 11,000 miles in 11 straight days.

1988 Tami Rice (Haase) along with Bonnie Warch developed the Women's Motocross Association. The events ran in conjunction with the California Racing Club program. In 1990, the association added Brenda Hannah, a well-known jet ski racer, and the organization was renamed the Women's International Motosport Association, developing women's motocross, jet ski, and auto racing events.

1992 The women's international motocross championships, La Franz Femme International, were held in Italy. Elaine Ruff organized and funded the team of Tami Rice (Haase), Nadine Holbert, Kristy Shealy, and Dee Ann Wood. The U.S. team placed in three of the top five positions.

1994 Debbie Matthews, whose 26 years in racing (20 of them ranked in the top 15 of U.S. professional racers) is the longest career by a woman, joined Elaine Ruff to help develop the Women's Motocross Team. In 1996, they changed the name to the Women's Motocross League (WML).

1996 Shelly Khan won the first WML national championship.

1997 The AMA hosted the first National Conference on Women and Motorcycling.

1997 Debbie Matthews petitioned the AMA Congress and won approval for an "A" class ranking for women.

1997 Cathy Templeton was a champion hill climber, won numerous races, and, at the end of her amateur career, was the national number one plate in the 250cc class. In 1997 she was the first woman to receive a professional hill-climbing racing license.

1999 Voni Glaves won the BMW Motorcycle Owner of America race, beating all men and women with a total of 82,268 miles. Her past history with the race included placing in the top three finishers eight times and being the top woman finisher four times.

1999 Seventeen-year-old Jackie Hudson, of Houston, was selected WML Rookie of the Year after she won the WML International Cup amateur championships. She was also the first woman to sign with a men's team, Plano Honda Professional Men's Motocross.

2000 Jessica Patterson finished the 2000 WML season ranked number one in the world. She was first at the WML national championships, first in points at the AMA-WML National MX Championship Series, and, in a dual repeat of 1999, Loretta Lynn women's champion and GNC champion.

2001 Out of six annual WML races, Sarah Whitmore, of Cheboygan, Michigan, placed in the top three three times—taking second at Budds Creek and Broome Tioga and third at Steel City.

MOUNTAIN BIKING

Mountain bikers have to move fast over rough terrain. They often reach speeds up to 60 miles per hour and negotiate bone-jarring jumps and bumps. Mountain biking as a sport has grown tremendously since the early 1990s, due in part to the electric personalities of competitors like Juli Furtado and Missy Giove. Furtado was a trailblazer and brought attention to the sport when she earned back-to-back World Cups in 1992 and '93. Giove, known for her dreadlocks, piercings, and tattoos, matched the feat in 1996 and '97—overcoming 39 broken bones received during training and competing.

1975 Gary Fisher and Joe Breezer introduced the first mountain bikes, the "clunker" and the "breezer," to a small group of riders in Marin County. The group (six men and one woman, Wende Cragg), quickly became known as the "Marinites." Cragg was the first woman to ride from Crested Butte to Aspen, Colorado, via Pearl Pass.

1976 On October 21, the Marinites held the first "official" timed mountain biking races, on Pine Mountain in Colorado. Wende Cragg's time of 5:27 is the fastest women's time down the east side of the mountain.

1980 Jack Ingram and many Marin County riders founded the National Off-Road Biking Association (NORBA). The first NORBA championships for men and women were held the next year. Jacquie Phelan won the first five NORBA championships.

1987 The first (but unofficially-timed) world championships were held in Mammoth, California, and won by Sara Ballantyne.

1988 The International Mountain Biking Association was formed. Membership grew slowly, but the opening of the Mountain Biking Hall of Fame, in Crested Butte, spread excitement about the sport. Jacquie Phelan, who dominated the early days of the sport, was the first woman inducted into the Hall of Fame in its inaugural year.

1989 The NORBA National Championships Series began. The championships included four events: cross-country, short-track cross-country, downhill, and dual slalom. In 1990, Juli Furtado became the first American to win the series; she then to won every year through 1993.

1990 The first Union Internationale Cycliste (UCI) world championships were held in Durango, Colorado. Juli Furtado won the cross-country, and Cindy Devine won the downhill.

1993 Juli Furtado won the world championship in cross-country for the second consecutive year, becoming the first woman to win back-to-back mountain biking World Cups in cross-country.

1994 Juli Furtado was the first female named Cyclist of the Year by *Velo News*. She won 17 consecutive national and international races, including two World Cups and four national series.

1994 Missy Giove won the world championship in the downhill event.

1996 Mountain biking made its Olympic debut in Atlanta. Susan DeMattei, of San Rafael, California, became the first U.S. medalist when she captured the bronze. She was the only U.S. biker to medal.

1996 Susan DeMattei finished in the top three at the NORBA championships for the seventh consecutive year, 1991–'96.

1996 Legendary mountain biker Juli Furtado announced her retirement after she was diagnosed with lupus. In her career, Furtado won two world championships, three World Cup championships, and five national championships.

1998 Marla Streb won the Winter X-Games "Biker X" competition. In her career, Marla has won four national series races.

1998 In September, Missy Giove captured her third world title in four years at the World Cup Downhill Series, in Hawaii. UCI, the sport's governing body, ranked Giove number one in the world after the victory. She later won the downhill event at ESPN's inaugural Winter Xtreme Games and the U.S. downhill championship in 1999 and 2000.

2000 Sue Haywood won the 24 Hours of Moab (Utah) race for the second year in a row. In 1999 she covered 180 miles and in 2000, 165 miles—beating an impressive group of male and female riders.

2001 Leigh Donovan retired after nine years of rigorous competition. Donovan broke onto the scene after winning the U.S. Downhill Series championship in 1995. Also in 1995, she became the only person to win the U.S. slalom championships, the downhill world championships, and the U.S. Downhill Series. Donovan has won more U.S. championships than any other female rider.

2001 Allison Tucker won the World Championships of Mountain Biking, held in Vail, Colorado.

2001 The Luna Chix, Alison Dunlap, Marla Streb, Kelli Emmet, and Gin Hall, became the first all-women mountain biking team.

2001 Alison Dunlap, at the world championships in Vail, Colorado, placed first in cross-country. She is a national champion in three disciplines: road, mountain biking, and cyclo-cross.

OLYMPICS

The Olympics are regarded as the premier venue for the best athletes in the world. The International Olympic Committee (IOC) is the governing body for the worldwide Olympic movement. This committee is responsible for rules, regulations, adding new sports, choosing the host city, and all other aspects of the Olympic games. Most countries have national committees that act as the governing authority over their own country's Olympic athletes, teams, and training. The United States Olympic Committee (USOC) is the governing body for the U.S. Olympic and Pan American teams.

One of the pivotal events in Olympic history that helped bring more attention to women athletes occurred in 1960 in Rome. The IOC approved television rights for the games, and over time women athletes gained more international exposure. In addition, it is now mandatory that any new event added to the Olympic Games have competitions for both men and women.

This chapter treats the Summer Games and Winter Games in separate sections.

Summer Olympics

1896 The first modern Olympic Games, held in Athens, Greece, included 245 male participants but no women. Women first competed unofficially in 1900 in Paris. The sports comprised tennis—singles and mixed doubles—golf, and yachting.

1900 In Paris, golfer Margaret T. Abbott became the first American woman to win an Olympic gold medal.

1904 Archery double rounds became an Olympic sport at the games in Saint Louis. Lydia Howell, from the Cincinnati Archery Club, became the first American female to win three gold medals in one Olympics.

1908 Figure skating made its debut as an Olympic event in London, the first time winter sports were included in the Olympics.

1908 The IOC officially recognized women's events for the first time at the games in London. Women competed in tennis, archery, and figure skating, but American women did not participate in the London games. The all-male U.S. Olympic Committee opposed American women's participation in events in which women did not wear long skirts. There were also no women competing from Great Britain, Germany, or Sweden.

1912 At the games in Stockholm, Sweden, three contests for women became official events: two swimming—the 100-meter freestyle and the 4×400-meter freestyle relay; and one diving—platform. Forty-two women competed but none from the United States. Equestrian events were also added, but the United States did not compete.

1916 The games in Berlin were canceled due to World War I.

1920 The first Olympic flag and Olympic oath were introduced at the games in Antwerp, Belgium. New women's events included swimming—300-meter freestyle; springboard diving; yachting—mixed Finn; tennis doubles; and figure skating.

1920 The United States sent its first team of women athletes to the Olympics. The team consisted of 15 swimmers and 2 figure skaters.

1920 In Antwerp, Belgium, Ethelda Bleibtrey was the first American woman to win a gold medal in swimming, winning the 100-meter freestyle. Aileen Riggin, age 14, won the gold in springboard diving.

1922 Alice Milliat, of France, in an effort to counteract the difficulty women had in being recognized for international competition, organized the Federation Sportive Feminine Internationale to stage a separate Women's Olympic Games. Three hundred women from five countries competed from 1922 to 1934 in four successful games. The United States took part in 11 track-and-field events. These games promoted the inclusion by the IOC of track-and-field events for women in the Olympics.

1924 At the Olympics in Paris, new events included fencing—foil and individual—and the 200-meter breaststroke in swimming; also in swimming, the 300-meter freestyle became the 400-meter freestyle.

1924 The United States sent its first official team to the Olympics. The U.S. women's swimming team won four gold, three silver, and three bronze medals. The United States also swept springboard diving and won gold and silver in platform.

1924 The United States did not medal in fencing, but one of the U.S. entrants was Adeline Gehrig, sister of the great New York Yankee baseball player Lou Gehrig.

1924 In tennis, Helen Wills Moody won the gold and teamed with Hazel Hotchkiss (Wightman) to win the doubles title. Hotchkiss teamed with R. Norris Williams to win the mixed doubles. After a dispute with the International Lawn Tennis Association, the IOC dropped tennis from the Olympics until 1988.

1924 Adding to her 1920 Olympic gold, Aileen Riggin won the bronze in the 100-meter backstroke and a silver in springboard diving, making her the first Olympian to win medals for both swimming and diving.

1928 The games were held in Amsterdam, Holland. New events for women included track and field—100 meters, 800 meters, 4×100-meter relay, high jump, and discus throw—and team combined gymnastics.

1928 Sixteen-year-old Betty Robinson won the 100-meter race, the first women's track-and-field event. She also won silver in the 4×100-meter relay, an event in which she won gold in 1936.

1928 In Amsterdam, equestrian team dressage became an event, with men and women on the same team. The United States did not enter. In 1949, the U.S. equestrian team was formed.

1928 The Olympic high jump was introduced. Mildred Wiley won the bronze. In 1932, Jean Shiley and Mildred "Babe" Didrikson tied for the gold, setting a world record of 5 feet, 5¼. Alice Coachman (Davis) won the gold in 1948, and Mildred Davis won gold in 1956.

1928 Women's gymnastics team competition made its Olympic debut in Amsterdam. It wasn't until 1948 that the United States medaled, taking the bronze in London. The United States won the silver in Los Angeles in 1984, silver in '92 in Barcelona, Spain, and gold in '96 in Atlanta.

1928 Lillian Copeland, a student at the University of Southern California, won a silver medal in the first Olympic discus event. Her best event, the javelin, was not yet in the Olympics.

1928 The women's 800 meters was included in the Olympics for the first time but was canceled afterward because officials felt it was too strenuous for women.

1932 The first Olympic Games held in the United States were in Los Angeles. The first Olympic Village (a residential area for athletes and coaches) was created, but it was for men only. New events for women included the 80-meter hurdles, the javelin throw, and the mixed star class in yachting.

1932 Medal ceremonies with national anthems played for the winners of the gold medal were held for the first time.

1932 Louise Stokes and Tidye Pickett were the first two African American women to qualify for the games, but they were not allowed to participate due to racial prejudice. They qualified again in 1936.

1932 Setting an Olympic record in the discus of 133 feet, 2 inches, Lillian Copeland won the gold, with Ruth Osburn taking the silver.

1932 Georgia Coleman became the first woman in Olympic history to complete a two-and-a-half forward somersault in springboard diving.

1932 Babe Didrikson set an Olympic record in the javelin throw of 143 feet, 4 inches, winning the gold. A U.S. woman didn't medal again in javelin until 1972 in Munich, when Kathryn Schmidt won the bronze; she won it again in 1976.

1932 The first 100-meter hurdle race was won by Babe Didrikson, who set a world record of 11 feet, 7 inches. Evelyn Hall took the silver. Didrikson is the only athlete in history to win individual medals in running, throwing, and jumping.

1936 The Olympics were held in Berlin. No new women's events were added.

1936 Helen Stephens won the gold in the 100 meters, and the U.S. 4×100-meter relay team also won gold.

1940 The games in Tokyo were canceled due to World War II.

1944 The games in London were canceled due to World War II.

1948 The games were held in London. New events included the 200 meters, long jump, and shot put in track and field, and the kayak singles and 500 meters in canoeing.

1948 Alice Coachman (Davis) became the first African American to win an Olympic gold medal, high-jumping 5 feet, 6 inches.

1948 Audrey Patterson won the first 200-meter event in track and field.

1948 The long jump was held for the first time, but the United States did not medal. In 1956, Willye White became the first U.S. woman to medal, taking the silver in Melbourne, Australia. A U.S. woman didn't medal again until Kathy McMillan won the silver in 1976 in Montreal.

1948 Kayaking became an event for the first time in London, but it was not until 1964 in Tokyo that a U.S. woman medaled, when Marcia Jones won the bronze in the single 500 meters.

1948 Victoria "Vicki" Draves became the first woman in Olympic diving history to win both diving medals in the same games—gold in springboard and gold in platform.

1948 Shot put became an Olympic event. It wasn't until 1960 in Rome that a U.S. woman placed, when Earlene Brown won the bronze.

1948 Maria Cerra (Tishman) finished in fourth place in fencing, the highest finish to date for a U.S. woman in the event.

1948 The U.S. gymnastics team captured the bronze—the first medal ever for the United States in gymnastics.

1952 At the Games in Helsinki, Finland, individual gymnastics events were medal events for the first time. Women competed in the uneven bars, side horse vault, all-around, balance beam, and floor exercise.

1952 Soviet athletes participated in the Olympics for the first time in 40 years. In gymnastics, they won the gold medal in team combined and won three out of four gold medals in individual events.

1952 For the first time in Olympic history, women competed directly with men in equestrian events. The U.S. equestrian team, which included Marjorie Haines, placed sixth.

1956 The Melbourne games marked the first time in the modern era that the Olympics were held in the southern hemisphere. A new swimming event for women was the 100-meter butterfly, which the U.S. swept.

1956 Women participated in show jumping for the first time. Although the official games took place in Melbourne, the equestrian events were held in Stockholm, due to strict quarantine regulations.

1956 Patricia "Pat" McCormick repeated her gold-medal victories of 1952 in the platform and springboard, becoming the first woman to win both diving events in consecutive Olympics.

1960 The games were held in Rome. New events for women included reinstatement of the 800 meters in track and field; the kayak 500-meter doubles; the team foil in fencing; the 4×100-meter medley relay in swimming; and the mixed Flying Dutchman in yachting.

1960 Earlene Brown's bronze was the first medal for a U.S. woman in shot put. Brown is the only American shot-putter to compete in three consecutive Olympics: 1956, '60, and '64.

1960 The games in Rome marked the first worldwide television coverage and the first time the Olympics were televised in Europe. Television coverage was instrumental in creating an ongoing interest in the achievements of female athletes.

1960 Wilma Rudolph became the first woman to win three gold medals in track and field in one Olympics, by winning the 100 meters, with a time of 11.0; the 200 meters, with a time of 24.0; and the 4×100-meter relay. Rudolph was selected the Associated Press Female Athlete of the Year and became an international celebrity.

1964 Tokyo was the first Asian city to host the games. New women's events included both the 400 meters and the pentathlon (which included 100-meter hurdles, shot put, high jump, long jump, and 800 meter run) in track and field; the 400-meter individual medley in swimming; and volleyball.

1964 Kathy Kusner placed sixth in equestrian jumping, the highest finish at that time for a U.S. woman.

1964 The U.S. won its first medal in kayak doubles as Francine Fox and Gloriane Perrier took the silver with a time of 1:59.16.

1964 Donna de Varona won the first 400-meter individual medley, with a six-second margin of victory over U.S. teammate Sharon Finnerman.

1968 The Games were held in Mexico City. New sports for women were mixed skeet shooting and a roster of swimming events: 200-meter freestyle, 800-meter freestyle, 200-meter backstroke, 100-meter backstroke, 200-meter butterfly, and 200-meter individual medley.

1968 With the 800 meters again a medal event, Madeline Manning was the first U.S. woman to medal, setting a world record of 2:00.9 and capturing the gold.

1968 The IOC implemented gender testing in order to protect women from unfair competition.

1968 The first woman to carry the U.S. flag in the opening ceremonies was fencer Janice Lee York Romary, of San Mateo, California, who, at age 40, was competing in her sixth Olympics.

1968 Norma Enriqueta Basilio was the first woman to carry the Olympic torch and to light the Olympic flame in the stadium, in Mexico City. This was also the first Olympics to provide live broadcasts in the United States and the first to require drug testing.

1968 Wyomia Tyus was the first runner, male or female, to win a sprint event in two consecutive Olympics. She won the 100 meters in 1964 with a time of 11.4 and won again in 1968, setting a world record of 11 seconds.

1968 With her performance on the balance beam, Linda Metheny was the first U.S. woman to finish as high as fourth in an individual gymnastics event.

1968 Donna de Varona, a former Olympic swimmer, was the first woman to become a television commentator of the Olympics.

1972 At the Games in Munich, new events for women included the increase of the 80-meter hurdles to 100 meters as well as the addition of the 1,500 meters and the 4×400-meter relay in track and field; the return of archery for the first time since 1920, with individual single rounds; the slalom singles in kayak; and the mixed sailing class in yachting.

1972 The Games were marred when Palestinian terrorists broke into the Olympic Village, killing two Israeli athletes and taking nine Israeli athletes and coaches as hostages. The Olympians were killed along with the terrorists at a shoot-out at the airport. The games were postponed for 34 hours.

1972 The first time a U.S. fencing team placed as high as seventh was in Munich, with team members Tanya Adamovich, Natalia Cloris, Harriett King, Ann O'Donnell, and Ruth White.

1972 In archery, Doreen Wilber won the gold, setting a record with 2,424 points.

1972 U.S. women swimmers broke every existing Olympic record and won eight gold medals; Melissa Belote won three.

1972 Margaret Murdock, a 33-year-old nurse from Topeka, Kansas, won the silver medal in the small-bore rifle. Murdock was the first woman to win a medal in direct competition against men. Lanny Basham, who won the gold medal, narrowly beat Murdock and at the medal ceremony pulled her up to the first-place platform to stand with him.

1972 Kathy Hammond was the first to medal in the 400-meter sprint for the United States, winning a bronze with a time of 51.64.

1972 The U.S. basketball team, with players Ann Myers, Nancy Lieberman (Cline), and Pat Head Summitt, won the silver. The Soviets won the gold.

1976 The games were held in Montreal. New events for women included basketball, team handball, the mixed tornado class in yachting, and, in rowing, the single scull, double sculls, quadruple sculls, pairs without coxswain, fours with coxswain, and eights.

1976 A U.S. equestrian team with a woman member—Hilda Gurney—medaled for the first time, capturing the bronze.

1978 President Carter signed the Amateur Sports Act into law, which imposed changes in the structures of the Olympic movement, including the training and development of athletes. The main objective was to make U.S. athletes more competitive.

1980 President Carter imposed a boycott on U.S. participation in the Olympics in Moscow, in protest of the Soviet Union's invasion of Afghanistan. This was the first time the Olympics were held in Russia.

1980 Field hockey was introduced as an Olympic sport.

1983 The U.S. Olympic Hall of Fame was founded to honor outstanding U.S. Olympians.

1984 The Games were held in Los Angeles. Women competed in four new track-and-field events: the 3,000 meters, marathon, 400-meter hurdles, and the heptathlon replaced the pentathlon when the javelin and the 200 meters were added to the event. In addition, the all-around in rhythmic gymnastics and the road race in cycling were added.

1984 The Olympics were boycotted by the Soviet Union in retaliation for the U.S. boycott in 1980.

1984 The first separate Olympic Village strictly for women was constructed in Los Angeles.

1984 Darlene May was the first woman chosen to officiate in Olympic basketball. She was also the first woman to be a basketball referee in an international men's game, when she worked the World University Games in 1977 in Bulgaria.

1984 In her first international competition, Mary Lou Retton became the first U.S. gymnast to score a perfect 10, doing so in the vault and floor exercise in the all-around competition. She won the all-around gold medal, took silver in the vault and team competitions, and earned bronze in the uneven bars and floor exercise.

1984 The women's 3,000-meter race became one of the notable stories of the Olympic Games. Competing in the medal race were U.S. pioneer middle-distance runner Mary Decker (Slaney) and South African teenager Zola Budd. Budd had been banned from the games because of racial policies and obtained British citizenship in order to compete. With two laps to go, the two runners bumped each other; Decker fell, and Budd finished seventh, and controversy over "fault" was ongoing.

1984 Joan Benoit Samuelson won the inaugural Olympic marathon. She pulled ahead of the pack after 14 minutes and led for the remainder of the race. Her entry into the Los Angeles Coliseum for the last lap remains one of the all-time great moments in Olympic history for U.S. women. Her time was 2:24:52.

1984 Karen Stives became the first U.S. woman to win an individual equestrian medal, taking silver astride Arthur in the three-day event.

1984 Connie Carpenter Phinney became the first woman to compete in both Winter and Summer Olympics. After competing in speed skating in 1972, she won the gold medal in cycling in 1984 in the first Olympic cycling road race, beating Rebecca Twigg by half a wheel.

1986 The IOC appointed former Olympic rower Anita DeFrantz to lifetime membership on the IOC. DeFrantz, a champion rower who won a bronze medal at the 1976 games, became the only American woman and one of only five women on the 91-member committee. She was also the first African American woman to serve on the committee. In 1993, she was elected to the executive board.

1988 At the Games in Seoul, South Korea, new events for women included team competition in archery; the 1,000-meter sprint in cycling; air pistol; 50-meter freestyle in swimming; singles and doubles in table tennis; singles and doubles in tennis; and the 470 class in yachting.

1988 Jackie Joyner-Kersee set a world record in the heptathlon with 7,219 points and an Olympic record in the long jump (24 feet, 3¼ inches). Louise Ritter won the gold medal in the high jump with an Olympic record at 6 feet, 8 inches.

1988 Florence "Flo Jo" Griffith-Joyner set a world record in the 200-meter dash and an Olympic record in the 100 meters. She also was part of the 4×100-meter relay team, winning three gold medals.

1988 Allison Jolley and Lynn Jewell won the gold medal in yachting.

1992 The Games were held in Barcelona, Spain. Judo made its debut. Jackie Joyner-Kersee became the first woman to win the heptathlon in consecutive Olympics. In track and field, Gail Devers won the gold in the 100 meters, Gwen Torrence won the gold in the 200 meters, and the 4×100-meter relay team won gold. Janet Evans won the gold in swimming in the 800-meter freestyle. In gymnastics, Shannon Miller won the silver in the all-around competition and the bronze for the balance beam.

1996 The United States hosted the Olympics in Atlanta. Since the first modern Olympics in 1896, the United States has hosted the Games more than any other country: Saint Louis in 1904, Lake Placid and Los Angeles in 1932, and Los Angeles again in 1984, and Atlanta in 1996.

1996 New Olympic events included beach volleyball, fast-pitch softball, modern pentathlon, soccer, team synchronized swimming as a replacement for solo and duet, and the 4×200-meter freestyle relay.

1996 The United States Olympic Committee (USOC) honored the U.S. women's basketball gold-medal team as Team of the Year—the first such award ever given.

1996 The U.S. gymnastic team won the team gold for the first time, and Shannon Miller won gold in the balance beam. In swimming, Amy Van Dyken took the gold in the 50-meter freestyle, 100-meter butterfly, 4×100-meter freestyle relay, and the 4×200-meter freestyle relay. Brooke Bennett won gold in the 800-meter freestyle.

1996 Gail Devers defended her Olympic gold in the 100 meters, and the 4×100-meter relay won gold for the fourth consecutive Olympics. The

U.S. soccer, basketball, softball, and synchronized swimming teams all won the gold. In shooting, Jayne Dickman took the gold in the three-position rifle.

1997 Anita DeFrantz was the first woman to be elected IOC vice president in the organization's 102-year history.

2000 Marla Runyan became the first legally blind member of a U.S. Olympic team, finishing third in the 1,500 meters at the Olympic trials.

2000 The Games were held in Sydney, Australia, for the first time, and women competed in the same number of team sports as men. New events included white-water slalom in canoe/kayak, the 500-meter track in cycling, ball trap and skeet in shooting, duet synchronized swimming, taekwondo, trampoline, triathlon, water polo, and weightlifting.

2000 On September 30, Marion Jones became the first woman to win five medals in one Olympics. Jones won gold in the 100 meters and 200 meters and as a member of the 4×400-meter relay team, and took bronze in the long jump and as a member of the 4×100-meter relay team.

2000 On October 1, Emily Deriel became the first American woman to medal in the modern pentathlon—taking the silver. The all-day pentathlon includes shooting 20 shots at 20 targets with a 4.5 millimeter air pistol; fencing, consisting of a 24-person round robin of one-minute bouts; a 200-meter freestyle swimming race in a 50-meter pool; horseback riding through a course that includes 12 jumps; and a 3,000-meter cross-country race.

2000 Teresa Edwards became the first U.S. player, male or female, to compete on five Olympic basketball teams. She won gold in 1984, '88, and '96 and a bronze in '92.

2000 Joetta Clark Digger competed in her fourth Olympics, 1988–2000, in the 800 meters. She was indoor champion six times from 1988 to

1998 and a five-time U.S. champion. At the University of Tennessee, Digger won four straight NCAA championships.

2000 Other Olympic achievements included Nancy Johnson's gold in air rifle, Kimberly Rhode's bronze in double trap shooting, bronze in lightweight double sculls, bronze in pair rowing without coxswain, and Marie Holden's silver in the cycling individual time trial.

2000 Jesseca Cross was the first American woman to make an Olympic team in both the shot put and hammer throw.

2000 When Sandra Baldwin was elected president, the highest position within the USOC, she became the first female president in the organization's 106-year history.

Winter Olympics

1924 The first Winter Olympics were held in Chamonix, France. Sixteen nations participated, with five sports on the program, only one of which was open to women: figure skating. Thirteen women competed in singles and mixed pairs. Herma von Szabo-Planck, of Austria, won the gold; Beatrix Loughran, of the United States, won the silver; and Ethel Muckelt, of Great Britain, won the bronze.

1928 The Olympics were held in Saint Moritz, Switerland, with no new events for women. In figure skating, Beatrix Loughran won the bronze, while Norwegian great Sonja Henie won the gold.

1932 The Olympics in Lake Placid, New York, marked the first time figure skating events took place indoors; Maribel Vinson won the bronze. Speed skating was a demonstration sport, with the 500 meters, 1,000 meters, and 1,500 meters. Five U.S. women entered, finishing first in the 1,000 meters and 1,500 meters, second in the 500 meters, and third in all three events. Speed skating did not become a medal event until 1960.

1936 The Olympics were held in Garmisch-Partenkirchen, Germany. New events for women included alpine combined downhill and slalom skiing.

1940 The Games in Saint Moritz were canceled due to World War II.

1944 The Games in Cortina d'Ampezzo, Italy, were canceled due to World War II.

1948 The Olympics returned to Saint Moritz. New events included the downhill and slalom in alpine skiing. Gretchen Fraser, of the United States, won the inaugural slalom event.

1952 The Olympics were held in Oslo, Norway. Two new events were the giant slalom and the 10 kilometers in cross-country skiing. The alpine combined was discontinued. Andrea Mead (Lawrence) won the gold in the giant slalom and alpine, becoming the first American skier to win two gold medals in a Winter Olympics. Tenley Albright won the silver in figure skating.

1956 The Olympics were held in Cortina d'Ampezzo, Italy. In cross-country skiing, the 3×5-kilometer relay was added. Tenley Albright became the first American to win an Olympic gold medal in figure skating and Carol Heiss took the silver. No other American women medaled.

1956 For the first time, the Winter Olympics were televised.

1956 The Olympic oath was recited by a woman for the first time, by 1952 downhill-skiing bronze medalist Guiliana Minuzzo, of Italy.

1960 The Olympics took place in Squaw Valley, California. New events were added in speed skating: the 500 meters, 1,000 meters, 1,500 meters, and 3,000 meters. Carol Heiss won the gold in figure skating, and Barbara Roles won the bronze. Jeanne Ashworth won the bronze in the 500 meters in speed skating, and Penelope Pitou took silver in both downhill and giant slalom, and Betty Smite won silver in the slalom.

1964 The Olympics were held in Innsbruck, Austria. New events included single luge and the five kilometers in cross-country. Jean Saubert won the bronze in the giant slalom and slalom.

1968 The Olympics were held in Grenoble, France. There were no new women's events. Peggy Fleming won the gold medal in figure skating—the only U.S. gold at the games. In speed skating, the U.S. team scored a rare triple in the 500 meters, with three skaters finishing in a tie for silver: Jennifer Fish, Dianne Holum, and Mary Meyers, with a time of 46.3.

1972 The Olympics were held in Sapporo, Japan. Dianne Holum was selected as the flagbearer for the opening ceremonies—she was the first woman to do so in the Winter Games. Speed skaters Anne Henning and Dianne Holum won gold medals in the 500 meters and 1,500 meters, respectively, Barbara Cochran won the gold in slalom skiing, and Susan Corrock won the bronze in the downhill.

1976 The Olympics returned to Innsbruck. Ice dancing was an event for the first time, and in cross-country skiing, the 3×5-kilometer race was replaced by the 4×5-kilometer. Women participated in 14 out of 37 events. Dorothy Hamill won the gold in figure skating. In speed skating, Sheila Young won the gold in the 500 meters, the silver in the 1,500 meters, and the bronze in the 1,000 meters—coming in just behind Leah Poulous, who took the silver. Cindy Nelson won the bronze in downhill skiing.

1980 The Olympics returned to Lake Placid. The U.S. women did not win a gold medal, although speed skater Leah Poulous won silver medals in the 500 meters and 1,000 meters, and Beth Heiden won the bronze in the 3,000 meters.

1984 The Olympics were held in Sarajevo, Yugoslavia. The 20-kilometer race was added in cross-country skiing. In the giant slalom, Debbie Armstrong won the gold, and Christin Cooper won the silver. Linda Fratianne won the silver in figure skating.

1988 The Olympics were held in Calgary, Alberta. New women's events in Canada included the 5,000 meters in speed skating and the super giant slalom in alpine skiing; also, the alpine combined was resumed. Debi Thomas became the first African American to medal in figure skating, taking the bronze. Speed skater Bonnie Blair was the only double medal winner, taking gold in the 500 meters and bronze in the 1,000.

1992 The Olympics were held in Albertville, France, where new events included short-track speed skating, the 5,000 meters, freestyle skiing (moguls, ariels, cross-country), and the biathlon.

1992 Speeding and bumping down the ski slopes over the moguls, Donna Weinbrecht took the gold. Cathy Turner won the gold in the 500 meters speed skating short-track race.

1992 Gold medal winners included Bonnie Blair in 500-meter and 1,000-meter speed skating, Cathy Turner in 500-meter short track speed skating, Donna Weinbrecht in moguls, and Kristi Yamaguchi in figure skating. Silver medal winners were Diane Roffe in giant slalom, Hilary Lindh in downhill, and the 3,000-meter speed skating relay team. Nancy Kerrigan earned a bronze in figure skating.

1994 The Olympics were held in Lillehammer, Norway, only two years after the previous Olympics, under a new schedule whereby the Summer and Winter Games are held two years apart.

1994 U.S. women excelled at the Olympics. Gold medal winners included Bonnie Blair in 500-meter and 1,000-meter speed skating, Cathy Turner defended her gold in the 500-meter short track speed skating, Diane Roffe-Steimotter in the super-G (skiing). Silver medalists were Picabo Street in the downhill and Nancy Kerrigan in figure skating. Amy Peterson was a bronze medalist in 500-meter short track speed skating.

1998 The Games were held in Nagano, Japan, where new women's events included curling, ice hockey, and half-pipe snowboarding.

1998 In a thrilling final game to win the gold medal, the U.S. ice hockey team beat Canada for the first time ever. In figure skating, Tara Lipinski won the gold, and Michelle Kwan took silver.

1998 Speed skater Jennifer Rodriguez was the first Hispanic athlete to compete in the Winter Olympics, finishing fourth in the 3,000 meters. Also in speed skating, Chris Witty won the silver in the 1,000 meters and bronze in the 1,500 meters.

1998 Cammy Myler was the first woman to be a four-time Olympian in luge. She finished fifth in 1988—the highest U.S. finish ever in women's luge. Picabo Street took the gold in the super-G, Nikki Stone won gold in ariels, and Shannon Dunn took bronze in half-pipe snowboarding.

2002 At the Olympics in Salt Lake City, Utah, new events included skeleton, 1,500-meter short track speed skating, the 1.5-kilometer sprint in freestyle cross-country skiing, the parallel giant slalom in snowboarding, and bobsled.

2002 U.S. women won more medals than in any previous Winter Games. Gold medal winners included Kelly Clark in half-pipe snowboarding, Chris Witty in 1,000-meter speed skating, Sara Hughes in figure skating, Jill Bakken and Vonetta Flowers in bobsled, and Tristan Gabe in skeleton. Silver medalists included the ice hockey team, Lea Ann Parsley in skeleton, and Shannon Bahrke in moguls. Figure skater Michelle Kwan

KELLY CLARK. (PHOTO © CLIVE BRUNSCKILL/GETTY)

and speed skater Jennifer Rodriguez won bronze medals. Rodriguez medaled in two events—1,000 meters and 1,500 meters.

2002 Chris Witty was the third U.S. woman to qualify for the Olympics in two sports. Connie Carpenter Phinny (1972 and '84), Connie Paraskevin-Young (1984 and '88) and Witty (1998 and 2002) all competed in the same events: speed skating and cycling.

RACQUETBALL

THE CREATION of racquetball is credited to Joe Sobek, who, in 1949, combined the rules of squash and handball on a Connecticut handball court to create a fast-paced, easy-to-learn game that is played on a court in room that is 20 feet wide, 40 feet long, and 20 feet high. Players use a short racket that resembles a tennis racket. The server bounce-hits a soft rubber ball off the front wall. The ball should land behind a short line on the court. The other walls can then be used, but the ball cannot bounce twice. The first player to 15 points wins.

1968 The United States Racquetball Association (USRA) was founded, and the first men's national championship was played.

1968 The International Racquetball Federation (IRF) was established, with the United States as a charter member.

1970 Fran Cohen, playing in her home state of Missouri, won the first U.S. National Singles Women's Open Championships, in Saint Louis.

1972 Kimberly Hill and Jan Pasternak won the first U.S. National Doubles Women's Open Championships, in Memphis, Tennessee.

1974 Jan Pasternak, of Texas, won her second National Singles title and the first USRA Female Athlete of the Year Award.

1974 Peggy Steding, of Odessa, Texas, was the first woman inducted into the USRA Hall of Fame. Before taking up racquetball, Steding competed in tennis, basketball, volleyball, and fast-pitch softball. Steding, who won three National Singles titles beginning in 1973 and was ranked number one on the women's pro tour for three years, is credited with having elevated the game of racquetball for women during her reign as champion.

1975 Martha Byrd, representing the University of Florida, won the first U.S. National/World Intercollegiate Championships, held in Memphis.

1975 Janet Marshall and Debbie Vinson, representing Memphis State University, won the first U.S. National/World Intercollegiate Women's Doubles title. Memphis State began its domination of intercollegiate racquetball, winning the first of a record-setting seven consecutive U.S. National/World Championship Women's Team titles.

1981 The U.S. women won the first of 10 consecutive IRF World Championship Women's Team titles. As of 2001, they were undefeated in international team competition.

1981 Cindy Baxter won the first IRF women's division World Championship by defeating fellow American player Barbara Faulkenberry in Santa Clara, California. Mary Ann Cluess and Karen Borga, of the United States, won the first women's IRF World Championships Doubles title by defeating Miriam Wielheesen and Dineke Kool, of Holland.

1981 Sharon Fanning won the first U.S. National Doubles Mixed Open title with partner Jack Newman, in Monroeville, Pennsylvania.

1987 Heather Stupp, of Canada, won the first Women's Pan American Racquetball Confederation (PARC) Tournament of the Americas singles title, in Caracas, Venezuela. Stupp also became the first non-U.S. woman to win the IRF World Championships women's singles crown.

1989 The USRA became a member of the United States Olympic Committee.

1989 Michelle Gilman (Gould), of Ontario, Oregon, began her assault on the racquetball record books when, at age 19, she won the first of eight U.S. National Singles Women's Open titles—covering 1989–'93 and 1995–'97—and, with partner Cindy Doyle, won the first of her six U.S. National Doubles Women's Open titles—covering 1989–'91, '93, '95, and '96.

1990 Jackie Paraiso, of California, won the first of her record four women's IRF World Championship Doubles titles, covering 1990, '94, '96, and '98.

1992 Michelle Gould continued her domination of women's racquetball as she won the first of her record three consecutive women's IRF World Championship titles, besting the field in 1992, '94, and '96.

1994 Memphis State won its record 11th U.S. National/World Championship Women's Team title.

1994 With her first National Singles Women's Open title, Robin Levine ended Michelle Gould's record streak of five consecutive titles.

1995 Racquetball was included in the Pan American Games for the first time. Michelle Gould won the gold medal in singles in Buenos Aires, Argentina.

1996 The first "grand slam" event of professional racquetball was played in Memphis, as Michelle Gould won the inaugural U.S. Open championships.

1997 Tammy Brockbank, representing Treasure Valley Community College (Ontario, Oregon), tied the record for consecutive and overall U.S. National/World Intercollegiate titles, with three, in 1995–'97, matching Barbara Faulkenberry's streak at the Air Force Academy in 1979–'81.

1997 Michelle Gould won her record eighth USRA Female Athlete of the Year Award.

1998 Gould won her record fourth PARC Tournament of the Americas women's singles title, following wins in 1988, '90, and '91.

1998 Gould, the most dominant women's racquetball player to date, retired after winning 46 pro titles, 7 pro season titles, 18 national doubles and singles titles, and 11 international doubles and singles titles.

2001 Kristen Walsh became the first woman to earn concurrent appointments to the U.S. national team and the U.S. junior national team, by qualifying with a Junior National Championship title and a U.S. National/World Championship Women's title.

2001 Jackie Paraiso tied Michelle Gould for the most overall Women's PARC Tournament of the Americas titles, with six. Paraiso won the singles in 1993 and won five doubles—1991, '97–'99, and 2001. Gould won four singles—1988, '90, '91, and '98—and two doubles, 1994 and '96.

2001 After winning the last five professional tournaments of the 2001 season, Cheryl Gudinas, of Illinois, achieved the world number one ranking in May.

2001 Mary Low Acuff, of North Carolina, won the 80-plus USRA National Championship, giving her a grand total of 21 age-group championships.

ROWING

SPORTS HAVE the power to instill courage and leadership in athletes. Anita DeFrantz, a former rower from the University of Connecticut, took the lessons rowing taught her and applied them to life. In 1997, DeFrantz became the first woman elected vice president of the International Olympic Committee (IOC). Although rowing looks almost effortless, an intense amount of energy is required to force the boat through the water while keeping the oars in perfect sync. Even the coxswain, who sits in the front of the boat and shouts a cadence to maintain the rowing pace, is under great physical and mental pressure.

1875 Women's college and recreational rowing clubs were founded at Wellesley College (Massachusetts). Early boats at Wellesley were large enough to fit 10 women dressed in long full skirts.

1892 ZLAC, a rowing club in San Diego, California, was formed by a group of teenage women who used their initials to name the club: Zulette Lamb, Lena Agnes, and Caroline Polhamus.

1936 Sally Brown, of Rollins College (Florida), was the first woman coxswain of a men's collegiate varsity rowing team. Rollins defeated Marietta College (Ohio) in a race on New York's Harlem River.

1938 One of the first clubs organized for women on the East Coast was the Philadelphia Girl's Rowing Club. The PGRC was founded by Ernestine Bayer, who, with several other women, rented a skating club along the Schuylkill River. Bayer taught hundreds of girls and women to row at PGRC and is still competing (as of 2001) at the age of 93.

1938 On July 4, three entries for the PGRC entered a regatta on the Schuylkill River in Philadelphia. This was the first time that women's boats raced on the Schuylkill. Ernestine Bayer and Jeanette Waetjem Hoover won the women's race.

1954 The European Championship Regatta was established and became the leading international rowing event for women.

1960s Women's rowing continued to grow throughout the 1940s and '50s with new clubs and increasing numbers of college teams. The older clubs continued to grow as well—in the early part of the decade, the Philadelphia Girls' Rowing Club was the first women's rowing club to purchase their own facility on Boat House Row on the Schuylkill River.

1962 The National Women's Rowing Association (NWRA) was founded.

1966 The first NWRA national championships were held on June 18, at Greenlake, in Seattle. Ten clubs competed in 13 events. The Philadelphia Girls' Rowing Club won the heavyweight eight, and the Lake Washington Rowing Club won the points trophy.

1966 The first intercollegiate race was between Wellesley College and Massachusetts Institute of Technology.

1967 An NWRA boat of eight entered the European Championship for the first time and finished sixth. The team was invited to the championship after the PGRC team of eight, coached by Bayer, beat an elite men's team at the St. Catherine's Regatta in Ontario, Canada.

1969 Gail Pierson (Cromwell), former U.S. oarswomen and NWRA president, was the first woman to row in the classic Head of the Charles Regatta, in Boston, when she entered the men's single sculls event.

1971 The women's single event was added to the Head of the Charles Regatta, with five entries. In 1972, the eight was added.

1972 The IOC voted to include women's rowing in the 1976 Olympic Games. The United States Olympic Committee established the first United States Women's Olympic Rowing Committee.

1973 The first Ivy League Women's Rowing Championships were held.

1973 In Moscow, Joan Lind became the first American to reach the finals of the European championships.

1974 The first women's world championships were held in Lucerne, Switzerland.

1975 At the world championships in Nottingham, England, the U.S. eight crew took a silver, the first international rowing medal for the United States. The team included Carol Brown, Chris Ernst, Carie Graves, Gail Pierson, Wiki Royden, Claudia Schneider, Nacie Storrs, Ann Warner, and coxswain Lynn Silliman.

1975 At the championships held on Lake Carnegie, the international racing rules and elimination systems were employed for the first time in women's competition.

1976 The first women's crew competition at the Olympics took place in Montreal, Canada. Six new rowing events were added to the Olympic schedule: single sculls, double sculls, quadruple sculls with coxswain, pair-oared shell without coxswain, four-oared shell with coxswain, and eight-oared shell with coxswain. A total of 60 Olympic medals were awarded to women in the sport—second only to track and field.

1976 The first U.S. woman to win an Olympic medal in single sculls was Joan Lind, who took the silver. The U.S. women also won the bronze in the eight.

1976 At Yale University, the women's rowing team protested against the way they were treated as compared to the men's team. Led by captain Chris Arnst, they marched into the athletic director's office, stripped off their clothes, and revealed the phrase "Title IX" written across their chests and backs. The protest worked; the school soon added a women's wing to the boathouse.

1977 ZLAC became was the first junior women's rowing program to send a team from the United States to compete in European regattas.

1977 Elizabeth Hills and Lisa Hansen received the bronze at the world championships, the first world medal for a U.S. team in a tandem event.

1978 The mixed eight was added to the program at the Head of the Charles Regatta in Cambridge, Massachusetts.

1979 The United States took the bronze in the eight at the world championships.

1979 The first women's collegiate national championship event was the varsity eights race, held during the NWRA nationals. Yale was the first national champion.

1980 The first women's collegiate championship was held in Oak Ridge, Tennessee. UC Berkeley won the varsity eight.

1981 The United States won the bronze medal in the eight at the world championships.

1981 Susan Brown broke a 152-year male tradition by coxing in the prestigious Oxford-Cambridge University race.

1982 By this time there were over 100 NWRA organizations. They united with the National Association of Amateur Oarsmen to form U.S. Rowing, a member of the USOC and of the Federation Internationale des Societes D'Aviron (FISA).

1983 Virginia Gilder won a bronze medal at the world championships.

1984 The U.S. women's eight team won its first Olympic gold medal in Los Angeles. The team included coxswain Betsy Beard, Carol Bower, Jeanne Flanagan, Carie Graves, Kathy Keeler, Kristine Norelius, Kris Thornes, Holly Metcalf, and Shyrl O'Skeen.

1987 The first combined men's and women's national championship regattas were held in Indianapolis.

1987 Between 1981 and 1987, Holly Metcalf, a graduate of Mount Holyoke College (South Hadley, Massachusetts), won three silver medals and one bronze in the world championships. She also won the gold at the Olympics in 1984 in Los Angeles. Metcalf, a six-time national and Olympic team member, coached the U.S. national team to a silver at the world championships in 1990.

1988 The women's racecourse was extended to 2,000 meters, the same as the men's. Prior to 1988, women rowed on 1,000-meter courses.

1989 Kris Karlson was the first woman ever to win two sculling events at the same world championships. She won the gold medal in both the lightweight single and double sculls.

1992 The U.S. women's four won the silver medal at the Olympics in Barcelona.

1995 At the World Championship competition in Tampere, Finland, the women's teams won gold medals in the four, eight, the lightweight four, and the lightweight pairs and silver in the pairs. This was the best show-ing ever for the U.S.

1996 At the Olympics in Atlanta, Teresa Bell and Lindsay Burns took the silver medal in the lightweight double sculls, with a time of 7:14.65. Missy Schwan and Karen Kraft took the silver medal in pairs without coxswain, with a time of 7:01.78. The women's eight placed fourth.

1997 The World championships were held in Aiguebelette, France. Sarah Garner won the gold in single skulls and Michelle Borkhaus and Linela Muri took the silver in the lightweight pairs.

1997 The first National Collegiate Athletic Association (NCAA) women's rowing championships were held on Lake Natoma, in Rancho Cordova, California. The University of Washington won the team cham-pionship, followed by Princeton, Yale, Virginia, Rutgers, Oregon State, and Dartmouth. The University of Washington also won the eight.

1998 Sarah Garner and Christine Smith Collins won the gold medal in the lightweight double sculls at the World Championships in Cologne, Germany. U.S. women also won two silver and two bronze medals.

1998 Michelle Whitcomb Borkhaus won the lightweight pairs at the national championships and took silver in 1997. She won the bronze in 1998 at the world championships.

1998 The University of Washington won its second straight NCAA championship and won again in 2001.

1999 Monica Michini, of Billings, Montana, won her second silver medal in the eight at the world championships in St. Catharine's Canal, having won the first in 1994. She won the bronze in the quadruple skull in 1993 and a gold in the eight in 1995. Michini also is a seven-time national champion.

1999 The U.S. women's teams earned gold in lightweight pairs and quad; silver in eight, lightweight single, and lightweight double; and bronze in four at the World Championships in St. Catherine's, Ontario Canada.

2000 Brown University (Providence, Rhode Island) won its second straight NCAA championship, placing first in the variety eight race. In the second race, the team set a championship record with a time of 6:49.10, besting the mark set by Virginia in 1999.

2000 At the Olympics in Sydney, Australia, Karen Kraft and Missy Ryan teamed up to win bronze in the pairs without coxswain race.

2000 Christine Smith Collins has won more world titles than any other female rower in history—four. She competes in lightweight double sculls and lightweight pairs. Paired with Sarah Garner, they won the lightweight double sculls at the Olympics.

2000 Amy Fuller has won more medals than any other U.S. rower—seven world championship medals and an Olympic silver. She is a ten-time member of the U.S. national team and a three-time Olympian.

2001 At the World Championships in Lucerne, Switzerland, the openweight quadruple scull team won the bronze medal. The lightweight pair with coxswain team brought home a silver.

2001 Sara Hall, age 48, who started rowing at 42, won the gold medal in the Head of the Charles race in the 50 double with Judy Davis. She also took gold at the Head of the Schuylkill with Marie Hagelstein in veteran's doubles in 2000 and '01. In 1998 at the World Masters games, she won gold in the women's C singles and doubles with Carie Davis.

RUGBY

ORIGINATING IN England, rugby is frequently compared to American football. A full-contact sport with continuous play, the game pits two 15-member teams against each other. The ball resembles a large football. Women play with exactly the same rules as men. Games have two 45-minute periods. "Tries," worth five points, are scored by running the ball past the goal line. U.S. women have become actively involved in the international development of the sport.

1970s Women began playing rugby in the United States.

1972 The first college women's rugby teams were formed at the Universities for Colorado, Missouri, and Illinois. By 1976 there were teams in Boston, Chicago, Hartford, Philadelphia, and Kansas. These were all considered "club" teams.

1975 The United States of America Rugby Football Union (USARFU) was established and represented both men's and women's rugby.

1977 The first American exhibition game was played in the United Kingdom.

1979 Florida State University defeated Wisconsin at the first USA Rugby women's club championship.

1980s Club teams continued to be formed across the country, with official club championships held for the first time.

1981 The first U.S.-sanctioned nationals were held.

1987 The first USA Rugby national team was founded.

1987 The Canadian Rugby Board set up women's first test matches in Vancouver. The United States played its first international rugby match, defeating Canada by a score of 22–3, and England played Wales.

1990 The international women's Rugby Fest was held in New Zealand, and the USA Rugby national team adopted the name of the Eagles.

1991 In Cardiff, Wales, the United States won the first Women's World Cup, defeating England, 19–6. Twelve other countries participated in the tournament.

1991 The first National Collegiate Athletic Association national championships were held.

1994 The second Women's World Cup was held in Edinburgh, Scotland. The United States, the defending champion, lost to England in another 19–6 game.

1996 Princeton University won the national championship in 1995 and '96 and set a new standard for collegiate players. Princeton was upset by Penn State in '97.

1997 The United States formed a national team for women under 23 years old, called U-23.

1997 The first International Sevens were held in Hong Kong, in March.

1998 The third Women's World Cup was held in Amsterdam, Holland. Sixteen teams competed, with New Zealand defeating the United States in the final.

1998 In August, Eastern Illinois University became the first college to grant varsity status to its women's rugby program.

2001 More than 172 women's teams nationwide belonged to USA Rugby.

2002 The fourth Women's World Cup will be held in Barcelona, Spain.

SAILING

T̲H̲E̲ M̲O̲S̲T̲ important of nature's elements as far as sailors are concerned is the wind. Sailboats move in two directions related to the wind: upwind or downwind. The sail creates pressure that moves the boat, much like the wings of an airplane. Sailboats come in many sizes and can be navigated by a single sailor, a pair of sailors, or a team. The boats also are made in many styles, for recreational enjoyment and for racing.

1896 Olympic yachting was introduced at the games in Athens, Greece, but it took another 92 years before women were allowed to compete.

1897 On October 30, the United States and Canada joined to form the North American Yacht Racing Union (NAYRU) to promote the sport and to unify racing and rating rules throughout the yachting world. The organization attempted to agree upon international standards with the Yacht Racing Association of the United Kingdom, but no settlements could be reached. NAYRU was dormant from 1898 to 1925.

1924 The first U.S. women's sailing championship, the Hodder Cup— later changed to the Adams Trophy—was held at the Boston Yacht Club. Crews of two, age 12 years and older, competed in 14-foot Marconi catboats. Ruth and Ester Sears were the first winners and repeated in 1925.

1925 NAYRU was reestablished by Clifford D. Mallory. The organization administered 17 national championships and negotiated with the International Yacht Racing Union (IYRU) to form international rules.

petition—junior, collegiate, and adult—enjoyed a period of growth and recognition.

1985 The Rolex International Women's Keelboat Championship was inaugurated through the efforts of the USYRU Women's Championship Committee. Skipper Betsy Alison and crew won the first event, hosted by the Ida Lewis Yacht Club, in Newport, Rhode Island. The championship, held every two years, has become the premier women's sailing event in the world.

1985 The America's Cup began under another name in Britain (1851), but was later renamed the America's Cup because the American teams dominated the race. It was not until 1985 that women were allowed to participate for the first time.

1988 The first women's-only Olympic yachting event, the women's 470—a single-handed dinghy—took place in Seoul, South Korea, with more than 30 nations competing. There were seven races, with points awarded according to place of finish. Allison Jolly and Lynne Jewell, of the United States, took home the gold.

1989 Dawn Riley was a part of the first all-women crew to compete in the nine-month-long Whitbread Round the World Race. In 1991, she became the first woman to sail in an America's Cup series, in an otherwise all-male crew. After serving as captain on another all-female boat in the Whitbread race of 1993, she headed the first co-ed syndicate in America's Cup history, aboard the *America True* in 2000.

1991 The USYRU voted to change its name to the United States Sailing Association (U.S. Sailing). U.S. Sailing maintains national standards for sailing and fields teams in the Olympics and Pan American Games.

1992 Two women's events—mistral (windsurfer) and Europe dinghy (single-handed dinghy)—were added to the Olympics in Barcelona,

Spain. Julia Trotman won the bronze medal in the first Europe dinghy race. Courtney Becker-Day placed sixth.

1992 Allison Jolly and Lynne Jewell, overcoming 30-mile-an-hour winds and 30-foot waves in the final race, won the inaugural 470 competition in Barcelona. Jennifer "JJ" Isler and Pam Healy won the bronze.

1994 Dawn Riley became the first U.S. woman to skipper an all-women boat—the *Heineken*—in the Whitbread race. The Whitbread, a 32,000-mile, five-day event, is considered one of the most grueling races. It was established in 1975 by the Royal Navy Sailing Association of Great Britain and is held every four years.

1994 Bill Koch announced that his boat, the *America³*, would race in the 1995 America's Cup with an all-women team.

1995 *America³* sailed as the first all-women's team to compete against men for the America's Cup, a five-month-long sailing contest. The team drew enormous attention to women sailors as 650 women competed for the 25 available places. The *America³* team won the first race in round one, against Dennis Connor. They were one of three teams to make it to the final round, but they eventually lost to Connor's team.

1996 At the Olympics in Atlanta, Courtney Becker-Day won the bronze medal in Europe dinghy.

1997 The Women's International Match Racing Association was formed. The association developed three major international races. By 1998, Betsy Alison, of Newport, had the top-ranked match-racing team.

1997 Alison, considered the most dominant competitor in women's team sailing, won her fourth consecutive and fifth overall Rolex International Women's Keelboat Championship, spanning 1991–'97. The event hosts more than a dozen nations, yet America has been the sole champion since its inception in 1985.

1997 Lanee Butler won the gold medal at the Pan American Games. She also won gold in 1991 and took the bronze in '95.

2000 Lanee Butler, at the Olympics in Sydney, Australia, was the first female sailor to represent the USA in three consecutive Olympics. She won.

2000 Olympic sailors competed in the one-design class. The International Sailing Federation set strict standards for the "one-design" boats, allowing the best sailor to win, as opposed to the best boat.

2000 Jennifer (JJ) Isler became the first American to win two Olympic medals in women's sailing, when she teamed with Pease Glaser to take the silver in the 470 at the Sydney Olympics. Her previous win was the bronze in 1992.

2001 On September 28, the Rolex International Women's Kneelboat championships were held in Anapolis, Maryland. *Sertl*, skippered by Cory Sertl of Rochester, New York, was the winning boat.

SHOOTING

I N 1967, when Margaret Murdock won the small-bore rifle competition at the Pan American Games by shooting a score of 391, she set a world record and became one of the first women to surpass a men's record in any sport. Nine years later, at the Olympics in Montreal, Murdock finished in a tie with teammate Lanny Basham, but the judges awarded the gold to Basham on a rules technicality. In a poignant moment at the medal ceremony, Basham pulled Murdock to the gold-medal stand as the national anthem played.

Shooting with the rifle, pistol, and shotgun has been practiced in many countries since the Middle Ages. During the 19th century, however, shooting also developed into a sport. Associations formed in various countries to ally shooters and clubs in local, regional, and national organizations.

Today, Olympic competition consists of four primary disciplines: pistol, shooting, running target, and shotgun. One of the few sports in which men and women have competed together, shooting has developed over time to provide for separate men's and women's competitions.

1880s Phoebe Ann Mosey, who changed her name to Annie Oakley, was a legendary stunt shooter who brought international attention to women. She became famous on her own but developed an international following when she joined Frank Butler, whom she later married, on barnstorming shows, including the Buffalo Bill Wild West Show. Oakley performed trick acts with unprecedented precision. In 1884, she broke 943 out of 1,000 glass bottles thrown in the air, using a .22 caliber Stevenson rifle. In 1922, she shot 100 clay targets in a row—claimed to be a record for women.

1966 The women's world championships were held and included both rifle and pistol events. Margaret Thompson Murdock won a gold medal in the small-bore rifle and repeated in 1970.

1967 In a sport requiring a sharp eye and mental toughness, Margaret Thompson Murdock was a pioneer for women and one of the best shooters in history, winning numerous small-bore riflery championships. At the Pan American Games, in open competition against men, she won the small-bore gold medal and won it again in 1975. Not only was her 1967 win a first for female competitors, but in the process of achieving it, Murdock set a world record with a score of 391, becoming the first woman to break a men's world record in any sport.

1968 Women were eligible to compete at the Olympics for the first time, but none qualified. In 1984, some events were broken out by sex.

1969 Margaret Murdock won the national women's small-bore prone and three-position titles; she won the prone title again in 1972.

1970 Margaret Murdock was the first woman to win an open competition against men at the world championships. She was four months pregnant at the time.

1976 Margaret Murdock was the first woman to become a member of the U.S. Olympic shooting team, at the Montreal Olympics. She was also the first U.S. woman to win a medal, a silver in small-bore three-position rifle.

1984 Ruby Fox was the first U.S. medalist in sport pistol, winning the silver at the Los Angeles Olympics. She also won the bronze in the three-position rifle.

1984 At the Olympics in Los Angeles, shooting events were separated by sex. Women's air rifle and 50-meter three-position rifle were medal events for the first time. The first gold medal in Olympic competition was won by Pat Spurgin in small-bore rifle, who hit 393 out of 400 shots.

1988 Air pistol became an event for women at the Olympics in Seoul, South Korea.

1990 Constance Petiacek set a national record in the 25-millimeter sport pistol, with 600 points.

1992 At the Olympics in Barcelona, Spain, Launi Meili won a gold medal in the 50-meter three-position rifle.

1993 Deena Minyard set a national record in women's trap, with 181 points out of 200.

1995 Deena Minyard (Wigger) won the gold medal in the Pan American Games, a repeat of her 1983 performance. In 1987, she led her college team, Murray State University (Kentucky), to the National Collegiate Athletic Association championships. In 1988, Wigger qualified for the Olympics.

1995 In the 50-meter three-position rifle Elizabeth Boutland set a national record of 590 points out of 600.

1996 Rhonda Bright set a national record of 387 points in women's air pistol.

1996 At the Olympics in Atlanta, all shooting events were separate competitions for women and men.

1996 Kim Rhode, who had just turned 17, became the youngest person to win a medal in Olympic shooting, when she won gold in the inaugural double trap competition. In addition to her Olympic gold, Rhode is a four-time national champion, was voted USA Shooting Female Athlete of the Year in 1996, '97, and '98, has a gold medal from the Pan American Games, and was a strong competitor in the 2000 Olympics.

1999 Lauryn Ogilvie set a national record in women's skeet of 274 points out of 300.

1999 Jayme Dickman won gold medals in the Pan American Games in air rifle and three position rifle. She also took bronze in these events at the U.S. Championship, earning her a spot on the 2000 Olympic team.

1999 Jean Foster was another member of the 2000 Olympic team after having won the U.S. Championship in three position rifle and prone and taking second in air rifle.

1999 Cindy Gentry won both the U.S. Championship and the World Championship titles in trap. She also won the silver in the Pan American Games and was named USA Shooting Female Shotgun Athlete of the Year.

1999 Rebecca Snyder won the gold medal in air and sport pistol at the U.S. championships. She also won a silver in sport pistol at the Pan American games and was a two-time Olympian, 1996 and 2000.

1999 Nancy Johnson, a two-time Olympian (1996 and 2000), won the gold at the U.S. National Championships in air rifle. She also took the silver in the three-position rifle competition at the Pan American Games.

2000 At the U.S. National Championships, in the 50-meter three-position rifle Jean Foster won gold, Thrine Kane won silver, and Tanny Foster took bronze.

2000 At the national championships in trap, Cindy Gentry won gold, Teresa DeWitt took silver, and Deena Minyard won the bronze. Minyard was also a world cup gold medalist.

2000 In Sydney, Australia, women's skeet and women's trap made their first Olympic appearance, although women competed against men in 1998 and 1992. Nancy Johnson won the gold in the 10m air rifle, the first U.S. gold medal at the Olympics, and Kimberly Rhode took the bronze in the double trap.

2000 The U.S. national champions in skeet medalists were Cindy Shenberger—gold, Connie Schiller Smotek—silver, and Linda Ferrence—bronze. Connie Schiller Smotek also won a world cup gold in 1999 and another gold in '99 at the Pan American Games.

2000 Kim Rhode, at the Olympics, won the bronze medal in double trap—added to her gold in 1996.

2001 Haley Dunn, competing at the World Clay Target championship in Cairo, Egypt won the junior world title in women's skeet.

2001 Rebecca 'Becki' Snyder at the Championships of the Americas in Fort Benning, Georgia won the gold medal in both women's air pistol and sport pistol. Snyder was a two-time Olympian.

SKIING

I N ALPINE racing, it's the clock that counts, with winning determined by times in hundredths of a second. Skiers are judged not on form but on how quickly they come down the mountain.

Alpine races are skied in four events: downhill, slalom, giant slalom, and super giant slalom—or "super G." Downhill and super G are one-run speed events over a long course, about two miles in length, with gates (specifically placed poles) that skiers must negotiate as they go down the mountain. The slalom and giant slalom are two-run events and are more technical. The slalom has the shortest course and closest gates. The giant slalom has bigger turns, and an increased emphasis is put on control.

One of the most famous skiers of all time is Picabo Street. In the 1994 Winter Olympics, she took the silver medal and in 1998 she claimed gold in the Super-G. In 1995, she became the first U.S. woman to win a World Cup downhill title. After recovering from several career threatening injuries, she came back for one more Olympics; however, she failed to medal in Salt Lake in 2002.

This chapter presents separate listings under the headings Downhill, Freestyle, Moguls, Aerials, and Cross-Country.

1908 The first women's international ski race was held at Chamonix, France.

1920s Competition for women existed mainly in ski clubs and college-sponsored teams. The Lake Placid Club, in New York, held events in cross-country, downhill, and slalom.

1924 The first Winter Olympics were held in Chamonix, but the only events for women were in figure skating.

1924 The International Ski Federation (ISF) was founded, and the federation sanctioned downhill and slalom as international events for both men and women.

1931 World championships sponsored by the ISF were held for women for the first time.

1931 The first alpine ski championships for women were held in Muren, Switzerland. Esme McKinnon won both the alpine and slalom events.

1932 Lake Placid was the site of the first Winter Olympics held in America. The exposure from the games boosted the popularity of skiing in the United States, and resorts began opening all over the country.

Downhill

1936 Alpine, or downhill, skiing was given Olympic recognition for the first time.

1936 The first U.S. women's Olympic ski squad was formed and sent to Garmisch-Partenkirchen, Germany. Four women competed: Elizabeth Woolsey, Clarita Heath, Helen Boughton Leigh, and Mary Bird, but they were no match for the highly experienced European women. Betty Woolsey placed highest among the Americans at 14th.

1941 Gretchen Fraser won the U.S. national downhill and alpine combined championships, and in 1942, she won the national slalom.

1948 On February 5, in Saint Moritz, Switzerland, 29-year-old Gretchen Fraser, skiing in the first position, became the first U.S. skier to win an

Olympic medal, capturing the gold in the slalom with a time of 1:57.2 and ending the European dominance. Fraser had qualified for the U.S. Olympic team in 1940, but the games weren't held because of the war.

1950 Andrea Mead Lawrence, who learned to ski at her parents' resort in Pico Peak, Vermont, was 17 when she won the downhill slalom and combined at the U.S. nationals. In 1951, she placed first in 10 international competitions, which later became the World Cup.

1952 At the Olympic Games in Oslo, Norway, the giant slalom became a medal event. Nineteen-year-old Andrea Mead Lawrence was the first American to capture two gold medals in a single Olympics, winning the slalom in 2:10.6 and the giant slalom in 2:06.8.

1956 Andrea Mead Lawrence became the first American skier to compete in three Olympics. As a mother of three, she placed fourth in the giant slalom in Cortina d'Ampezzo, Italy, with a time of 1:58.3.

1960 At the Olympics in Squaw Valley, California, Penelope Pitou won the silver medal in the giant slalom with a time of 1:40.0 and won another silver in the downhill.

1963 Jean M. Saubert was the first woman to win six of a possible eight national championship races. In the 1964 Olympics, she tied with Christine Gortshel, of France, for the silver in the giant slalom, with a time of 1:53.11, and she took the bronze in the alpine slalom, with a time of 1:31.36.

1967 The first World Cup was held. In 1969, Kiki Cutter became the first U.S. skier to win a World Cup title.

1967 Suzy Chaffee placed fourth in the downhill at the world ski championships in Portillo, Chile. She was the highest-ranked American in alpine competition.

1972 On an extremely icy course on which only 19 out of 42 entrants finished both runs, Barbara Cochran won the gold medal in the slalom at the Olympics in Sapporo, Japan, with a time of 1:31.24. Susan Corroch won the bronze in the downhill in 1:37.68.

1972 The ISF sanctioned the giant slalom as an international event.

1974 Cindy Nelson was the first U.S. skier to win a World Cup downhill title.

1976 At the Olympics in Innsbruck, Austria, Cindy Nelson won the bronze in the slalom with a time of 1:47.50. She is considered one of the best downhill racers ever and was a 13-year member of the U.S. Team (1971–'84). She won the downhill national championship in 1973 and '78, the slalom championship in 1975 and '76, and qualified for four Olympic teams.

1980 At the Olympics in Lake Placid, the women's giant slalom was held as a two-run competition for the first time.

1983 Tamara McKinney became the first American woman to win the biggest prize in skiing, the overall World Cup title, at the world championships in Furano, Japan. In 1981, she won the giant slalom title. McKinney, one of history's most accomplished alpine skiers, had a decade-long career in the '80s, winning 18 World Cup events—9 in slalom and 9 in giant slalom. The youngest of seven children, she grew up traveling on the skiing circuit.

1983 The first National Collegiate Athletic Association men's and women's skiing championships with combined scoring were held at the Bridger Bowl, in Bozeman, Montana, hosted by the University of Montana. Beth Heiden, also a great speed skater and cyclist, won the championship.

1984 Seattle native Debbie Armstrong, at age 20, had competed in only a few races when she won the gold medal in the giant slalom at the Olympics in Sarajevo, Yugoslavia, defeating the best skiers in the world. In 1983, she won the silver medal in the combined at the U.S. nationals, and in 1987, she was the U.S. national champion in the slalom.

1984 Christin Cooper won the Olympic silver medal in the giant slalom. In 1982, she won silver in both the slalom and giant slalom at the world championships. Cooper was also a member of the 1980 Olympic team.

1987 The super G was sanctioned as an international event by the ISF.

1989 Tamara McKinney made a memorable comeback after experiencing several personal crises, losing her parents and a brother and watching another brother and a sister suffer severe injuries. Her gold medal in the combined at the world championships in Vail, Colorado, was all the more gratifying under the circumstances. In both the 1985 and 1987 world championships, she won the bronze in the combined.

1994 Diann Roffe-Steinrotter won the gold medal in the super G at the Olympics in Lillehammer, Norway. In 1992, she won the silver medal in the giant slalom. When she was 16, she finished second in the giant slalom at the world junior championships in Sugarloaf, Maine, the first U.S. skier to win a medal in that competition. In 1985, at the world championships in Italy, she won the giant slalom.

1994 Picabo Street won the silver medal in the downhill at the Olympics, and in 1993, she won the silver medal in the combined at the world championships. Even before her career on the U.S. ski team, at age 17, she won the national junior downhill and super G titles.

1995 Picabo Street was the first American woman to win the World Cup downhill title. In 1994–'95, she won six out of nine races, and in the

CINDY NELSON.

1995–'96 season, Street became the first woman to win six straight down-hill events.

1998 Picabo Street won the gold medal in the super G by one-hundredth of a second at the Olympics in Nagano, Japan. This was a remarkable win considering Street had just recovered from tearing her ACL (a tendon in the knee), and her chances of competing at a top level after that were bleak. Also in 1998, she became Nike's only female winter-sport endorsement athlete, with her own signature sneaker. In 2001, she marked 14 years on the U.S. ski team.

1998 Paralympic skier Muffy Davis won the bronze medal in the down-hill at the Olympics in Nagano.

1998 Hillary Lindh retired from competition after an impressive career. In 1986, she was the world junior downhill champion, and in both '86 and '89, she was U.S. downhill champion. In 1992, Lindh became the first

Alaskan to win an individual Olympic medal, when she won the silver in the downhill, missing the gold by six-hundredths of a second. Earlier that year, she also won the combined U.S. championship.

1998 In January, the first U.S. Ski Team Gold Cup competition was held in Lake Placid. Skiers competed in cross-country, alpine, and aerial events for cash prizes, and winners earned spots on the U.S. Olympic ski team.

1999 Between 1991 and '99, Megan Gerety, of Anchorage, Alaska, placed in the top three for a record 11 times in U.S. title competitions. Gerety's other highlights include three top-eight finishes in international competition.

2000 Caroline Lalive finished the season ranked second in the World Cup combined competition.

2001 At the world championships in Saint Anton, Austria, Kristen Clark won the combined downhill. She was the first to win four straight U.S. downhill titles, 1998-2001.

2002 Caroline Lalive finished the season ranked second in the World Cup downhill.

2002 At the Chevy Truck U.S. Alpine championships, Sara Schlepin defended her U.S. title in the slalom, and Jonna Mendes defended her U.S. title in the giant slalom.

Freestyle

Freestyle skiing, introduced in the United States by Stein Eriksen (an Olympic champion who immigrated from Norway) in the early 1950s, combines acrobatics and skiing and is judged for style and creativity.

1966 The first freestyle competition took place in Attitash, New Hampshire.

1971 Suzy Chaffee joined the men's professional freestyle tour, because no women's tour existed. She won three consecutive world championships in co-ed competition in 1971–'73. Chaffee appeared in advertisements, becoming well known for the Suzy Chapstick commercial, and was active in promoting legislation to benefit women.

1973 The International Freestyle Ski Association, including a woman's division, was formed.

1979 The Federation Internationale de Ski, the sport's governing body, sanctioned freestyle.

1980s World Championship and World Cup competitions were held.

1988 Freestyle skiing was an exhibition sport at the 1988 Olympic Games and was added to the program as a medal sport in 1992.

Moguls

Formerly known as ballet, the moguls competition requires a skier to take a quick dash down a 270 yard course while negotiating a field of snowy bumps (moguls). Mogul skiers also take two jumps during the run. Scoring is by a panel of judges based on the amount of time the skier is on the course and the execution and difficulty of turns. The turns count for 50 percent, aerial and speed count for 25 percent each.

1988 The Federation Internationale de Ski voted to have mogul skiing as a full-medal sport at the 1992 Olympics, in Albertville, France.

1988 At the U.S. freestyle championships at Stratton Mountain, Vermont, Donna Weinbrecht was named World Cup Rookie of the Year.

1990 Between 1986 and 1990, Diana Golden won 10 gold medals at the World Handicapped Championships. When Golden was a young teenager, her right leg was amputated due to cancer. Afterward, she became an international inspiration, competing on one leg and winning 19 U.S. titles. In 1987, she won the gold medal in the downhill at the Winter Paralympics and also made the top 10 in an open slalom race, the only disabled skier in the event. The United States Olympic Committee named her Female Skier of the Year in 1988. Golden died in August 2001.

1991 Donna Weinbrecht won the world championship in moguls. From 1988 to 1992, she was the U.S. mogul champion. Between 1989 and 1997, she had 46 World Cup wins.

1992 At the Olympics in Albertville, France, moguls became an official medal event. Donna Weinbrecht won the first gold medal and brought international attention to mogul skiing.

1994 Donna Weinbrecht won the U.S. championship—her sixth.

1994 Liz McIntyre won the silver medal at the Olympics in Lillehammer, Norway.

1998 In March, three-time Olympian Ann Battelle and Garth Hager became the first U.S. dual moguls champions, in Carrabassett Valley, Maine.

1999 Ann Battelle won the world championship and bronze medal in the dual event. A two-time World Cup champion (1999 and 2000), she won six U.S. titles and is a three-time Olympian (1992, '94, and '98).

2001 Hannah Hardaway won the U.S. mogul championship for the second consecutive year. She also won two World Cups.

2002 Shannon Bahrke won the first U.S. medal of the Olympic Games in Salt Lake City, Utah, by taking the silver.

2002 Ann Battelle appeared in her fourth Olympics, placing seventh. Her teammate Hannah Hardaway placed fifth.

Aerials

In the aerials competition, skiers without poles descend a concave ramp that launches the skier 50 feet or more into the air. While airborne, the skiers perform a variety of twists, flips, and somersaults (in less than four seconds) before landing on a steep slope and finishing the run. Seven judges evaluate competitors based on the air and form of the jump and how well it was landed.

1994 Women's aerial skiing made its debut as an Olympic sport on February 21 at the games in Lillehammer, Norway.

1998 At the Olympics in Nagano, Nikki Stone won the gold medal after recovering from a serious back injury that had threatened her career two years earlier.

1999 Marissa Berman won the U.S. Championship.

2000 Kelly Hillman won the U.S. Championship.

2001 Emily Cook won the U.S. Freestyle Championship and would have been a strong contender for an Olympic medal had she not been injured.

2002 Tracy Evans competed in her third Olympics in Salt Lake City.

Cross-Country

Cross-country skiing is a mix of speed and endurance. Races of various distances over courses that are one-third rolling, one-third uphill, and one-third downhill are skied in one of two styles: classic and freestyle. Classic cross-country skiers keep each ski in a separate, pre-cut track and move the skies straight ahead. In freestyle cross-country, the skiers move the skies in a skating motion. The skis themselves are longer and thinner than downhill skies.

1952 Cross-country events were added to the Olympics in Oslo.

1956 The cross-country skiing 3×5-kilometer relay became an Olympic event for women in Cortina d'Ampezzo.

1964 Individual Olympic events were held for the first time.

1966 The first U.S. skier to win an unofficial cross-country World Cup race was Alison Owen (Kiesel), at age 13. She was the only girl competing. At the time, the national alpine and junior championships were held together, and the cross-country races were all one division.

1968 The first U.S. women's cross-country championships were held in Durango, Colorado. Martha Rockwell, who became a premier U.S. racer, won the event. She won 15 individual titles in her career.

1969 The first national women's team was formed.

1975 Martha Rockwell won her seventh consecutive 10-kilometer freestyle at the national championships.

1978 In December, the first official World Cup race was held at Telemark Resort, in Wisconsin. Alison Owen (Kiesel) won the 5-kilometer run in 7:14.43, finishing 14 seconds ahead of Marie Johannson, of Sweden. Lesley Bancroft, of the United States, was eighth.

1979 At the first World Cup for women, Alison Owen (Spencer) placed seventh. The official World Cup began in 1981–'82.

1981 Alison Owen (Spencer) won her fourth consecutive title in the 5-kilometer classic stride. The same year, she retired, after competing in two Olympics and eight national championships.

1982 The first official World Cup season began. Women's races ranged from 5k (3.1 miles) to 30k.

1992 The 30K race became an Olympic even in Albertville, France.

1993 Laura McCabe won the 30k freestyle at the U.S. Nationals and repeated the feat in 1997.

1996 The sprint race became part of the World Cup schedule of events.

2000 Nina Kemppel earned enough points to break into the World Cup standings in five separate events: three sprints and two long-distance races.

2002 Kemppel won the Nordic Gold Cup in Midway, Utah, becoming the first woman skier to qualify for four U.S. Olympic teams (1992–2002). She is the all-time U.S. record holder with 18 national titles.

2002 At the U.S. championships, Kemppel won her eighteenth U.S. title by winning the 30k with a time of 1:48:21.8.

2002 The 1.5 kilometer sprint was added to the Olympic cross-country events for the first time, representing the sport's shortest race.

2002 The U.S. had the largest cross-country ski team in its history competing in the Olympics in Salt Lake City, Utah. The team was picked based on international standings from the past year and included Tessa Benoit, Kristina Joder, Barb Jones, Nina Kemppel, Aelin Peterson, Kikkan Randall, Wendy Wagner, and Lindsey Weier.

SNOWBOARDING

There's plenty of drama in snowboarding, which has added new excitement to winter sports. The half-pipe, has made it all the way to the Olympics. Introduced at the 1998 games in Nagano, Japan, snowboarding already had a huge following. According to the Sporting Goods Manufacture Association, snowboarding is the fastest growing segment of downhill snowsports.

Athletes are judged in five categories: standard airs, or tricks that have less than 360-degree rotations; rotations; amplitude; landings; and technical merit. In Olympic competition each rider takes one run, and the top six automatically advance to the final round. Then finishers 7 through 14 take a second run. The top six from that round advance to the finals as well.

Competitive snowboarding consists of two types of riding: alpine and freestyle. Alpine snowboarding closely resembles alpine skiing, with the purpose being to get down the course as quickly as possible. The half-pipe, on a supersized u-shaped course, is a freestyle event. A typical pipe is about 110 meters long and is placed on a slope of about 15 degrees. Riders slide back and forth from one side to the other, performing tricks at the top of each side.

The parallel giant slalom was introduced in the 2002 Olympic Games. Two snowboarders race down parallel courses at the same time, taking two runs and switching sides for the second run.

1994 The first Federation Internationale de Ski (FIS) snowboarding season was created.

1996 Aurelie Sayres, of East Haddam, Connecticut, won her second gold medal in the half-pipe at June Mountain, California. Sayres placed second in the half-pipe at the 1997 world championships.

1997 Sondra Van Ert won the giant slalom in the world championships and had seven World Cup top-three finishes in the course of the season.

1997 Christy Barrett won the U.S. Open in the half-pipe.

1998 Snowboarding became an Olympic sport at the Nagano Games. Two-time world champion, Shannon Dunn, was the first American to medal, winning the bronze in the women's half-pipe with 72.8 points.

1997 At the World Championships, Rosey Fletcher, of Girdwood, Arkansas, finished third in the giant slalom and Shannon Dunn finished fourth in the half-pipe.

1999 Fletcher, won her third U.S. title in the slalom. She captured her first and second in 1997 in the slalom and giant slalom. In 1999, Fletcher also placed second in the parallel giant slalom at the FIS worlds. Fletcher was the first female to make the first U.S. Olympic snowboard team.

1999 At the X-Games in Crested Butte, Colorado, Michele Taggart won the half-pipe. She is also a four-time ISF overall champion.

2000 At the Olympics in Nagano, snowboard was a medal event for the first time in the half-pipe. Shannon Dunn won the bronze medal.

2000 Sondra Van Ert was a member of the U.S. team for the seventh year. She won the alpine title on the grand prix tour.

2000 Tricia Bryner won five World Cup events, finishing second on the World Cup points list behind Sab Wehr Hasler, of Germany. Bryner also won the gold medal at the Goodwill Games the first time the event was held; Kelly Clark, of Mount Snow, Vermont, finished second.

2000 Clark won the junior world championship in the half-pipe. She was also the U.S. champion in snowboard cross, which is the equivalent of skiing's downhill races.

2000 Kim Stacy won the pipe contest at the Sims Invitational World Snowboarding Championship and took first place at the U.S. championships.

2001 In January, 367 athletes from 36 nations, the largest number of participants ever, attended the fourth FIS world championships in Madonna Di Compigllo, Italy. Sondra Van Ert was the highest-placing American in the giant slalom, finishing fourth with 500 points.

2001 Rosey Fletcher took first in the slalom at the U.S. national snowboard championships in River, Maine. She finished a record 9.47 seconds faster than runner-up Stacia Hookom.

2002 In January Kelly Clark finished first at the U.S. Snowboarding Grand Prix.

2002 At the Olympics in Salt Lake City, the parallel giant slalom was a medal event for the first time.

2002 Kelly Clark won the first U.S. gold medal in the sport and the first U.S. gold medal in the 2002 Games by winning the half-pipe with a score of 47.9 out of 50. Her teamates Shannon Dunn and Tricia Byrnes were fifth and sixth, respectively.

2002 Stacia Hookum won the parallel giant slalom and the giant slalom at the U.S. Snowboarding Championships in Truckee, California.

SOCCER

Mia, Julie, Brandi, Kristine, Michelle, Briana, Tiffeny, and Carla are all instantly recognizable names that don't need to be attached to surnames—they belong to the members of the U.S. national women's soccer team. After winning the 1996 Olympic gold medal and the 1999 women's World Cup, the team rose to a level of prominence they never dreamed possible . . . and they just kept going.

In 2000, they won a record 26 matches and outscored their opponents 124–31. Kristine Lilly and Mia Hamm were the first two players, male or female, to compete in 200 international games. The following year the Women's United Soccer Association (WUSA), a professional league was launched. The 20 women on the 1999 World Cup team were founding members and many play in the league.

1950s Soccer became an intramural sport in many women's colleges as well as high schools.

1960s Interest among a range of age-groups, with school and club teams forming at all levels in several areas of the country. The first college varsity team was established at Castleton State College (Vermont) in the mid-'60s. Other schools, including Johnson State College (Vermont) and Lyndon State College (Lyndonville, Vermont), followed.

1970s The sport continued to expand in colleges and as a club sport. Areas such as Dallas, northern Virginia, and Seattle became well known for developing women players.

1977 The first women's team was formed at Brown University (Providence, Rhode Island), and other Ivy League schools followed. In 1979, the first Eastern Regional Championship was held at Brown. Harvard beat Brown in the final game.

1980 The first national tournament was held at Colorado College, in Colorado Springs, and was won by State University of New York College at Cortland.

1981 On April 27, Betty Ellis became the first female official hired by the North American Soccer League.

1981 More than 50 women's collegiate teams were in existence across the country. The collegiate championship was held under the auspices of the Association for Intercollegiate Athletics for Women (AIAW) at the University of North Carolina, which won the title. The championship was organized by UNC coach Anson Dorrance and Colorado coach Chris Lidstone. Twelve teams participated.

1982 The National Collegiate Athletic Association (NCAA) took over the national collegiate tournament, as the University of North Carolina at Chapel Hill defeated the University of Central Florida, 2–0, to become the first champions of the NCAA Division I tournament. UNC won the last AIAW and first three NCAA tournaments.

1983 Jan Smisek, at age 26, was the first woman in the United States to be awarded a United States Soccer Federation (USSF) coaching license.

1985 In July, the United States Olympic Committee and USSF hosted the first Olympic Festival for women's soccer, in Baton Rouge, Louisiana. Players were chosen from each state to compete at a regional level, and then regional players were sent to the festival, where a national team was selected. The U.S. team made its international debut on August 18, in

Jessolo, Italy; the team lost a 3–0 game to England, tied Denmark, and then lost to Italy, 1–0.

1986 Anson Dorrance was hired by the USSF to select and coach the national team.

1986 The first North American championship for women was held. The United States defeated Canada, 2–0.

1986 The first NCAA Division III women's soccer championship was held at State University College of New York at Cortland in November. The University of Rochester (New York) defeated Plymouth State (New Hampshire), 1–0, for the title.

1987 Lisa Cole, of Southern Methodist University (Dallas), set a season mark of 37 goals, establishing an NCAA Division I record.

1987 The University of North Carolina set an NCAA record for shutouts in a season, with 22. The 1999 UNC team tied the record.

1987 Mariel Margaret "Mia" Hamm became the youngest woman to play for the U.S. national team, playing her first international match at age 15.

1988 The first NCAA Division II women's championship was held at Barry University (Miami Shores, Florida) in November. California State University at Hayward defeated Barry, 1–0, for the title.

1988 The Herman Trophy was established, which awards the best female Division I player as determined by a vote of coaches and sports writers.

1989 The USSF established the under-20 women's national team, which became the under-21 team in 1998.

1991 Michelle Akers, legendary forward for the U.S. team, set records for the most goals in a match, with 5, against Taiwan at the world championships; the most goals in a season, with 39; and most points in a season, with 47. She was the first player named U.S. Soccer Female Athlete of the Year in two consecutive years (1990 and '91).

1991 The USSF granted money for the U.S. team to hold its first three-week training camp in Florida.

1991 In November, the Federation Internationale de Football Association (FIFA), soccer's international governing body, staged the first women's world championships (the name became World Cup in 1999), which were equivalent to the men's World Cup. The championships were held in Guangzhou, China, with 12 teams competing. Playing before 65,000 fans, the U.S. team, captained by April Heinrichs, defeated Norway, 2–1, for the title. Carin Jennings Gabarra led the team in scoring and was named MVP of the tournament. The women's world championship is held every four years.

1993 The International Olympic Committee voted to admit soccer as an official sport for women in 1996. Marilyn Childress, of Atlanta, deserves much of the credit for convincing the committee that women were "ready."

1994 The USSF set up a six-month residential training camp in Florida, and for the first time, postcollegiate players earned a small salary.

1994 Mia Hamm, the University of North Carolina forward, was the first soccer player to win the Honda-Broderick Cup, which recognizes the top NCAA Division I athlete. She was the leading career scorer for the Tar Heels, with 39 points and 15 goals, and led her team to four NCAA championships. As a three-time all-American, she was the first woman to receive two Neiman Trophies.

1994 Colette Cunningham became the first woman to play in a professional soccer league in the United States. She played for the Washington Warhogs as a midfielder.

U.S. WOMEN'S WORLD CUP SOCCER TEAM. (PHOTO © AP PHOTO/MICHAEL CAULFIELD.)

1994 On October 2, the University of North Carolina's 92-game winning streak came to an end when UNC and Notre Dame battled to a 0–0 tie in Saint Louis. This was the longest streak ever for any team.

1994 Carla Overbeck became the first player, male or female, in U.S. soccer history to play all 90 minutes in more than 30 consecutive games.

1994 The NCAA Division I women's championship field expanded to 16 teams.

1994 The University of North Carolina won its ninth consecutive NCAA title. This is the longest championship streak in Division I history for any men's or women's sport.

1994 Tony DiCicco became coach of the U.S. team. Lauren Gregg continued as an assistant coach.

1995 The field for Division I women's championships was expanded to 24 teams.

1995 At the second women's world championships, in Sweden, the U.S. team placed third behind China and Norway, which won the title. Joy Fawcett was the only woman to play every minute of every game.

1996 The soccer bracket expanded in all three divisions of the NCAA. Division I went to 32 teams, Division II to 12 teams, and Division III to 24 teams.

1996 The University of North Carolina scored nine goals for a record third time: the first in 1989 against Hartford, 9–0; again in 1992, against Duke, 9–1; and in 1996 against Florida, 9–0.

1996 At the Olympics in Atlanta, soccer became a medal sport. Eight teams competed.

1996 The U.S. team won the first game in Olympic history on July 21, beating Denmark, 3–0. Tisha Venturini scored the first goal by a U.S player in the 35th minute. The U.S. team was captained by Carla Overbeck, with Julie Foudy cocaptain.

1996 On August 1, at Sanford Stadium, in Athens, Georgia, before 76,481 fans, the United States defeated China, 2–1, to win the first Olympic gold medal. At the time, this was the largest crowd ever to attend a women's sporting event.

1996 Sarah Cameaux, of the University of Mississippi, set a Division I record in scoring seven goals in one game, against Northwestern.

1996 The University of Nebraska's record-setting 19th corner kick came against the University of Minnesota in double overtime for the 3–2 win. The Cornhuskers finished the season with 19 wins and 2 losses, and made it to the third round of the NCAA championships.

1997 Holly Manthei, of Notre Dame, achieved an NCAA-record 15 career assists.

1998 On May 20, Kristine Lilly became soccer's career leader in international appearances among both men and women. She scored her 57th international goal and played in her 152nd match, breaking the record held by Heidi Stoere, of Norway.

1998 In August, Nancy Lay and Sandra Hunt became the first female senior referees in Major League Soccer (MLS) history. The MLS and the National Basketball Association are the only major professional sports leagues to have women as senior officials.

1998 Becky Burleigh became the first woman to coach an NCAA Division I women's soccer champion, when the University of Florida defeated 15-time champion North Carolina on December 6.

1998 Julie Foudy, star midfielder and cocaptain of the U.S. national team, became the first woman and the first American to receive FIFA's Fair Play Award, for her "commitment to bringing an end to the use of child labor in the manufacture of soccer balls." Foudy played for Stanford and was a four-time all-American; she played on the first world championship team in 1991. She also was cocaptain of the Olympic gold-medal team in 1996, the 1999 World Cup team, and the 2000 Olympic team.

1998 The U.S. Soccer Federation became U.S. Soccer and the U.S. team won the gold medal at the Goodwill Games.

1998 U.S. Soccer established a national under-18 team, which became the under-19 team in 2001.

1999 The final draw to determine the four groups of four nations to compete in the women's World Cup was conducted on February 14, during halftime at the first FIFA women's all-star match, at Spartan Stadium, in San Jose, California.

1999 The third FIFA women's World Cup was held in the United States, the first time America hosted the tournament. ABC and ESPN televised all 32 matches, the first time every game was televised worldwide.

1999 On May 22, Mia Hamm became the leading scorer of all time, male or female, surpassing the record held by Italian player Elisabetta Vignotto, of 107. Hamm was U.S. Soccer's Player of the Year five straight years.

1999 The United States was the first host country to play in the final game of the women's World Cup and win. The game, on July 10, against China, was also the first time that a World Cup championship was decided by a shoot-out, after the full regulation game and two overtime periods ended in a scoreless tie. The U.S. team won the historic shoot-out by a score of 5–4 on Brandi Chastain's goal before 90,185 fans, the most ever to see a women's sporting event. Kristine Lilly, who made a dramatic defensive header off the goal line in the final, played every minute of all six games.

1999 For the first time in women's World Cup history, all officials were women.

1999 Goalkeeper Briana Scurry, the only African American starter on the U.S. team, became a hero in the World Cup finale's shoot-out, blocking Lio Ying's kick to give the United States the victory.

1999 The U.S. team was the first to be both Olympic champion, with the 1996 gold, and World Cup champion.

1999 The World Cup set an event record of 36 matches, 123 total goals, and total attendance of 660,159.

1999 The U.S. team was the first to win two world championships—1991 and 1999.

1999 Brandi Chastain was the first athlete to make the cover of three major national magazines—*Time*, *Newsweek*, and *Sports Illustrated*—within a week's time frame. The image of Chastain in a sports bra holding in the air her shirt, which she'd pulled off in excitement after making the championship-winning kick, is one of the most famous sports photographs in history.

1999 Lauren Gregg, the assistant coach of the U.S. national team since 1989, also coached the U.S. women's under-21 team. The team won two Nordic Cups, the unofficial world youth title. Gregg was also an assistant on the 1991 and 1999 World Cup teams and the 1996 Olympic team.

1999 Wendy Gebaurer became the first woman to play in a men's league, when she played 17 minutes for the Raleigh, North Carolina, Capitals in a men's A-league match. Raleigh lost, 3–0, to Boston.

1999 *Time* magazine named the U.S. national team the top sports story of the year.

1999 FIFA named Michelle Akers and Sun Wen the Players of the Century.

2000 At the Olympics in Sydney, Australia, the U.S. team won the silver medal; Norway won the gold.

2000 On July 16, Mia Hamm played in her 200th international game, following Kristine Lilly, who had played her 200th two months earlier, on May 7.

2000 Julie Foudy, cocaptain of the U.S. national team, became president of the Women's Sports Foundation, the first soccer player to hold this position.

2000 April Heinrichs became the first female player inducted into the United States Soccer Hall of Fame, in Oneonta, New York. She also was named coach of the U.S. national team, the first woman in the 15-year history of the program, taking over from longtime coach Tony DiCicco. She was a three-time all-American at the University of North Carolina—1984, '85, and '86—and the captain of the U.S. team that won the first women's world championships, in 1991. She finished her national team career with 38 goals in 47 games. She is the all-time NCAA leader in points scored, with 225—87 goals and 51 assists; UNC's record was 85 wins, 3 losses, and 2 ties.

2000 The U.S. national team played a record 41 matches, with 26 wins, 6 losses, and 9 ties. A record five players reached double figures in goals scored: Cindy Parlow—19, Tiffeny Milbrett—15, Mia Hamm—13, Shannon MacMillan—12, and Christie Welsh—11. The United States also won the Algarve Cup for the first time in six tries.

2000 Joy Fawcett became the highest-scoring defender in U.S. national team history, with 24 points.

2000 Carin Gabarra became the second female player inducted into the Soccer Hall of Fame.

2000 As of September 25, Mia Hamm's 127 goals and 109 assists made her the leading goal scorer in history.

2001 The under-19 team completed its first year. The team will compete in the first FIFA World Youth Championships in 2002.

2001 The first women's professional league, the WUSA, was established, with eight franchises: Atlanta Beat, Bay Area CyberRays, Boston Breakers, Carolina Tempest, New York Power, Philadelphia Charge, San Diego Spirit, and Washington Freedom. The 21-game season ran from April to September. The league was founded by John Hendricks, chairman and CEO of Discovery Communications, and 20 players who have an equity stake in the league.

2001 In an unprecedented move for team sports, the WUSA named a player representative, Julie Foudy, to its board of governors. Foudy was selected by the other founding players.

2001 The first WUSA draft was held in San Jose, and the first selection was Sun Wen, a star Chinese forward.

2001 The inaugural WUSA game was held at RFK Stadium, in Washington, D.C., on April 14. The Washington Freedom beat the Bay Area CyberRays before 34,148 spectators.

2001 On June 22, Tiffeny Milbrett, of the New York Power, became the first WUSA player to earn a hat trick, when she scored three times against the Boston Breakers in a 3–1 game.

2001 Mia Hamm became captain of a team for the first time, with the Washington Freedom. She scored six goals and had four assists in her first year.

2001 In June, Julie Foudy played in her 200th game on the women's national team, joining Kristine Lilly, with 226, and Mia Hamm, with

217, as the only players with 200 or more appearances on the national team.

2001 In the Independence Day series in Blaine, Minnesota, Cindy Parlow, 23, became the youngest U.S. player to make 100 international appearances. The American team defeated Canada, 1–0, in front of a crowd of 15,614, which set a National Center attendance record.

2001 Christine Welsh a junior at Pennsylvania State University was awarded the Hermann Trophy as the nation's top female college soccer player. She is the first Penn State woman to win the trophy. Welsh broke Penn State's and the Big Ten conference's career records for goals (69), assists (39), points (177), and game-winning goals (22).

2001 In July, the U.S. Youth Soccer national championships were held in Lawrence, Indiana. There was an under-17 division and an under-14 division. The Bethesda Fury (Maryland) defeated the defending champions, the Southern California Blue, 1–0, in the second overtime, for the under-17 title. The Fury's Kelly Hammond won the Golden Boot Award. In another 1–0 game, the K.C. Dynamos (Kansas City) defeated Chantilly Milan (Virginia) in the under-14 division. Chantilly Milan was previously undefeated in postseason play, with 31 straight victories.

2001 On July 31, the U.S. women's under-21 team won its third straight Nordic Cup, defeating Sweden in Gjovik, Norway. Finland took third place by defeating Germany, 3–2.

2001 Joy Fawcett, who plays professionally with the San Diego Spirit, gave birth to her third daughter. She was the only U.S. national team player to be on the field every minute of the 1995 and 1998 women's World Cups and the 1996 and 2000 Olympic matches.

2001 As of August 1, Kristine Lilly and Mia Hamm were the all-time international leaders in caps, with 227 and 218, respectively.

2001 CyberRays goalkeeper LaKeysia Beene led the WUSA in saves, with 95 in 20 matches, and in save percentage, with 83.3. Beene had a run of six consecutive shut-outs, and eight solo shut-outs overall, and was named the league's best goalkeeper.

2001 Briana Scurry, who was the U.S. goalkeeper in the World Cup, played professionally for Atlanta. She was team captain and the WUSA league leader in goals-against average, with 0.82. LaKeysia Beene was second, with 0.97. Scurry had seven shut-outs.

2001 The Philadelphia Charge ranked as the highest-scoring team in the first WUSA season, with 35 goals.

2001 WUSA Most Valuable Player Tiffeny Milbrett, of the New York Power, won the scoring title in the inaugural season. She scored 55 percent of the Power's 29 goals, with 16 goals and 35 points.

2001 Philadelphia's Doris Fitschen was named the league's most outstanding defensive player.

2001 In the first WUSA play-offs, a single-elimination game on August 18, the CyberRays defeated the Power, 3–2, and the Atlanta Beat defeated the Charge by the same score. Cindy Parlow scored in sudden-death overtime to lead the Beat into the championship game.

2001 On August 25, the first WUSA championship game was played in Foxboro Stadium (Massachusetts) between the Bay Area CyberRays and the Atlanta Beat. After 90 minutes of regulation and two overtimes, the score was tied at 3. In a thrilling finale, the CyberRays won the shoot-out, 4–2, and were the inaugural Founders Cup champions.

2001 The WUSA's Coach of the Year was Ian Sawyer, of the Bay Area CyberRays.

2001 Santa Clara defeated the University of North Carolina, 1–0, to win the Division I championship and end UNC's 34-game winning streak. UNC has won 16 of the 19 NCAA Division I women's national championships, more than any other Division I program in the nation in any sport. From 1986 to 1994, the Tar Heels won 9 championships in a row. Anson Dorrance began the varsity program in 1979 and is still the coach of one of the great dynasties in college sports. George Mason in 1985, Notre Dame in 1995, and Florida in 1998 are the only other teams to have won the championship since it was first held in 1982.

2001 Mia Hamm was the first FIFA World Woman Player of the Year.

2001 Tiffany Milbrett was selected as the United States Soccer Federation's female athlete of the year for the second straight year. Aleisha Cramer was the under-21 female athlete of the year.

2002 The WUSA will add an all-star game in the league's second year.

2002 The first under-19 World Championship game will be held.

2003 The women's World Cup will be held in China.

SOFTBALL

SOFTBALL WAS invented by George Hancock on Thanksgiving Day in 1887, in a gym in Chicago and was originally called "indoor baseball." Eight years later, the first women's team was organized at Chicago's West Division High School, marking the beginning of the women's game.

The modern game has two versions: fastpitch and slowpitch. Each version of the game has seven innings, but the similarities end there. Fast pitch has nine players, slow pitch has ten; fast pitch throws high-speed pitches from a distance of 40 feet; slow pitch is slower and has a defined arch from 46 feet; fast pitch places 60 feet between the bases and 200 feet to the outfield fence; slow pitch has a larger field—65 feet between bases and 250 feet to the fence.

1888 The game moved outdoors and was called "indoor-outdoor."

1906 "Kitten ball" was an early name for softball until 1922, when the name changed again, to "diamond ball."

1925 The Committee on Women's Athletics, formed in 1917 to oversee rules for women's sports, formed a committee for women's softball.

1933 "Softball" was adopted as the official name of the sport. The Amateur Softball Association of America (ASA) was founded in Chicago.

1933 The first ASA women's national fast pitch championship was held in Chicago.

1943 The New Orleans Ajax Maids, led by the Savona sisters, won their first of three consecutive ASA national fast pitch championships.

1950 Bertha Reagan (Tickey), a member of the Orange Lionettes, a California team, pitched 143 consecutive innings. Tickey was also a star pitcher for the Raybestos Brakettes, of Stratford, Connecticut. Her career record was 757 wins and 88 losses. She won 11 national titles, was selected for the all-star team 18 times, and won eight MVP awards. In 1968, the Bertha Tickey Award was established; it is given annually to the ASA outstanding pitcher in the national championship.

1951 Madeline Lorton, of Bronx, New York, became the first licensed woman umpire in organized softball.

1957 In response to the popularity and growth of softball, the ASA established a separate division of championship play for company teams.

1957 The ASA established the National Softball Hall of Fame, and Marie Waldow was the first woman elected. In 1973, an actual Hall of Fame building opened in Oklahoma City.

1961 The first ASA Major Slow Pitch championship was held. It was an international tournament prior to 1961.

1965 The Federation Internationale de Softball (ISF) was established as softball's international governing body.

1965 The first international competition for the U.S. team was the world championships in Melbourne, Australia. Five teams competed. The

Raybestos Brakettes represented the United States and lost their first game 1–0, to Australia. The U.S. team made it to the title game but lost again to Australia and took home the silver medal with an 8–3 record.

1965 Legendary basketball player Nera White, of Nashville, was also an outstanding softball player who could run the bases in 10 seconds. She was on the all-American fast-pitch softball team from 1959 to 1965. In 1965, she received the first Erv Lind Award, presented to the outstanding defensive player in the ASA women's fast-pitch national championship.

1970 Eleanor Snell, a legendary coach at Ursinus College (Collegeville, Pennsylvania), compiled a record of 125 wins and 20 losses. During the 10-year period from 1941 to 1951, her teams lost only one game.

1970 The ISF world championships were held in Osaka, Japan, with 10 teams competing. Pitcher Nancy Welborn set world records for most wins and most innings pitched, but the U.S. team lost a 1–0 heartbreaker in the title game to Japan, in front of 30,000 people.

1974 The United States won its first ISF world softball championship, in Stratford, Connecticut. The U.S. team posted nine consecutive shutouts, outscoring opponents by 75–0. U.S. pitcher Joan Joyce set tournament records for most strikeouts—76; lowest earned run average—0.00; most consecutive scoreless innings—36; most no-hit, no-run games—3; and most perfect games—2.

1979 The U.S. team won the gold medal at the Pan American Games in San Juan, Puerto Rico—the first time it was an official Pan Am sport.

1982 The ISF world championships were held in Taipei. For the first time, the U.S. team did not medal.

1982 The first National Collegiate Athletic Association (NCAA) Division I women's softball championships were held at Creighton Univer-

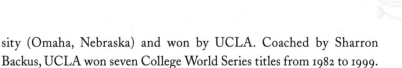

sity (Omaha, Nebraska) and won by UCLA. Coached by Sharron Backus, UCLA won seven College World Series titles from 1982 to 1999.

1982 The first NCAA Division II championships were held in May at Sacred Heart University (Bridgeport, Connecticut). Sam Houston State University (Huntsville, Texas) defeated California State University at Northridge, 3–2. Northridge won the next three championships, 1983–'85.

1982 Also in May, the first NCAA Division III championships were held at the College of New Jersey (Trenton), which lost to Eastern Connecticut State, coached by Clyde Washburne, 2–0.

1987 The U.S. team won the gold medal at the Pan American Games.

1987 Michelle Granger became the first player to compete in one season in the international junior world championships, the U.S. Olympic Festival, the Pan American Games, and the ASA national championships.

1988 Playing for the Raybestos Brakettes, Sheila Douty set a season record for triples, with 19.

1989 Dot Richardson was named the NCAA Player of the Decade for the 1980s, as a shortstop. She was a four-time collegiate all-American for Western Illinois and UCLA and 17-time ASA all-American selection.

1991 On June 13, the International Olympic Committee approved fast-pitch softball as a medal sport, to begin in the 1996 Olympic Games.

1992 The Raybestos Brakettes won their 23rd ASA women's fast-pitch national championship, beating the Redding, California Rebels.

1992 Donna Lopiano became executive director of the Women's Sports Foundation. Lopiano won six national titles with the Raybestos

Brakettes. She was tournament MVP three times and is a member of the ASA National Softball Hall of Fame.

1993 During her career at UCLA, Lisa Fernandez compiled a 93-and-7 pitching record, for a .930 winning percentage. She batted .381 and posted a 42-game winning streak from February 5, 1992, to April 4, 1993. Fernandez was a three-time Honda Award winner, 1991–'93. She was the first softball player to win the award, presented to the nation's outstanding female collegiate athlete. On the U.S. national team, she was a starting pitcher, reliever, and third baseman.

1996 On July 21, softball debuted in the Olympics in Atlanta. Dot Richardson hit the first home run in Olympic history, and Lisa Fernandez had the first run batted in. The U.S. team routed Puerto Rico, 10–0. In the gold-medal game against China, Richardson hit a two-run homer in the third inning. The United States won the game, 3–1, to claim the first Olympic softball gold medal.

1996 Dot Richardson was named the ASA Sportswoman of the Year for her outstanding performance at the Olympics. A member of the U.S. national team since 1979, mostly as a shortstop, Richardson was an all-American 14 times, earned seven ASA Best Defensive Player Awards, and was ASA national champion MVP three times. At UCLA from 1981 to '83, she was an all-American all three years. Richardson was named NCAA Player of the Decade for the '80s.

1996 The College of New Jersey advanced to the College World Series for the 17th time—a Division III record—and won its sixth NCAA Division III championship, with titles in 1983, '87, '89, '92, '94, and '96.

1997 Jan Hutchinson, head softball coach at Bloomsburg University of Pennsylvania for 20 years, doubled as Bloomsburg's field hockey coach. She earned her 1,000th career coaching victory when her team swept a twin bill from Dowling College (Oakdale, New York).

1997 By the end of the season, the South Carolina Lady Gamecocks had established an NCAA Division I record with 38 straight wins.

1997 The Women's Professional Fastpitch League was established with 8 teams. In 1998, the first all-star game was held. In 2000, the league changed its name to the Women's Professional Softball League (WPSL). John Carroll was the first commissioner and CEO of the WPSL.

1998 DeeDee Weiman pitched the league's first perfect game as a member of the WPF Tampa Bay FireStix.

1998 The U.S. team won its fourth consecutive ISF world championship, in Fujinomyia, Japan. The other titles were won in 1986 in Aukland, New Zealand; 1990 in Normal, Illinois; and 1994 in Saint John's, Newfoundland. In 1998, Lisa Fernandez pitched the title game against Australia, a one-hit shutout that included 14 strikeouts and no walks. She also hit a home run, for the only U.S. score.

1999 The United States won the gold medal at the Pan American Games in Winnipeg, Canada.

1999 On May 29, Courtney Blades, of the University of Southern Mississippi, allowed second-seeded Arizona just two hits, ending her season with 497 strikeouts, an NCAA record.

2000 Lisa Fernandez, on the "Central Park to Sydney Tour," threw five straight perfect games, believed to be unprecedented in the history of the sport. She struck out 100 batters in recording 122 straight outs, finishing the streak by fanning 21 batters, en route to the U.S. gold medal at the Olympics. Fernandez joined the U.S. team in 1990.

2000 Lori Harrigan pitched the first solo no-hitter in Olympic softball history, dispatching Canada, 6–0. Harrigan retired 20 consecutive batters after an error in the first inning.

LISA FERNANDEZ. (PHOTO © DONALD MIRALLE/ALLSPORT.)

2000 The U.S. softball team had a consecutive winning streak of 112 games, a national team record, before facing Japan on September 18, in

Sydney. The 11-inning battle ended in a 2–1 victory for Japan. The previous loss for the Americans was in the 1998 world championships.

2000 In April, Fresno State coach Margie Wright broke the NCAA Division I record for victories, with her 941st.

2000 On May 29, the University of Oklahoma won the Women's College World Series, defeating UCLA, 3–1, in Oklahoma City, making it the first host institution in Division I softball history to win the title.

2000 The California Commotion, of Woodland Hills, won its fourth straight ASA women's fast-pitch national championship.

2000 The ASA Junior Olympic program established national championships in girls Class B fast pitch and women's 23-under fast pitch.

2001 On May 28, the University of Arizona Wildcats won their sixth NCAA Division I championship by defeating UCLA, 1–0, in Oklahoma City. Wildcats pitcher Jennie Finch set an NCAA record for victories in a season, with 32.

2001 At the NCAA Division III championships in Eau Claire, Wisconsin, Muskingum College (New Concord, Ohio) won its first national title, defeating Central College (Pella, Iowa). The victory extended the Muskies' consecutive-game win streak to 34, breaking the Division III record held by Saint Mary's University of Minnesota since 1998.

2002 Michele Smith, pitcher and two-time Olympian played professionally in Japan and was a five-time Japan Professional Softball League Champion and five-time MVP.

SPEED SKATING

COILED TO explode at the sound of the starter's pistol, the speed skater is ready to charge down the ice. As the gun goes off, her arms begin to swing back and forth, working with the powerful strides of her legs. Gaining speed as she rounds the track, racing the clock, she is focused at all times on the finish line. Speed skaters compete on an oval rink and race long track and short track events. Both events rank skaters based only on their times. Long track events are held on a 400-meter track with two skaters in two lanes. The inside lane is shorter than the outside lane, so the skaters change lanes after each lap. Women can compete in 500, 1,000, 1,500, 3,000, and 5,000 meter races. Short track events are held on a standard hockey rink (111 meters), and packs of four to six skaters race at the same time. Bonnie Blair, the most decorated U.S. athlete in winter Olympic history (earning five golds and one bronze between 1988 and 1994), was instrumental in increasing the sport's popularity.

1927 The Amateur Speed Skating Union was established as the governing body for the sport in the United States.

1936 On February 2, Kit Klein Outland, who medaled in four events, won the first world championships. It wasn't until 33 years later, in 1979, that a U.S. skater, Beth Heiden, won the title again.

1938 Maddy Horn, at the World Championships in Oslo, Norway, won two silver medals in the 500 meter and 1,000 meter races.

1960 Women's long track speed skating became an Olympic event in Squaw Valley, California. Jeanne Ashworth won the bronze medal in the 500 meters with a time of 46.1. Her career includes nine indoor and outdoor titles. Other Olympic events were the 1,000, 1,500, and 3,000 meters, but the U.S. women did not medal.

1966 At age 14, Dianne Holum became the youngest skater to compete in the world championships.

1968 In the 500-meter race at the Olympics in Grenoble, France, U.S. skaters Jennifer Fish, Dianne Holum, and Mary Meyers finished in a three-way tie for the silver medal.

1968 In Grenoble, Dianne Holum became the first U.S. skater to medal in the 1,000 meters. She took the bronze with a time of 1:33.4. She also tied for the silver in the 500 meters, making her the first skater to win two medals in the same Olympics.

1971 At the first world sprint championships, Anne Henning won the gold in the 500 meters in 42.75 seconds.

1972 Dianne Holum became the first American woman to earn an Olympic gold medal in speed skating, winning the 1,500 meters in Sapporo, Japan, with a time of 2:20.4, an Olympic record. She also won a silver in the 3,000 meters with a time of 4:58.67, becoming the first American to place in this event. She won eleven world championship medals in senior events, and was the first woman ever to be selected as the U.S. flagbearer for the opening ceremonies.

1972 Jeanne Omelenchuk was the first American woman to compete on three Olympic speed-skating teams—1960, '68, and '72—the last at age 40. Between 1957 and 1965, she won ten U.S. and North American championships. She was also the first woman to win a national title in more than one sport—she won six national bicycle racing titles.

1973 Sheila Young (Ochowicz) became the first athlete to hold world championship titles in two sports at the same time—speed skating and track cycling. She also was the first woman to win three world sprint speed-skating championships—in 1973, '75, and '76. Bonnie Blair later won three world sprint championships in speed skating—in 1989, '94, and '95.

1973 The junior world championships were held for the first time. Kay Lunden won silver in the 500 and 1,000 meter races and Connie Carpenter won bronze in the 500 meter race.

1976 Sheila Young (Ochowicz) became the first U.S. athlete to win three medals at a single Olympics: gold in the 500 meters, silver in the 1,500 meters, and bronze in the 1,000 meters, in Innsbruck, Austria. Between 1973 and '76 she won seven world championship medals—six gold and one bronze.

1976 The first World Championships in short track racing were held in Champaign, Illinois.

1980 Nancy Swider Peltz set the U.S. record in the 10,000 meters with a time of 17:37.35, in Savalen, Norway.

1980 Between 1980 and '85, Lydia Stephens was a member of eight world teams in long and short track, winning two bronze medals in short track and making the Olympic long track team in 1984. She had already won the national indoor title in short track in 1982, and in 1983 she was the North American indoor champion.

1980 Leah Poulous (Mueller) won two world sprint championships, in 1974 and '79, and three silver medals in Olympic competition—the 1,000 meters in 1976, and the 1,000 and 500 meters in 1980.

BONNIE BLAIR.

1980 Beth Heiden won the bronze in the 3,000 meters at the Olympics. In her career, she won twenty-two medals at world championship events and 14 senior, 8 junior, and several national titles.

1981 The first world short track championships were held.

1986 At the world short track championships, Bonnie Blair won the 500 meter and 1,000 meter titles. Other wins include the 1,000 meter title in 1984 and the 1,500 meter in 1985 and '86.

1988 Bonnie Blair was the first woman in Olympic competition to skate the 500 meters in less than 40 seconds. With a time of 39.10, she won the gold medal and set a world record in Calgary, Alberta. She also won the bronze medal in the 1,000 meters.

1988 Short track speed skating was introduced as a demonstration sport at the Olympics in Calgary, Canada.

1992 Short-track races became a medal sport at the Olympics in Albertville, France. Women raced in the 500 meters and 3,000-meter relay. Cathy Turner won the gold medal in the 500 meters and a silver in the 3,000-meter relay. In 1994, in Lillehammer, Norway, Turner won the gold again in the 500 meters and a bronze in the 3,000-meter relay with teammates Cathy Turner, Amy Peterson, Darcie Dohnal, and Nikki Ziegelmeyer.

1994 At the Olympics in Lillehammer, Norway, the 1,000 meter short track race became a medal event.

1994 Bonnie Blair, considered the matriarch of women's speed skating, was the first person in U.S. history to win gold medals in three consecutive winter Olympic games. She won the 500 meters in 1988, the 500 meters and 1,000 meters in 1992, and the 500 and 1,000 again in 1994. Blair also gained international celebrity by becoming the first American woman to win five gold medals. She was named *Sports Illustrated* Sportswoman of the Year in 1994 and was the USOC women speed skater of the year every year from 1985 to 1992.

1996 Moria D'Andrea won her third straight U.S. All-Around championship in long track skating.

1997 Short track skater Julie Goskowicz set the junior American record in the 1,000 meters with a time of 1:33.530, and the junior American record in the 1,500 meters with a time of 2:30.55. She also won the bronze medal in the World Championships.

1998 The Olympic 500 meters became a two-day race in Nagano, Japan. Each skater starts in the inner lane on one day and in the outer lane on the other. Combined times determine the results.

1998 Jennifer Rodriguez was the first female in-line skater to make the U.S. long-track Olympic team. She was also the first Hispanic (Cuban

American) to represent the U.S. in the winter Olympics. She took fourth in the 3,000 meter race.

1998 Cathy Turner appears in her third Olympics.

1998 Kirstin Holum, daughter of former champion Dianne Holum, set the American 5,000 meter record with a time of 7:14.20, at the Nagano Olympics, which also qualified as the junior world record. She placed seventh overall at the Olympics.

1998 In March, Chris Witty set the world all-around 500-meter record, 39.45, in Heerenveen, Netherlands. In the 1,000 meters she holds the world record of 1:15.43 in Calgary, Canada. Witty also holds the U.S. record of 38.36 in the 500 meters, set in March 2001 in Salt Lake City, Utah.

1998 On November 8, Amy Peterson recorded the fastest time by a U.S. skater in the 500 meter short track, with a 44.844 finish in Szekesfehervar, Hungary. On February 21, in Nagano, she recorded the fastest time for an American in the 1,000 meters, 1:33.530. Peterson also holds the record for the fastest American time in the 3,000 meters, 5:05.362, set in Burnio, Italy, on March 27. She is an eight-time U.S. champion.

2000 On February 17, Julie Goskowicz, Caroline Hallisey, Sarah Lang, and Amy Peterson set an American 3,000-meter-relay record of 4:21.875 in Lake Placid, New York.

2000 On February 18, Caroline Hallisey set the junior American record in the 500 meters, 45.900, in Lake Placid, New York.

2000 Elli Ochowicz (Sheila Young Ochowicz's daughter) set a new junior U.S. sprint samalog record of 159.221, in Calgary. In 2002 she competed in Salt Lake City, becoming a second generation Olympian.

2001 Also in Calgary, Jennifer Rodriguez set a new U.S. record in the 1,500 meters, 1:55.30, and another in the 3,000 meters, 4:06.59.

2001 In March, Sarah Elliot set a new junior world and junior U.S. record of 1:59.24 in the 1,500 meters, in Calgary, Canada.

2002 Amy Peterson, a short-track champion was chosen by her fellow athletes to be the official flagbearer for the U.S. teams at the opnening ceremonies. This was Peterson's fifth time as an Olympian—she won a silver for the 3,000 meter race in 1992 and bronze in both the relay and 500 meter race in 1994.

2002 The 1,500 meter short track race became an Olympic medal event in Salt Lake City. The event consists of 13½ laps around the 111.12 meter indoor track.

2002 At the Olympics, Chris Witty won the 1,000 meter long track race, setting a world record of 1:13.83. This was a stunning achievement since Witty was recovering from mononucleosis in the weeks prior to the Olympics and had been training only occasionally.

2002 Jennifer Rodriguez won bronze medals in the 1,000 and 1,500 meter races. She placed seventh in the 3,000 meters and broke her own American record by 1.5 seconds with a time of 4:4.99.

2002 Catherine Ramey placed ninth in the Olympic 5,000 meter race, setting a new U.S. record of 7:06.89.

SQUASH

SQUASH WAS originally played in England outdoors as players waited to get on the racquets court. It was introduced to the United States at the turn of the 20th century as an indoor sport, and the first court was built at Saint Paul's School, in New Hampshire. The U.S. version is played on a four-walled court measuring 18 and one-half feet wide, with a small hard rubber ball. The American game, known as "hardball," is scored to 15, with points being earned on each serve. The international game, "softball," is played on a 21-foot-wide court with a softer ball and is scored to 9. By the mid-1980s, softball had replaced hardball as the predominant game in the United States.

1926 Eleanora Sears, a founder of U.S. squash, helped secure playing privileges for women at Boston's Union Boat Club and Harvard Club. She also organized the first women's tournament at the Union Boat Club.

1928 Eleanora Sears, at the age of 37, won the first women's national singles championship, played at the Round Hill Club, in Greenwich, Connecticut. She also won the Massachusetts state championship, a title she won again in 1929, 1930, and 1938.

1932 The United States Women's Squash Racquets Association (USWSRA) was incorporated, and Mrs. Edgar Arnold served as president.

1933 Eleanora Sears became president of the USWSRA, a position she held until 1947. She was also captain, for five successive years, of the U.S. team for the Wolfe-Noel Cup matches, played against England.

1933 Ann Page and Sarah Madeira, of Philadelphia, teamed up to win the first women's national doubles championships. Page went on to win another title, in 1936, with Agnes Lamme, of New York. She also won the 1947 national singles championship.

1949 An age-group championship was held for the first time. Sue Peterson, of Philadelphia, was the inaugural 40-plus titleholder.

1955 The national team championship was officially named the Howe Cup, in honor of Margaret Howe and her twin daughters, Betty and Peggy. The Howe women won nine national singles championships.

1956 Peggy Carrott, of Greenwich, Connecticut, and Blanche Day, of Philadelphia, were the first women's senior doubles champions. Carrott also won the national 40-plus singles championship for four consecutive years, beginning in 1956.

1965 The first women's intercollegiate championship was held at Wellesley College (Massachusetts). Katherine Allabough, of Vassar (Poughkeepsie, New York), was the first women's intercollegiate champion and won a second title in 1968.

1969 Jane Stauffer, of Philadelphia, won the first mixed doubles national championship with Daniel Pierson. She won a women's doubles national championship the following year.

1970 Princeton University coach Betty Howe Constable and University of Pennsylvania coach Ann Wetzel organized the Women's Intercollegiate Squash Association.

1972 Princeton won the first intercollegiate division of the Howe Cup, played at the New Haven Lawn Club.

1973 At Yale, seven teams competed in the inaugural intercollegiate Howe Cup, the women's national intercollegiate championship. Princeton, coached by Betty Howe Constable until 1991, won the first of its record 14 championships. Although the tournament grew to include 28 teams, only four other universities have claimed the championship: Harvard, with 11 titles; Yale, with 3; the University of Pennsylvania, with 1, and Trinity University (Connecticut) with 1.

1974 New Zealand native Marigold "Goldie" Edwards, a psychology professor at the University of Pittsburgh, won the national championship in the 40-plus draw. It was the first of 28 national age-group championships for Edwards, who did not lose a national championship match until 1992.

1976 The first world open championship was held in Brisbane, Australia.

1977 Gail Ramsay, of Pennsylvania State University, the only player of either sex to win four national intercollegiate singles championships, won her first intercollegiate title.

1980 Alicia McConnell, of Brooklyn, New York, won the world junior championship in Sweden, the first and only world singles championship won by a U.S. player.

1982 In February, University of Pennsylvania freshman Alicia McConnell completed an unprecedented sweep of three national singles championships: the U.S. junior championship, the national intercollegiate championship, and the women's national championship. McConnell went on to win six consecutive national hardball championships, one national softball championship, six national women's doubles championships, and three world doubles championships and represented the United States at five world team championships.

1985 The USWSRA merged into the United States Squash Racquets Association (USSRA), the national men's squash organization. Also, the Women's American Squash Professionals Association was incorporated, and a 13-city women's professional hardball tour was created.

1985 Sue Cogswell, the former number one player in the world, moved from England to New York and challenged Alicia McConnell for the top U.S. ranking.

1988 Alicia McConnell attained a ranking of number 15 in the world, the highest placement achieved by a U.S. player internationally.

1989 Demer Holleran, a senior at Princeton, won her first national hardball singles championship as well as her third national intercollegiate singles championship. Holleran went on to win five consecutive hardball championships and, beginning in 1992, eight consecutive national softball singles championships. She also represented the United States at five world team championships.

1991 Squash joined the United States Olympic Committee (USOC) as a member of the national governing body. Ellie Pierce, of Newport, Rhode Island, winner of the national singles softball championship, was named by the USSRA as USOC Athlete of the Year.

1994 In Toronto, Demer Holleran and Alicia McConnell teamed up to win the first women's world open doubles championship, a title that they successfully defended twice. Holleran also won the first of her seven women's and eight consecutive mixed national doubles championships and was named USOC Athlete of the Year.

1994 The national women's intercollegiate championship switched to softball, leading the American transition to the game as it was played internationally.

1994 In Guernsey, England, the U.S. women's national team of Demer Holleran, Ellie Pierce, Shabana Khan, and Karen Kelso achieved the highest placement of a U.S. team in international competition when it cracked the top eight at the women's world team championships.

1995 Squash was included in the Pan American Games for the first time. The U.S. team of Demer Holleran, Alicia McConnell, Ellie Pierce, and Shabana Khan won a silver medal in the team championships in Mar del Plata, Argentina. In the singles competition, Holleran won a silver medal, and McConnell and Pierce earned bronze medals.

2001 Julia Beaver of Brooklyn, New York, won her third National Intercollegiate Singles title and ended her college career at Princeton University undefeated in dual match play.

2001 Shabana Khan of Seattle defeated her younger sister Latasha, already a two-time national champion, to win her first national singles championship.

2001 Demer Holleran and Alicia McConnell won their sixth consecutive national women's doubles championship, in Portland, Oregon. Holleran has won a record 33 national championships, including junior, intercollegiate, women's, and doubles titles.

2001 The U.S. junior women's team of Michelle Quibell, Allie Pearson, Amy Gross, and Kate Rapisarda recorded the best finish ever for a U.S. team in international competition as they reached the semifinals at the world junior team championships in Panang, Malaysia. Quibell's quarterfinal finish in the world junior singles championship was the best showing by an American in international singles competition since Alicia McConnell won the title in 1980.

2002 The Trinity University team became the first non-Ivy League women's squash team to win the Intercollegiate Howe Cup National Team Championship when they defeated Harvard, 5–4.

SWIMMING

THE FIRST Amateur Athletic Union (AAU) competitions for women were in swimming, as were some of the earliest Olympic events. Competitive swimming is one of the most grueling disciplines, where microseconds make a difference. Janet Evans, one of the greatest swimmers of all time, not only was passionate about the sport but also had the talent to excel. She still holds world records set in 1987 at age 15 in the 800- and 1,500-meter freestyle. In 1988, she won three Olympic gold medals: the 400-meter individual medley, the 400-meter freestyle—in world-record time, and the 800-meter freestyle. At 5 feet, 6 inches, the 104-pound high schooler made women everywhere realize that size doesn't matter, as long as you reach the end of the pool faster than the competition.

This chapter includes separate sections for endurance swimming and synchronized swimming.

1887 The first municipal swimming pool was built in Brookline, Massachusetts, and soon after, New York City built public pools. Within a few years, pools were constructed in many other cities around the country.

1910 The International Swimming Federation became the first international sports group to accept events for women in its competitions. U.S. women did not go to the Olympics until 1920.

1912 Women's swimming competitions were held for the first time at the Olympics in Stockholm, Sweden. Events included the 100-meter freestyle and 4×100-meter freestyle relay.

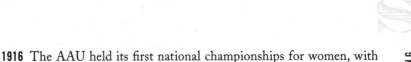

1916 The AAU held its first national championships for women, with four events: 440 yards, 880 yards, one mile, and a diving contest.

1917 The Women's Swimming Association of New York was formed to promote interest in the sport. The association held competitions and provided lifesaving instruction. Swimmers from the New York club primarily made up the Olympic teams during the early years of women's competition.

1917 Gertrude Ederle, as a 12-year-old, set a world record in the women's 880-yard freestyle, with a time of 13 minutes and 19 seconds, in Indianapolis. She was the youngest person ever to set a world record.

1920 The 400-meter freestyle was added to the Olympics in Antwerp, Belgium.

1920 At age 18, Ethelda Bleibtrey became the United States' first international swimming champion, when she won all three events open to women at the Antwerp Olympics: the 100-meter freestyle, 300-meter freestyle, and 400-meter freestyle relay. She was never defeated in amateur events and held national titles in every distance open to women. In 1919, she received a ticket for violation of laws against nude bathing when she took off her stockings on a New York beach.

1924 Helen Wainwright and Aileen M. Riggin were the first women to win Olympic medals in both swimming and diving. Wainwright won the silver in the 3-meter springboard in 1920 and the bronze in the 400-meter freestyle in 1924, in Paris. Riggin won a bronze in the 100-meter backstroke and silver in springboard diving in Paris. The 4-foot-8-inch, 70-pound Riggin was nicknamed "Tiny." In 1922, the first slow-motion and underwater coaching films starred Riggin. Riggin is now in her 90s and still swimming.

1924 Going into the Olympics, Sybil Bauer held world records in every backstroke distance. She won the first gold medal in the 100-meter backstroke at the Olympics in Paris and won 10 national titles between 1921 and 1926. Bauer set 23 world records during her six years of competition.

1924 Seventeen-year-old Ethel Lackie won two gold medals in Paris, in the 100-meter freestyle and 4×100-meter freestyle relay. She was the first woman to swim the 100-yard freestyle in less than 1 minute and the first to break the 1-minute-and-10-second barrier in the 100-meter freestyle.

1924 Gertrude Ederle won the Olympic bronze in the 100-meter freestyle.

1924 Agnes Geraghty won the silver medal in the first Olympic 200-meter backstroke, with a time of 1:11.4.

1924 Martha Norelius (Wright), Helen Wainwright, and Gertrude Ederle swept the gold, silver, and bronze in the 400-meter freestyle at the Olympics. The U.S. won the gold in the 4×100-meter freestyle relay.

1928 Albina Osipowich and Eleanor Saville (Garatti) won the gold and silver in the 100-meter freestyle at the Olympics in Amsterdam. The U.S. team won the gold in the 4×100-meter relay.

1928 Martha Norelius (Wright) became the first woman to win the gold medal in the same event in two consecutive Olympics. In Paris in 1924, she won the 400-meter freestyle with a time of 6:02.2. In 1928, she captured gold again, breaking her own record with a time of 5:42.8.

1930 During a 16-and-a-half-month period in 1930 and '31, Helene Madison broke all 16 world records at distances from 100 meters to one mile. In 1932, she won three gold medals—two individual and one relay—at the Olympics in Los Angeles.

1932 Helen Madison won the gold in the 100-meter freestyle with an Olympic-record time of 1:06.8, and Eleanor Saville (Garatti) won the bronze. In the 400-meter freestyle, Helene Madison won gold, and Lenore "Lenne" Wingard (Knight) took the silver.

1932 Eleanor Holm won an Olympic gold medal in the backstroke, but she received more attention in 1936 for her suspension from the Games for drinking a glass of champagne at a pre-Olympic party. During her swimming career, Holm won 20 national championships: 9 in individual medley, from 1927 to 1932, and 11 in backstroke, from 1929 to 1936.

1936 At the Olympics in Berlin, Lenore Wingard (Knight) won the bronze in the 400-meter freestyle, Alice Bridges won the bronze in the 100-meter backstroke, and the U.S. team won the bronze in the 4×100-meter freestyle.

1937 At the AAU championships, Katherine Rawls became the first woman to win four swimming championships in a single meet, winning the 400 yards, 880 yards, one-mile freestyle, and individual medley. She repeated this feat in 1938. From 1932 to 1938, she dominated U.S. swimming, winning more than 25 national championships. Rawls also won two silver medals in springboard diving in the Olympics.

1940s Esther Williams, a national champion in the 100-meter freestyle in 1939, also set a national record for the 100-meter breaststroke. During the 1940s and '50s, she did more to popularize swimming than any other woman of her era. Williams became famous starring in several MGM movies, many of which included majestic water ballets.

1944 Ann Curtis was the first woman in history and the first swimmer of either sex to receive the James E. Sullivan Award, honoring the outstanding amateur athlete of the year. Between 1943 and 1948, Curtis won 31 national championships, setting a women's record that stood for four decades, until broken by Tracy Caulkins.

1948 At the Olympics in London, Ann Curtis won the silver in the 100-meter freestyle and gold in the 400-meter freestyle.

1952 At the Olympics in Helsinki, Finland, Evelyn Kawamoto won the bronze in the 400-meter freestyle.

1956 The 100-meter butterfly became an Olympic event in Melbourne, Australia, and the United States swept: Shelley Mann won the gold, Nancy Ramey won the silver, and Mary Sears won the bronze. Sylvia Ruuska won the bronze in the 400-meter freestyle, and Carin Cone won the bronze in the 100-meter backstroke. The U.S. team took silver in the 4×100-meter relay.

1960 In Rome, Christina "Chris" von Saltza, a national and international champion, was the first woman to swim the 400-meter freestyle in under 5 minutes. She set an Olympic record, winning the gold in 4:50.6. She also won the gold in the 4×100-meter freestyle relay and the 4×400-meter medley, and the silver in the 100-meter freestyle.

1960 The 4×400-meter medley relay was a medal event in the Olympics for the first time, and the U.S. team won the gold medal.

1960 Lynn Burke set an Olympic record in the 100-meter backstroke, with a time of 1:09.3. Carolyn Schuler also set an Olympic record, completing the 100-meter butterfly in 1:09.5. The U.S. 4×100-meter relay team took the gold while setting a world record of 4:08.9.

1964 The U.S. women won nine medals at the Tokyo Olympics. The 4×100-meter relay team set a world record on their way to winning the gold, as did Sharon Stouder in the 100-meter butterfly. She also won a silver in the 100-meter freestyle; Kathleen Ellis took the bronze. Donna de Varona won gold in the 400-meter individual medley and on the 4×100-meter freestyle relay team. Cathy Ferguson won the gold in the 100-meter backstroke; Virginia Duenkel took the bronze.

1964 Along with her two gold medals, de Varona also won 13 national titles between 1960 and 1964. She became the first female sportscaster on national television, as a commentator for ABC, and she was the first woman to cover the Olympics.

1968 At the Olympics in Mexico City, the 200-meter freestyle, 800-meter freestyle, 100-meter breaststroke, 200-meter backstroke, 200-meter butterfly, and 200-meter individual medley races were held for the first time as medal events.

1968 Debbie Meyer became the first American swimmer, male or female, to earn three Olympic gold medals in individual events, winning the 200-meter, 400-meter, and 800-meter freestyle events. Between 1967 and 1971, she won 17 national championships at various freestyle distances and two individual medley titles. In Meyer's five seasons of competition, she set 24 American and 15 world records. She was also the first woman to swim the 500 meters in less than 8 minutes, swim 400 meters in less than 4.5 minutes, swim 500 yards in less than 5 minutes, and swim 1,650 yards in less than 17 minutes.

1968 Lillian "Pokey" Watson was the first Olympic gold medalist in the 200-meter backstroke. In 1972, Melissa Belote also won the gold.

1968 In the first-ever Olympic 100-meter breaststroke event, Sharon Wichman won the bronze medal. She also took gold in the 200 meters. The 100 meter freestyle was a U.S. sweep by Jan Henne, Susan Pendersen, and Linda Gustavson, as was the 200-meter freestyle by Debbie Meyer, Jane Henne, and Jane Barkman, and the 400-meter freestyle by Debbie Meyer, Linda Gustavson, and Karen Moras. Pamela Krause took silver in the 800-meter freestyle.

1972 At the Olympics in Munich, 15-year-old backstroker Melissa Belote earned three gold medals. She won the 100 meters; in the 200 meters, she set a world record of 2:20.64; and she swam backstroke for the gold in the 4×100-meter medley relay. At Arizona State University, she won four Association for Intercollegiate Athletics for Women (AIAW) titles.

1972 Catherine Carr won the gold medal at the Olympics in the 100-meter breaststroke and won team gold in the 4×100-meter medley relay. Claudia Kolb took the silver in the 200-meter breaststroke.

1973 The University of Miami awarded the first swimming scholarships to women: Jenny Bartz—breaststroke, Lynn Genesko—butterfly, and freestylers Nina MacInnis and Sharon Berg.

1973 The first Women's World International Swim Meet was held in February at East Los Angeles College.

1973 The first world championships were held in Belgrade, Yugoslavia.

1976 Shirley Babashoff won a total of eight medals at the 1972 and 1976 Olympics. In her career, she set six individual world records, won 27 national championships, and was on five world-record relay teams.

1978 USA Swimming was established as the national governing body.

1978 The 400-meter freestyle record of 4:02.59 was set by Cynthia "Sippy" Woodhead and still stands.

1978 At 16 years old, Tracy Caulkins became the youngest winner to date of the Sullivan Award, recognizing the nation's top amateur athlete.

1982 The first National Collegiate Athletic Association (NCAA) Division I championships were held. The University of Florida won the event. Since then, Stanford has won eight national championships, Texas seven, Georgia three, and Southern California one.

1982 The first 50-meter national championship was won by Diane Johnson, of the University of Arizona, with a time of 23.16. The current record holder is Amy Van Dyken, of the University of Colorado, with a time of 21.77, set on March 17, 1994.

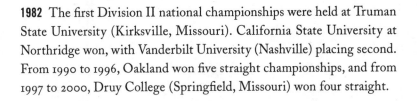

1982 The first Division II national championships were held at Truman State University (Kirksville, Missouri). California State University at Northridge won, with Vanderbilt University (Nashville) placing second. From 1990 to 1996, Oakland won five straight championships, and from 1997 to 2000, Druy College (Springfield, Missouri) won four straight.

1982 Katherine Eckrich, of Williams College (Williamstown, Massachusetts), still holds two records set in 1982: the 50-yard breaststroke at 31.09 and the 100-yard individual medley at 1:01.00.

1983 Trisca Zorn was the first blind woman to win a full athletic scholarship, competing in swimming for the University of Nebraska in the early 1980s. She won the Big Eight 200-meter breaststroke championship in 1983. In 1988, she became the first athlete, male or female, to win 12 gold medals at the Paralympic Games.

1984 Mary T. Meagher put the butterfly on the map for U.S. women, setting 7 world and 13 U.S. records and winning 21 national titles. At the Los Angeles Olympics, she won three gold medals: the 100- and 200-meter butterfly and the 4×100-meter freestyle relay. She made the Olympic team in 1980, but the games were boycotted. In 1981, she set world records in the 100-meter butterfly, with a time of 57.83, and the 200-meter butterfly, with a time of 2:05.96. In 1988, she won an Olympic bronze. At the University of North Carolina, Meagher won the 200-yard butterfly three years in a row at the NCAA championships and also won the 100-yard butterfly in 1985 and '87. She won the Honda-Broderick Cup as the nation's outstanding female athlete.

1984 Sandra Baldwin became the first woman president of USA Swimming. In 2000, she became the first woman president of the United States Olympic Committee (USOC).

1984 One of the world's great all-time champions, Tracy Caulkins won an incredible 48 national championships between 1977 and 1984 and is the only swimmer, male or female, to hold American records in every stroke. This winning record surpassed the previous women's record of 31 championships, held by Ann Curtis, as well as the overall record of 36, held by Johnny Weissmuller. Caulkins also won two Olympic medals in 1984, in the 200-meter and 400-meter individual medleys. Afterward, she retired from competition, having set 61 American and five world records. In 1990, Caulkins was named Swimmer of the Decade by *USA Today*.

1984 U.S. teammates Nancy Hogshead and Carrie Steinseifer tied for the gold in the first dead heat in Olympic swimming history, in the 100-meter freestyle. Hogshead also won two team golds and a silver in the 200-meter individual medley. In 2000, at the Olympics in Sydney, Jenny Thompson and Dara Torres tied for the bronze in the 100-meter freestyle.

1986 On June 27 in Orlando, Florida, Betsy Mitchell-Longhorn set an American record of 2:08.60 in the 200-meter backstroke, which still stands. American swimmers who have come close are Janie Wagstaff, with 2:09.09 in 1991; Lea Loveless, 2:10.65 in 1992; and Beth Botsford, 2:10.66 in 1996.

1986 Between 1981 and 1986, Tiffany Cohen won 16 national freestyle titles at distances ranging from 200 to 1,500 meters. She also won the butterfly in 1986. In 1984, Cohen won Olympic gold medals in the 400-meter freestyle and the 800-meter freestyle.

1987 Janet Evans broke three world records: the 400 meters, 800 meters, and 1,500 meters.

1988 Carol Zaleski became president of USA Swimming and was the first woman on the technical committee of FINA. In 1992, she reached another milestone as the first woman to chair the technical committee.

1988 The 50-meter freestyle was added as an Olympic event for the first time, in Seoul.

1988 Jill Sterkel was the first woman to make four Olympic swim teams—1976, '80, '84, and '88. She won a gold medal in 1976 in the 4×100-meter freestyle relay; the 1980 games were boycotted; she won another gold medal in 1984 in the 4×100-meter freestyle relay; and she won a bronze medal in the 50-meter freestyle in 1988. In 1981, she won the Honda-Broderick Cup as the nation's top female college athlete.

1988 Angel Martino was the first American woman to swim the 100-meter freestyle in less than 55 seconds.

1988 Janet Evans was the first American woman to win four individual Olympic gold medals in swimming. In Seoul, she won the 400-meter individual medley; the 400-meter freestyle, with a time of 4:03.85—a world and Olympic record that still stands; and the 800-meter freestyle. She also won the 800-meter freestyle in Barcelona, in 1992, giving her back-to-back golds in the same event. She also set a world record of 15:52.10 in the 1,500-meter freestyle at the Phillips 66 Spring National Championships, in Orlando, and was the first swimmer to break the 16-minute mark in the 1,500 meters, with a time of 15:52.70. In August 1989, Evans set a world record that still stands in the 800-meter freestyle, with a time of 8:16.22. Between 1987 and 1995, she won 14 national freestyle championships and four national championships in the individual medley.

1989 Ann Wycoff, of Army, won her third consecutive Division II 400-yard individual medley. She also won her second consecutive 200-yard individual medley and second consecutive 200-yard butterfly.

1989 Tina Schnare, of Cal State Northridge, won her third consecutive Division II 100-yard breaststroke and 200-yard breaststroke.

1989 At the world championships in Tokyo, Janet Evans set an 800-meter freestyle world record of 8:16.22, which still stands.

1990 Leigh Ann Fetter, of the University of Texas, was the first woman to break 22 seconds in the 50-meter freestyle, finishing in 21.92, at the NCAA championships. Fetter won the title all four years from 1988 to '91. In 1994, Amy Van Dyken, of the University of Colorado, broke Fetter's mark with a time of 21.77.

1992 On July 29, Nicole Haislett won the gold medal at the Barcelona Olympics and set the U.S. record in the 200-meter freestyle, which still stands at 1:57.90. She beat the previous U.S. record of 1:58.23, set by Cynthia Woodhead in Tokyo on September 2, 1979. Haislett was the only U.S. athlete to take home three gold medals from Barcelona, as she won in the 4×100-meter freestyle relay and the 4×100-meter medley relay.

1992 At the Olympics, Summer Sanders set an American record, which still stands, of 2:11.91 in the 200-meter individual medley. She also set the still-standing American record of 4:37.58 in the 400-meter individual medley.

1992 At the U.S. trials, Jenny Thompson set a world record of 54.07 for the 100 meters, becoming the first non–East German in 20 years to hold the record.

1992 The U.S. team of Nicole Haislett, Dara Torres, Angel Martino, and Jenny Thompson swam the 4×100-meter freestyle in a world-record time of 4:17.1, beating the 1956 record held by the Australians.

1994 At the world championships, Janet Evans won her 21st consecutive 800-meter event and second world title—1991 and 1994. In her career, she won 45 national titles, 17 international titles, and 5 NCAA titles. In 1994 she was named Female Athlete of the Year by U.S. Swimming and the USOC.

1996 In Atlanta, Amy Van Dyken became the first American woman to win four gold medals at a single Olympics, Winter or Summer. Her gold medals are in the 50-meter freestyle, 100-meter butterfly, 4×100-meter medley relay, and 4×100-meter freestyle.

1996 Brooke Bennett won Olympic gold in the 800-meter freestyle at age 14. In 1994, she won the bronze in the same event at the world championships.

1996 At the Atlanta Games, Beth Botsford won the gold in the 100-meter backstroke and in the 4×100 medley relay.

1998 On January 14, Leah Mauer set an American record that still stands of 1:00.77 in the 100-meter backstroke, in Perth, Australia. The previous American record was 1:00.84, set by Jamie Wagstaff in Indianapolis on March 3, 1992.

1998 At age 15, Natalie Coughlin placed among the world's 10 fastest swimmers in 12 events and qualified for all 14 individual events in the 1998 national championships. In August, she set an American record that still stands in the 50-meter backstroke, 29.01.

1998 U.S. national team member Kristine Quance-Julian qualified in four individual events for the world championships, becoming only the fifth woman to do so. The others are Shirley Babashoff in 1975, Cynthia Woodhead and Tracy Caulkins in 1978, and Janet Evans in 1995.

1999 The U.S. 4×800-meter freestyle relay record, 7:57.61, was set in August by Lindsay Benko, Ellen Stonebraker, Jenny Thompson, and Christina Teuscher.

2000 Kenyon College (Gambier, Ohio), under coach Jim Steen, won its 17th consecutive Division III women's swimming and diving title, starting in 1984.

2000 In September, when Jenny Thompson won three medals at the Olympic Games in Sydney, she became the most decorated U.S. woman in Olympic history in any sport, with ten medals, including eight gold. Thompson was the first swimmer to hold as many as 23 career national titles. Her 14 years on the U.S. national team is the longest tenure of any swimmer, male or female. On August 14, Thompson set a new 100-meter freestyle record, 54.07, at the Olympic trials in Indianapolis. She shaved two-hundredths of a second off her old record set in July, which broke her 1992 record.

2000 Competing in Sydney, Dara Torres became the first U.S. swimmer to compete in four Olympic Games—1984, 1988, 1992, and 2000.

2000 Misty Hyman set an Olympic and American record in the 200-meter butterfly with a time of 2:05.88. Hyman broke the 19-year-old American record of 2:05.96, held by Mary T. Meagher, and upset world record holder Susie O'Neill, of Australia, who hadn't lost a 200-meter race in six years.

2000 At the Sydney games, Kristy Kowal set an American record in the 200-meter breaststroke with a time of 2:24.56, winning the silver. She is an eight-time U.S. record holder, world record holder, two-time world champion, and seven-time NCAA champion at the University of Georgia.

2000 Brooke Bennett set an Olympic record in the 800-meter freestyle with a time of 8:19.67. She also won the gold in the 400 meters and Diane Munz took the silver.

2000 Christina Teucher won the bronze in the 200-meter medley at the Olympics.

2000 Dara Torres set an American record in the 50-meter freestyle with a time of 24.63 in Sydney, breaking Amy Van Dyken's record of 24.87 set at the 1996 Atlanta games. Torres also set an American record in the 100-meter butterfly, finishing in 57.58.

2000 The 400-meter relay team set a world and Olympic record of 3:36.6 in Sydney. The order was Amy Van Dyken, Dara Torres, Courtney Shealy, and Jenny Thompson.

2000 The 400-meter medley relay team set a world and Olympic record of 3:58.30. The order was B. J. Bedford, Megan Quann, Jenny Thompson, and Dara Torres.

2000 The 800-meter freestyle team set an Olympic record of 7:57.80. The order was Samantha Arsenault, Diana Munz, Lindsay Benko, and Jenny Thompson.

2000 Dara Torres, at age 33 years and 161 days, became the oldest U.S. gold medalist.

2000 On September 18 in Sydney, Megan Quann set an American record in the 100-meter breaststroke of 1:07.05, winning the gold medal and beating her own record of 1:07.12, set in August. On August 11, she set the American record in the 50-meter breaststroke with a time of 31.34.

2000 For the first time, swimmers in the NCAA championships were eligible for world records, which must be set in metric distances. The swimming and diving championships were held in Indianapolis. The University of Georgia relay team set a world record of 3:57.46 in the 400-meter medley, surpassing the mark of 3:57.62 set by Japan in 1999.

2000 Christina Teucher received the Honda-Broderick Cup, given annually to the nation's outstanding female collegiate athlete.

2001 The University of Texas shattered its NCAA championship record and the American record in the 200-meter freestyle relay. The Longhorns posted a time of 1:28.89, one-hundredth of a second faster than the previous record.

2001 At the NCAA Division I women's swimming championships, Maggie Bowen, of Auburn (Alabama), set a meet and American record of 1:55.49 in the 200-meter individual medley. Bowen lowered the record of 1:55.54 set by Summer Sanders, of Stanford, in 1992.

2001 In Fukuoka, Japan, at the world swimming championships, Haley Coup, of Chico, California, turned in a time of 28.51 in the 50-meter backstroke, two-hundredths of a second ahead of Germany's Antje Buschschulte. Coup's gold was the only medal won by an American woman.

2001 To date, the women with the most NCAA Division I titles are Tracy Caulkins, University of Florida, 12; Martina Moraveova, Southern Methodist (Dallas), 10; Jenny Thompson, Stanford, 9; and Marybeth Linzmeier, Stanford, 8.

2001 Four-time Olympian Jill Sterkel was named coach of the U.S. national swimming team at the world championships, becoming the first woman to hold this position.

2001 Natalie Coughlin of California set world and U.S. short course records at a World Cup meet in East Meadows, New York. She set a world record of 57.08 in the 100-meter backstroke and a U.S. record in the 50-meter butterfly with a time of 25.83. She also set a world record of 2:03.62 in the 200-meter backstroke.

2002 Coughlin set three records at the NCAA Swimming and Diving Championships. She broke her own 200-meter backstroke record in 1:49.52, which is also an American record. She also set American and NCAA records in the 100-meter backstroke (49.97) and the 100-meter butterfly (50.01).

Endurance Swimming

At age 33 on September 11, 1951, Florence Chadwick became the first woman to swim the English Channel from England to France, going against the tides and wind. The icy waters were considered virtually impossible in this direction, but Chadwick was determined and driven by the motto she had pasted in her scrapbook as a young girl: "Winners never quit; quitters never win." Fighting rough waters, stomach cramps, and heavy fog, she completed the 35-mile crossing in 16 hours and 19 minutes.

A year earlier, on August 8, 1950, she plunged into the water at Cape Gris-Nez, France, to begin her swim and waded ashore 13 hours and 20' minutes later in Dover, England, breaking the famous record of Gertrude Ederle by 1 hour and 11 minutes.

1926 On August 6, Gertrude Ederle, at the age of 19, became the first woman to swim across the English Channel from France to England. Her time of 14 hours and 31 minutes broke the men's record by more than 2 hours. Only five other people had crossed it prior to Ederle—all men. She returned to New York to a hero's welcome—a ticker-tape parade on Fifth Avenue attended by more than 2 million people.

1926 Three weeks after Gertrude Ederle's English Channel swim, Mrs. Clemington Carson, of New York, took one hour longer to make the trip. Disappointed at not being the first woman to make the swim, she pointed out that she was the first mother to do so.

1950 Florence Chadwick was the first woman to cross the English Channel in both directions. In August, she broke Gertrude Ederle's record by swimming the English Channel in 13 hours and 20 minutes, eclipsing Ederle's time by more than an hour. In 1951, she swam the more difficult England-to-France route in 13 hours and 55 minutes, a new record. In 1952, she also became the first woman to complete the swim of the Catalina Channel, a 26-mile stretch between San Diego, California, and Catalina Island. Chadwick completed the course in 13 hours and 47 minutes.

1972 Lynn Cox, a leading open-water swimmer, swam across the English Channel.

1975 On October 6, Diana Nyad, a major marathoner, swam around New York's Manhattan Island in 7 hours and 57 minutes, breaking a 50-year-old record held by Byron Somers. In 1970, in a 10-mile swim in Lake Ontario, Nyad finished 10th overall, setting a women's world record of 4 hours, 22 minutes. She set another women's record in 1974, swimming the Bay of Naples—a 22-mile distance—in 8 hours and 11 minutes.

1979 Diana Nyad set a world distance record of 89 miles, becoming the first person to swim from the Bahamas to Florida. She accomplished the feat in 27 hours and 38 minutes.

1987 Wearing nothing but a bathing suit, Lynn Cox swam the Bering Strait in water just above freezing, covering the 7 miles in 2 hours and 6 minutes.

1994 Lynn Cox, who used her swimming efforts to focus attention on the cause of world peace, made a symbolic swim of the 14 miles across the Gulf of Aqaba—against the current—in an effort to unite Israel, Egypt, and Jordon.

1999 On May 12, Susie Maroney was the first woman to swim from Cuba to Florida.

2001 On July 28, Marcella MacDonald, at age 37, became the first U.S. woman to swim the English Channel both directions, leaving Dover, England, in the morning for France and then returning. The round trip took 21 hours and 19 minutes.

Synchronized Swimming

The first time synchronized swimming was an Olympic team event was at the Atlanta games in 1996—with the United States winning the gold in the team competition. The event features eight women performing in nine feet of water. The swimmers are not permitted to touch the bottom of the pool at any time. In gracefully choreographed routines, including many acrobatic elements, set to music, the team strives for split-second synchronization.

1939 Synchronized swimming first became popular when well-known Olympic swimmer Eleanor Holm performed at the world's fair in New York.

1940 Esther Williams, the U.S. 100-meter freestyle champion, was instrumental in bringing national attention to the sport through her appearances at the San Francisco world's fair and her starring roles in several movies.

1945 The Amateur Athletic Union officially recognized the sport.

1946 The inaugural U.S. national championships were held.

1955 The Pan American Games included synchronized swimming events, and the world aquatics championships were held.

1973 At the world aquatics championships, Teresa Anderson won the solo and teamed with Gail Johnson to win the duet. In 1975, Johnson won the solo, and Robin Currer and Amanda Norriah won the duet. The United States won the team event.

1975 Gail Johnson won 11 national championships, including 4 consecutive outdoor solo titles, from 1972 to 1975. She was the indoor solo champion in 1972 and '75. Teamed with Teresa Anderson, Johnson won indoor and outdoor duet titles in 1972 and '73, and with Sue Baross she won the outdoor duet title in '74. Johnson's domination of the sport continued, as she won the world solo title in '75 and took the gold in solo at the Pan American Games.

1982 Tracie Ruiz (Conforto) was the world solo champion and won the silver with Candy Costie. Ruiz won gold medals in both events at the Pan American Games in 1983.

1984 After almost 40 years of effort and with the push of individuals such as coach Mary Jo Riggieri, of Ohio State University, synchronized swimming became an Olympic sport. Solo and duet events were held in Los Angeles. Tracie Ruiz was the sport's first gold medalist, in solo. She earned another gold, teaming with Candy Costie to win the duet competition.

1988 Tracie Ruiz (Conforto) won the silver medal in the solo competition at the Olympics in Seoul, South Korea. Twin sisters Karen and Sarah Josephson won the silver in duet.

1989 Walnut Creek Aquatics, of California, was the first team to win 10 consecutive national titles.

1992 At the Olympics in Barcelona, Spain, Karen and Sarah Josephson won the gold medal in the duet, making 16 straight titles for the Josephsons.

1992 Kristin Babb-Sprague won the gold medal in Barcelona—winning by a narrow margin over Tracie Ruiz-Conforto.

1994 Becky Dyroen Lancer won the world aquatics championship and won the duet with Jill Sudduth. Lancer and Sudduth won four international championships between 1993 and 1995.

1995 Becky Dyroen Lancer, considered the greatest solo performer in the history of the sport, was the World Cup solo champion and clinched her ninth consecutive "grand slam" by winning all major international events. No woman has won more international competitions.

1996 At the Olympics in Atlanta, the solo and duet events were dropped, and team competition became the medal event.

1996 The U.S. synchronized swimming team scored a perfect 10 and took the gold medal in the free routine in Atlanta, marking the first time a synchronized swimming team received a perfect score in any Olympic or international competition.

1998 On July 21, Kristina Lum and Bill May won the silver medal at the Goodwill Games, making them the first mixed duet team to medal in a major international competition.

2000 At the Olympics in Sydney, Australia, the United States failed to win a medal for the first time since the sport originally debuted in 1984.

2000 The duet competition was reinstated in Sydney.

2001 Tracie Ruiz (Conforto) was named Synchronized Swimmer of the Century by the International Swimming Hall of Fame.

TABLE TENNIS

TABLE TENNIS, also known as Ping-Pong, is one of the most popular recreational sports. On the elite level, table tennis is an incredibly fast-paced, action-packed sport. A skillful player can propel the ball over the net with lightning speed, using topspin, sidespin, and slices. Spectators are amazed to see such shots returned seconds later. Every 5 points, there is a change of serve, with the first person to reach 21 points the winner. The Chinese and South Korean women have dominated international play.

1926 The International Table Tennis Federation (ITTF) world championships began in London.

1928 The Parker Brothers' American Ping-Pong Association (APPA) was formed. Its first rival association was the New York Table Tennis Association (NYTTA), formed in 1931. In 1933, the NYTTA became part of the newly established United States Table Tennis Association (USTTA). The same year, the USTTA joined the International Table Tennis Association (ITTA). The first APPA national women's champion was Jessie "Jay" Purves, in 1933.

1933 Fan Pockrose won the first USTTA women's national championship, and the first and only NYTTA championship.

1934 The second and last APPA women's champion was Ruth Hughes Aarons. The first USTTA champion, also in 1934, was Iris Little. After

1934, the APPA had no players because they had all moved to the USTTA. In 1935, '36, and '37, Ruth Hughes Aarons was the USTTA women's champion.

1936 In Prague, Czechoslovakia, Ruth Hughes Aarons became the first and only American to win a world singles championship. She won four national singles titles from 1934 to 1937. Aarons also won the mixed doubles title in the same four years with four different partners.

1940 Sally Green Prouty was the first and only woman to win five consecutive U.S. Open championships.

1948 Peggy McLean won the U.S. Open, and in 1949, she won the English Open.

1948 Thelma Thall, nicknamed "Tybie," and partner Dick Miles won the world mixed doubles championships in Wembly Stadium, in London.

1950 Mildred Shahian won the English Open. In 1954 and again in 1962, she won the U.S. Open.

1952 Foam rubber rackets were introduced by Japan's Hiroji Satoh. They gave the game more speed and spin and reduced the noise.

1956 Leah Thall Neuberger, Thelma Thall's sister, with partner Erwin Klein won the world mixed doubles championships in Tokyo. Neuberger was a nine-time U.S. women's singles champion from 1947 to 1961 and an eight-time mixed doubles champion from 1942 to 1958.

1965 Patty Martinez won the U.S. women's singles championship at the age of 13, making her the youngest ever to win the title.

1966 The Hall of Fame was started with five inductees, including Ruth Hughes Aarons and Leah Thall Neuberger.

OCTOBER 1902　　　　　　　　　　　　　　　　TEN CENTS

1971 The United States had no diplomatic ties to China but sent a table tennis delegation to the country, including Leah Neuberger. The term "Ping-Pong diplomacy" made headline news. The year 2001 marked the 30th anniversary of the event.

1976 Eleven players participated in a closed championship for U.S. citizens only. Insook Na Bhushan was the winner.

1988 Table tennis made its Olympic debut in Seoul, South Korea. U.S. women have never won a medal in the event.

T

1993 U.S. Table Tennis Association was renamed USA Table Tennis. Since the early 1980s, the organization's headquarters have been in Colorado Springs as part of the U.S. Olympics training center.

1999 The U.S. team won the gold medal at the Pan American games.

1999 Gao Chang, originally from China, won the gold medal representing the U.S. in the women's singles at the Pan American games.

2000 The size of the table tennis ball officially changed from 38 millimeters to 40 millimeters. The ball is hollow and made from celluloid. It weighs only 2.7 grams, but a powerful player can smash it at speeds in excess of 100 miles per hour.

TAEKWONDO

TAEKWONDO, which means "way of kicking and punching," is the national martial art of Korea. Its roots lie in the art of *hwarang do* and reach back more than 2000 years. The free-fighting combat sport requires competitors to use only their bare hands and feet to repel opponents. Today taekwondo is the most recognized Korean martial art.

1973 On May 28, the World Taekwondo Federation was established.

1974 The United States Taekwondo Union (USTU) was established under the Amateur Athletic Union.

1984 The USTU was recognized as the national governing body of the sport and became a member of the United States Olympic Committee.

1987 In Indianapolis, taekwondo debuted at the 10th Pan American Games.

1987 On October 7, the first women's world taekwondo championships were held in Barcelona, Spain, 15 years after the biannual men's championships were first established.

1988 Taekwondo was a demonstration sport at the Olympics in Seoul and in 1992 in Barcelona. Lynnette Love won the gold medal in 1988 and then won the bronze in 1992. Love was a four-time world champion and a 10-time national champion.

1996 Barbara Kunkel was the first World Cup taekwondo championship medalist, earning a bronze in the middle division.

1999 In Winnipeg, Manitoba, Kay Poe captured the silver in the flyweight division at the Pan American Games. Poe was on four consecutive U.S. national teams and won four consecutive gold medals in the flyweight division. She was ranked number one in the world in the flyweight division for the 2000 Olympics in Sydney, Australia.

1999 Barbara Kunkel captained the U.S. team at the Pan American Games in Winnipeg and won a bronze medal in the welterweight division. She was a member of the U.S. national team for eight years, 1993–2000, and captained the team for six years, 1995–2000. Kunkel is a five-time Pan American taekwondo championship team member and four-time medalist: in 1994, she won the silver in the middle division; the bronze in the middle division in 1996; the gold in the welterweight division in '98; and bronze in the welterweight division in '99.

2000 At the U.S. Olympic team trials in Colorado Springs, flyweight favorite Kay Poe, undefeated prior to the championship match, defeated Mandy Meloon, of Texas, but suffered a dislocated patella. In the finals, Esther Kim, a friend of Poe's, disqualified herself so Poe could go to the Olympics. This gesture captured international media attention.

2000 In Sydney, taekwondo became an Olympic medal sport, with four weight divisions. Due to the limited number of competitors, only four athletes could represent each country. The two weight divisions chosen by the United States were the women's Olympic flyweight and the women's Olympic welterweight. Only six countries qualified a full team of four competitors. No American woman won a medal.

2000 Angela Prescott, 17, defeated Jessica Miron to win the U.S. Women's bantamweight national title. She also won the U.S. junior welterweight national title by defeating Eleni Kontsilianos. She was selected the USTU junior female athlete of the year for 2001.

TENNIS

Blinding serves, powerful ground strokes, and perfectly placed net shots formed the brand of tennis that Helen Wills brought to the sport in the 1920s. As she scrambled and lunged for balls, she became "America's tennis queen," winning Wimbledon eight times and never losing a set between 1927 and 1933.

> *"Public sentiment towards sport for women has correspondingly undergone a change. Our grandmothers didn't dream of the interest that we take in sport. Not many years ago it was believed that no lady would take part in a tennis game where the public was admitted as audience."*

—Helen Wills (Moody) 1930, first great U.S. tennis champion

1874 Mary Outerbridge, of Staten Island, New York, introduced tennis to the United States. Having seen the game played while on vacation in Bermuda, she laid out a tennis court at the Staten Island Cricket and Baseball Club and taught her brothers and friends to play.

1881 Smith College (Northampton, Massachusetts) introduced tennis as an outdoor sport at the collegiate level. On June 6, 12 women from Smith formed the first intercollegiate club.

1881 The United States Lawn Tennis Association (USLTA) was formed, and in 1889, it accepted women. The organization became the United States Tennis Association (USTA) in 1976.

1884 The singles competition for women debuted at Wimbledon. Maud Watson, of England, was the first winner, defeating her older sister Lilian. Maud won again in 1885. It wasn't until 1905 that a U.S. player, May Sutton (Bundy), won. She won again in 1907.

1887 Seventeen-year-old Ellen F. Hansell won the first official U.S. women's singles championship, which was held at the Philadelphia Cricket Club. Seven women entered the tournament. The Wissahickon Inn, whose grounds were adjacent to the club, provided the trophies for the winners, becoming the first sponsor of a women's tennis event. The Wissahickon Inn is now the Chestnut Hill Academy.

1890 A Young Ladies Lawn Tennis Club was recognized at the University of California at Berkeley.

1891 The first winner of the triple crown of singles, doubles, and mixed doubles titles in the U.S. women's championship was Mabel Cahill.

1892 Elisabeth Moore, of Brooklyn, New York, participated in the first five-set match ever played by women for the national championship. She lost to defending champion Mabel Cahill, but she won the title in 1896.

1892 Bryn Mawr College (Pennsylvania) played host to Vassar College (Poughkeepsie, New York) in the first intercollegiate invitational for women. This marked the first intercollegiate contest for women in any sport.

1900 American women entered the Wimbledon tournament for the first time. Marion Jones, the reigning U.S. champion, got as far as the quarterfinals.

1902 The U.S. national championship title game changed from the best of five sets to the best of three.

1905 May Sutton (Bundy) became the first American woman, and the first non-British player to win the ladies' singles championship at Wimbledon, by defeating Doris K. Douglas. She won the title again in 1907. She was also probably the only player in history to finish a match while using a crutch: at the U.S. Open in 1930, she slipped and fractured her leg; rather than conceding, she played out the match assisted by a crutch.

1909 Hazel Hotchkiss Wightman won the singles, doubles, and mixed doubles at the U.S. nationals and repeated this feat in 1910 and '11. Mary K. Browne accomplished the same in 1912, as did Alice Marble in 1938–'40.

1913 The first U.S. national ranking for women was instituted. Mary K. Browne was ranked number one in 1913 and '14.

1913 The women's doubles and mixed doubles became full championship competitions at Wimbledon.

1915 Molla Mallory Bjurstedt won the U.S. championship and subsequently became the first player to win the title four years in a row, 1915–'18. Helen Jacobs accomplished this feat in 1932–'35, and Chris Evert did as well in 1975–'78.

1917 By winning the inaugural women's singles title at the American Tennis Association (ATA) tournament in Baltimore, Lucy Stowe became the first African American woman tennis champion in the United States. Founded in 1916, the ATA was the African American counterpart to the all-white USLTA. Because of segregation, separate tournaments were held.

1921 The U.S. nationals moved from the Philadelphia Cricket Club to the West Side Tennis Club, in Forest Hills, New York. From 1921 to 1924, the women's tournament was a separate event. In 1924, the tournament was held in conjunction with the men's for the first time. Until 1974, the surface was grass; it changed to clay from 1975 to 1977 and then to hard courts.

1922 The Australian championships, which are now open, held a women's event for the first time. The men's championship began in 1905.

1923 Hazel Hotchkiss Wightman established the first international women's tennis team competition, between the United States and Great Britain, known as the Wightman Cup. It was held at New York's West Side Tennis Club, which had just been built. The United States beat Great Britain, 7–0. The following year, the event was held in Britain, and the British women won, 6–1. In her career, Wightman won 45 U.S. titles.

1924 In Olympic tennis competition in Paris, Helen Wills Moody won the gold by defeating Didi Viastro and teamed with Hazel Hotchkiss Wightman to win the doubles title. Wightman teamed with R. Norris Williams to win the mixed doubles. After a dispute between the International Lawn Tennis Association and the International Olympic Committee, tennis was dropped from the Olympics until 1988.

1924 Ora Mae Washington won her first of a record nine championships in the American Tennis Association (ATA)—1924, 1929–'35, and 1937. Segregation at the time prevented Washington and other black tennis players from competing in white tournaments.

1924 In the Wimbledon finals, Kathy McKane (British) defeated Helen Wills (Moody), the latter's only loss in 56 Wimbledon matches.

1926 Mary K. Browne was the first American woman to play professional tennis. In September, Browne, the sixth-ranked woman in the country, signed to play against France's Suzanne Lenglen for a reported $30,000. They played in New York's Madison Square Garden before 13,000 people, probably the largest crowd at that time to watch a match in the United States. Lenglen won, 6–1, 6–1.

1926 Molla Mallory Bjurstedt, at age 42, won the U.S. national title and became the oldest woman to win a major championship. Bjurstedt won eight U.S. championships—1915–'18 and 1920–'22—more than any other woman. She was the first player to achieve the number one ranking seven times, which she accomplished from 1915 to 1926. Helen Wills Moody matched this achievement during the 1923–'31 period, as did Billie Jean King, in 1966–'68, and 1971–'74.

1933 Helen Wills Moody was the country's first major woman tennis celebrity, known for her power game and dominance of the women's field. From 1927 to 1933, she won every set she played. Moody also won seven U.S. titles and won eight Wimbledon singles titles from 1927 to 1938, a record she held for 52 years, until Martina Navratilova won her ninth Wimbledon in 1990. In all, Moody won 19 singles titles. She also is credited with popularizing the visor.

1935 Helen Jacobs won her fourth consecutive U.S. championship. She also teamed with Sarah Palfrey Fabyan to win the U.S. doubles championships in 1934 and '35.

1938 Playing at Wimbledon, Helen Wills Moody won her 50th straight match—a record. It was her 55th win in 56 matches at Wimbledon.

1938 May Sutton's daughter, Dorothy Bundy Cheney, became the first American woman to win the Australian women's singles title. Sutton was the first U.S. woman to win Wimbledon, in 1905.

1939 Alice Marble, the first aggressive serve-and-volley player in women's tennis, was the first woman to score a "triple" victory in singles, doubles, and mixed doubles at both Wimbledon and the U.S. championship at Forest Hills, now the U.S. Open. Billie Jean King, another serve-and-volley player, duplicated this feat in 1967.

1946 Pauline Betz Addie won her fourth U.S. women's national championship, 1942–'44 and 1946, and also won Wimbledon in her first appearance there. She made the cover of *Time* magazine on September 2. Addie was an early pioneer in trying to establish a professional tour for women; when USLTA officials learned of her plans, they suspended her from amateur play.

1948 At the French Open, Patricia Todd was disqualified when she refused to play her semifinal match, which was moved to an outer court. She felt her matches should be played on center court, considering she was the defending champion.

1950 At the U.S. national tennis championships in Forest Hills, Althea Gibson broke the color barrier by becoming the first African American to play in a major USLTA event.

1951 Maureen Connolly, at age 14, was the youngest player to win the women's U.S. national championship.

1952 Louise Brough and Margaret duPont were the first doubles team to win 20 major tournaments, spanning 1942–'52. Pam Shriver and Martina Navratilova also won 20 major tournaments, during 1981–'87. In her career, duPont won 37 major tournaments—31 of them doubles and mixed doubles.

1953 Maureen Connolly became the first woman to win tennis's grand slam—the Australian Open, the French Open, Wimbledon, and the U.S. Open. She also went undefeated that year. The term *grand slam* was first used in tennis in 1938 to describe Don Budge's unprecedented sweep of all four major tournaments in the same year. The only other women to win the Grand Slam are Australian Margaret Smith Court, in 1969, and German Steffi Graff, in 1988.

1955 Doris Hart and Shirley Fry won the French doubles championship a record five straight times.

1956 Althea Gibson became the first African American to play in the All-England Tennis Championships at the All-England Club, in Wimbledon. In winning the doubles title with Angela Buxton, Gibson became the first African American to win a grand slam title.

1957 Althea Gibson became the first African American to win a grand-slam title, when she won Wimbledon, where she also won the doubles titles from 1956 to 1958. Gibson also won the U.S. nationals, now the U.S. Open, becoming the first African American to do so, and repeated both the U.S. Open and Wimbledon titles in 1958. In 1957, she reached the finals of the Australian Open and won the doubles title with Shirley Fry. Also in 1957, Gibson was the first African American to be selected as the Associated Press Female Athlete of the Year.

1957 Althea Gibson was the first woman featured on the cover of *Sports Illustrated*, appearing in the September 2 issue.

1960 For the first time, two women, Billie Jean King and Nancy Richey, were co-ranked number one by the USTA ranking committee.

1961 The youngest team in Wimbledon history—17-year-old Billie Jean Moffitt (King) and 18-year-old Karen Hantze Susman—won the doubles championship.

1962 Billie Jean King beat Margaret Smith Court in the opening round of Wimbledon, the first time a player with a number one ranking had lost so early in the tournament. At the time, King was unranked.

1963 In the longest singles set played by a woman—36 games—Billie Jean King defeated Christine Truman (British), 6–4, 19–17, in a Wightman Cup match.

1963 The Federation Cup tournament, known as the Fed Cup, was created by the International Lawn Tennis Federation to celebrate the organization's 50th anniversary and was played in London. Women's teams from several nations competed. The U.S. team defeated Australia, 2–1, to win the first competition.

1967 The steel racket was introduced by Wilson Sporting Goods, with the T-2000 model.

1968 Nancy Richey won her record sixth straight U.S. championship, on clay, making for 33 consecutive match victories.

1968 The British Hard Court Championships at the West Hants Lawn Tennis Club in Bournemouth, England, became the first "open" tournament in which amateurs and professionals competed against each other, with cash prizes awarded based on how far a player advanced in the tournament. Three of the four grand-slam events—the French, Wimbledon, and the U.S. Championships—also became open events that year.

1970 The U.S. Open became the first and only grand slam event to use the sudden death tiebreaker created by Jimmy Van Allen. Under this system, the player who wins the first seven points of the tiebreaker wins the set. However, the margin of victory must be at least two points, so the tiebreaker score may exceed seven points. Only one match at the U.S. Open has been decided by a tiebreaker in every set—Steffi Graf over Pam Shriver in 1985.

1970 The Virginia Slims, the first women's professional tennis tournament, was played in Houston. The event was established because the Pacific Southwest tournament, owned by Jack Kramer, wouldn't give women equal prize money; the cash ratio was 10–1 in favor of the men. Founders of the Virginia Slims tournament were *World Tennis* magazine publisher Gladys Heldman, Billie Jean King, and seven other players, who broke away from the USTA event in Los Angeles and signed $1 contracts with Heldman to play in Houston. The players in the inaugural tournament were Billie Jean King, Rosie Casals, Jane "Peaches" Bartkowicz, Judy Dalton, Valerie Ziegenfuss, Kerry Melville Reid, Nancy Richey, and Kristy Pigeon. Julie Heldman was also part of the original group to sign on, but she did not play due to an injury. Rosie Casals won the event.

1970 At Wimbledon, Margaret Court defeated Billie Jean King, 14–12, 11–9, in 46 games, the longest final in Wimbledon history.

1971 Billie Jean King was the first woman athlete in any sport to earn more than $100,000 in a single season, with a take of $117,000. She won 38 singles and doubles titles that year.

1972 Billie Jean King was named Sportswoman of the Year by *Sports Illustrated.*

1973 The Women's Tennis Association (WTA) was established. Billie Jean King served as the first president from June 1973 to September 1975 and served again from September 1978 to September 1981.

1973 On July 19, the USTA announced that equal prize money would be awarded to women and men at the U.S. Open. Australians Margaret Court and John Newcombe each won $25,000.

1973 One of the most famous and most hyped sporting events in history, the "Battle of the Sexes" between Billie Jean King and Bobby Riggs, was held at the Houston Astrodome. King defeated Riggs, 6–4, 6–3, 6–3, and launched women's athletics into a new arena of respect and opportunity. Attendance at the Astrodome was 30,472, and 50 million watched the telecast. King collected the $100,000 winner-take-all purse.

1973 One of the greatest rivalries in any sport began between Chris Evert, with her relentless baseline game, and Martina Navratilova, with her serve-and-volley style. The two champions met in 60 tournament finals, including 14 grand slams, with Navratilova winning 36 to Evert's 24. The rivalry lasted 15 years, ending in 1989, when Evert retired.

1974 The doubles team of Billie Jean King and Rosie Casals won five Wimbledon titles between 1967 and 1974, also winning the U.S. Open in both '67 and '74 and reaching the finals four other times—1966, '68, '73, and '75. They also reached the French Open finals in '68 and '70. In her career, Casals won 112 doubles titles and 11 singles titles.

1974 Chris Evert set a modern record by winning 56 consecutive matches.

1974 World Team Tennis, a co-ed league, was conceived by Billie Jean King and her husband, Larry King. It began in large U.S. cities, with home teams composed of both women and men. The season was three months long, and each team played 44 matches. Billie Jean King served as player-coach for the Philadelphia Freedoms, making her the first woman to coach a team on which men played. The league folded in 1978 but was started again in 1981 and is currently active as TYCO World Team Tennis.

1974 Chris Evert achieved the best record on clay, with 125 straight matches and 25 tournament wins between August 12, 1973, and May 12, 1974. Evert, renowned for her consistency, made the semifinals or better in a record 52 out of 56 grand-slam championships.

1976 The oversize racket was introduced by Prince.

1976 Chris Evert was selected *Sports Illustrated*'s Sportsman of the Year and was pictured on the cover of the magazine dressed in vintage tennis attire. She became the first American woman athlete to reach $1 million in career earnings.

1977 At the age of 14, Tracy Austin became the youngest player ever to enter Wimbledon and the U.S. Open and the youngest to be ranked in the top 10, at number 4.

1978 The U.S. Open moved from the West Side Tennis Club to the National Tennis Center, in Flushing Meadows, New York, and was played on hard courts for the first time, in Louis Armstrong Stadium. The facility was the largest tennis arena of its era, holding 20,000 spectators. In 1997, an even more commodious structure, Arthur Ashe Stadium, was built on the same site and is now the largest grand slam arena, with 22,911 seats.

1978 Chris Evert won the U.S. Open for the fourth consecutive year, the first player to do so since Helen Jacobs in 1935.

1978 Pam Shriver was the first amateur female finalist at the U.S. Open in the "open era" (i.e., since 1968). She was also the youngest finalist up to that point in time, at 16 years and 2 months.

1979 Billie Jean King won her 20th Wimbledon title, taking the doubles with Martina Navratilova. King won 10 doubles, 6 singles, and 4 mixed, breaking Briton Elizabeth Ryan's record of 19.

1979 Tracy Austin, at 16 years and 9 months, became the youngest U.S. Open champion.

1981 Tracy Austin and her brother Jeff became the only brother-sister team to win the Wimbledon mixed doubles title.

1982 In May, the first National Collegiate Athletic Association (NCAA) Division I tennis championships were held at the University of Utah. Stanford (California) won the team championship, and Stanford student Alycia Moulton won the individual championship. The Division II tournament was held at Southern Illinois University. California State University at Northridge won the first team championship, and Iwona Kuczynska, of California State University at Bakersfield, won the individual title. The Division III event was hosted by Millsaps College (Jackson, Mississippi). Occidental College (Los Angeles) won the team championship, and Beckie Donecker, of Elizabethtown College (Pennsylvania), won the individual title.

1983 In Beckenham, England, at age 39 and a half, Billie Jean King became the oldest woman to take a professional title. In her career, she won 39 major titles, including 6 Wimbledon singles titles between 1966 and '75 and 4 U.S. Open championships between 1967 and '74.

1984 Chris Evert was the first player to win 1,000 singles matches.

1984 Billie Jean King became the first female commissioner in professional sports history, governing Team Tennis, the first professional sports league in which women compete equally with men.

1984 On December 6, in the semifinals of the Australian Open, Helena Sukova snapped Martina Navratilova's record of 74 consecutive singles victories, including the French Open, Wimbledon, and the U.S. Open titles. The loss was Navratilova's third defeat in 167 matches.

1984 Pam Shriver and Martina Navratilova were the first women's doubles team to win all of the grand slam doubles championships in succession.

1985 Pam Shriver and Martina Navratilova were the first doubles team to compile a 109-match winning streak, which they accomplished during 1983–'85.

1986 In September, at the WTA tournament in Tampa, Florida, Lori McNeil and Zina Garrison played in the first all–African American final. McNeil won, 2–6, 7–5, 6–2.

1986 Chris Evert won the French Open for a record seventh time.

1987 Between 1982 and 1987, Martina Navratilova was ranked number one in the world for a record 150 weeks. Steffi Graf later surpassed that mark, with 186 consecutive weeks at the top.

1987 Martina Navratilova won a record ninth Wimbledon singles title. From 1982 to 1987, Navratilova won an unprecedented six consecutive singles championships. She was also the first woman player to compile a 74-match winning streak. Navratilova was instrumental in the promotion of conditioning training for women. She also became highly respected for her frankness and openness with the media.

1988 Tennis was reintroduced as a medal sport at the Olympics in Seoul, South Korea. Steffi Graf, playing for Germany, won the gold medal, defeating Gabriela Sabatini of Argentina. Tennis had been a medal sport from 1900 to 1924 and then was eliminated. In doubles, Zina Garrison and Pam Shriver won the gold medal, defeating Czech players Jana Novotna and Helena Sukova.

1989 Chris Evert achieved the highest career winning percentage in the open era, with a .900 record in matches, reflecting 1,309 wins and 146 losses.

1989 Martina Navratilova was named Female Athlete of the Decade by the Associated Press, United Press International, and *National Sports Review*.

1989 Chris Evert became the first 100-match winner in the 102 years of the U.S. national championship.

1990 At Wimbledon, Zina Garrison became the first African American to make it to the finals of a grand slam since Althea Gibson won the U.S. Open and Wimbledon in 1958. Garrison lost to Martina Navratilova.

SERENA AND VENUS WILLIAMS. (PHOTO © MATTHEW STOCKMAN/ALLSPORT.)

1990 On March 6, Jennifer Capriati, a few weeks shy of her 14th birthday, became the youngest woman to play a professional tennis match, in the Virginia Slims tournament in Boca Raton, Florida. She was the youngest player ever to turn pro. Also in 1990, she was the youngest player ever to reach the semifinals of a grand-slam tournament, playing in the French Open at 14 years and 2 months, as well as the youngest ever to win a match at Wimbledon.

1990 The Women's International Tennis Federation ruled that the earliest a player could become a professional was in the month the player would become 14 years old.

1991 Monica Seles, at age 16, was the youngest player to win a WTA event, and at age 17, she was the youngest player at the time to be ranked number one.

1992 Mary Joe Fernandez, of the United States, and Gigi Fernandez, of Puerto Rico, won the gold medal in doubles at the Olympics in Barcelona, Spain, defeating Arantxa Sanchez Vicario and Conchita Martinez, of Spain. Mary Joe Fernandez also won the bronze in singles.

1992 Jennifer Capriati beat Steffi Graf, 3–6, 6–3, 6–1, to win the Olympic gold medal.

1994 Martina Navratilova set the record for most years in the open era with at least one singles title, amassing 21 wins from 1974 to 1994. Chris Evert follows, with 18 titles from 1971 to 1988.

1994 NCAA Division II individual championships for women were suspended, but championships continued in Divisions I and III.

1995 When Monica Seles defeated Amanda Coetzer at the Canadian Open, 6–0, 6–1, the match broke the record for the least number of games played in a final.

1996 Mary Jo Fernandez and Lindsey Davenport won the doubles championships at the Australian Open and the French Open.

1996 Lindsey Davenport won the gold medal in singles, and Gigi Fernandez and Mary Jo Fernandez took the gold in doubles at the Atlanta Olympics.

1996 On the night of her official retirement from tennis in November, Martina Navratilova became the first woman athlete to have a retirement banner hang in Madison Square Garden.

1997 On September 7, Venus Williams, playing in her first U.S. Open, became the first unseeded player to reach the finals. Martina Hingis won the match, 6–0, 6–4. Williams was the first African American to make it to the finals since Althea Gibson won in 1957 and '58.

1997 In November, Serena Williams became the lowest-ranked player, at 304, to defeat two top 10 players—Monica Seles and Mary Pierce—in a singles event.

1998 On April 14, at the Lipton championships in Miami, Serena Williams set a WTA record by defeating five top 10 players in 16 matches. Monica Seles accomplished the same feat in 1989 in 33 matches.

1998 At Wimbledon, Venus Williams became the first woman ever to hit a serve 125 miles per hour.

1998 Lindsey Davenport won six tournaments, including Wimbledon and the U.S. Open, becoming the first U.S-born player to be ranked number one since Chris Evert in 1985.

1999 In January, Julia "Judy" Levering became the first woman president of the USTA.

1999 On February 28, Serena Williams won the Paris indoors championship, and Venus Williams won the Oklahoma City championships, making it the first time sisters won WTA-sponsored events on the same day.

1999 On March 28, Venus and Serena Williams became the first U.S. sisters to compete against one another, when they squared off in the finals of the Lipton championships. Eighteen-year-old Venus defended her 1998 Lipton title by defeating her younger sister in three sets: 6–1, 4–6, 6–4.

1999 In late March, following the Lipton championships, the WTA tour exceeded the one million mark in on-site attendance, the earliest point in any year that it had reached that level.

1999 On June 6, Serena and Venus Williams became the first sisters since 1890 to win a grand slam doubles title, when they won the French Open over Martina Hingis and Anna Kournikova, collecting $330,000. The Williamses join Grace and Ellen Roosevelt, who won the 1890 U.S. national doubles championships, as the only sisters to accomplish this feat.

1999 On July 3, 18-year-old Alexandra Stevenson became the first female qualifier to reach the semifinals of Wimbledon, when she defeated fellow teenage qualifier Jelena Dokic.

1999 Lindsey Davenport, at 6 feet, 2 inches, became the tallest woman to ever win Wimbledon.

1999 Serena Williams was the first African American to win the U.S. Open since Althea Gibson in 1957.

1999 In September, the richest tournament in tennis, the Grand Slam Cup, was played in Munich. It featured the 12 men and 8 women with the best records at the year's four grand-slam events. The women's champion received a record $800,000 in prize money.

2000 The United States continued to lead all countries by winning its 17th Fed Cup title, followed by Australia, with seven; Czechoslovakia and Spain, with five each; Germany two, West Germany two, East Germany one; and France one.

2000 Venus Williams became the first African American woman to win Wimbledon since Althea Gibson took the title in 1958. Williams defeated Lindsey Davenport, 6–3, 7–6.

2000 For the first time in Wimbledon history, there were five different winners in five consecutive years: 2000—Venus Williams, 1999—Lindsey Davenport, 1998—Conchita Martinez, 1997—Martina Hingis, and 1996—Steffi Graf.

2000 When Venus Williams won the Wimbledon title, the Williams sisters became the first sisters in tennis history to each own a grand slam title. Serena won the U.S. Open in 1999.

2000 In July, Serena and Venus Williams became the first sisters to capture the women's doubles championship at Wimbledon.

2000 On September 27, Venus Williams won the gold in Sydney and joined Steffi Graf (of Germany) as the only women to win Wimbledon, the U.S. Open, and an Olympic gold medal. On September 28, Williams became only the second American woman to earn two gold medals at the same Olympics, winning her second gold in doubles with her sister, Serena. Helen Wills won both the singles and doubles titles in the 1924 Olympics in Paris.

2000 Venus Williams's win at the U.S. Open gave the Williams family its second consecutive title, following Serena's win in 1999. This marked the first time siblings have won the women's singles title at the U.S. national championships, including the U.S. Open.

2000 For the first time ever at the U.S. Open, more women's matches than men's were played on center court.

2000 By coming out of retirement to compete in the women's doubles at the U.S. Open, Martina Navratilova became the only tennis player in the world to have played at the West Side Tennis Club, Louis Armstrong Stadium, and Arthur Ashe Stadium. In September, Navratilova also became the only player to have a WTA ranking in four decades—the '70s, '80s, '90s, and 2000. At age 43, she was ranked number 88 at the U.S.

Open. She is the winningest player, male or female, with 165 doubles championships and 167 singles championships.

2000 On December 21, Venus Williams signed an endorsement contract with Reebok for $40 million, the largest deal ever for a female athlete.

2000 An all-time-record 4.1 million fans attended Sanex WTA tournaments.

2000 Amy Jenson, of the University of California, won her record third straight NCAA Division I doubles title. In 1998 and '99, she teamed with Amanda Augustus, and in 2000, she teamed with Claire Curran.

2001 In January, Zina Garrison became the first African American woman to be selected to the board of directors of the USTA.

2001 Laura Granville, of Stanford, won the NCAA Division I title for the second straight year. Granville set a NCAA record with a 58-match winning streak. Lele Forood became the first female coach to win an NCAA tennis title. In 1986 and '87, Stanford's Patty Fendick also won back-to-back titles, as did Lisa Raymond, of the University of Florida, in 1992 and '93.

2001 Brigham Young University—Hawaii's 103-match winning streak from 1999 to 2001 was broken by Lynn University (Boca Raton, Florida) in the NCAA Division II championships.

2001 Stanford University won its 11th consecutive NCAA team title.

2001 In January Jennifer Capriati won the Australian Open (defeating Martina Hingis) and on June 10th, she took the French Open title by beating Kim Clyisters. The third set, which she won by a score of 12–10 was the longest third set in French Open history. Chris Evert was the last U.S. woman before Capriati to win the French Open, when she captured her seventh title in 1986. In October, Capriati reached the number one ranking for the first time, and the Associated Press named her Female Athlete of the Year. In 2002, Capriati won the Australian Open title again, in a thrilling come-from-behind win, she overcame four match points and defeated Martina Hingis in 100 degree heat.

2001 In June, after four days of meeting in Paris, the grand-slam tournaments ruled to double the number of seeded players to 32. The new system ensures that the top 32 players in the men's and women's rankings will be seeded, which makes early-round upsets less likely.

2001 Venus Williams won Wimbledon on July 8; it was the first back-to-back Wimbledon championship by an African American since Althea Gibson won in 1957 and '58.

2001 With Venus Williams capturing the Wimbledon title, the United States reached a leading total of 47 women's singles titles at Wimbledon. The British Isles is second, with 29, and Germany is third, with 8.

2001 Venus and Serena Williams made history at the U.S. Open by playing in the first all–African American final and the first prime-time women's singles final, held on Saturday night, September 8, with Venus defeating Serena, 6–2, 6–4. They also were the first sisters to play in a major singles championship since the Watson sisters (British) in 1884.

2001 The U.S. women have won 7 Australian Open titles, 7 French Open titles, 10 Wimbledon titles, and 10 U.S. Open titles.

2002 In February, 21 year-old Venus Williams was ranked number one, becoming the first African American woman to achieve the top spot since Althea Gibson in 1957. Williams became the tenth player to reach number one since the women's computer ranking began in 1975.

TRACK AND FIELD

I don't feel there's any hurdle too high or any obstacle in my life that I can't get over.

—Gail Devers, Olympic champion in the 100 meters and 100-meter hurdles, who recovered from a serious illness to compete

1880s Women began to compete in track-and-field events in women's colleges, club teams formed, and recreational running was growing in popularity.

1916 The Amateur Athletic Union (AAU) authorized track-and-field competitions.

1923 The first major outdoor track-and-field meet for women was held in Newark, New Jersey.

1928 Track-and-field events were held for the first time at the Olympics in Amsterdam, Netherlands. The events for women were the 100 meters, 800 meters, 4×100-meter relay, discus throw, and high jump.

1928 In Amsterdam, Mildred Wiley tied Carolina Gisolf for the silver in the high jump, with a mark of 5 feet, 5¼ inches. Jean Shiley won the bronze. In 1932, Shiley and Mildred "Babe" Didrikson (Zaharias) tied for the gold in the event, setting a world record at 5 feet, 5¾ inches.

1928 Elizabeth Robinson, a 16-year-old high school student from Riverdale, Illinois, was the first woman to earn an Olympic gold medal in track and field. She won the 100-meter sprint in Amsterdam in world-record time. The Olympics were only the fourth track meet of her career.

1928 Lillian Copeland, a student at the University of Southern California, won a silver medal in the first Olympic discus event. In 1932, she won the gold in the event. Copeland won two national championships in javelin, two in discus, and five in shot put.

1932 Babe Didrikson qualified for five out of six track-and-field events at the Olympic Games in Los Angeles, but rules passed after the 1928 games allowed women to participate in only three events.

1932 The 80-meter hurdles became an Olympic event. Babe Didrikson captured the gold medal with a time of 11.7, a world record at the time. Evie Hall was also timed at 11.7 but won the silver, coming in a hair shy at the tape. Like Didrikson, Hall won AAU events from 1930 to 1935.

1932 The 800 meters was not held after 1928 because it was thought too strenuous for women. No race longer than 200 meters was permitted in the Olympics for 32 years.

1932 The javelin throw was held for the first time in Los Angeles. Babe Didrikson set an Olympic record to win the gold, with a mark of 143 feet, 4 inches. A U.S. woman didn't medal again until 1972 in Munich, when Kathryn Schmidt won the bronze; she won it again in 1976.

1932 Jean Shiley won the gold medal in the high jump after a controversial victory over Babe Didrikson, who went over the bar backward. The mark—5 feet, 5¾ inches—matched the world record at the time. Shiley was the AAU high-jump champion from 1929 to 1931, and in 1932, she tied with Didrikson. She also won the indoor title from 1929 to 1932.

1932 Louise Stokes and Tidye Pickett were the first two African American women to qualify for the Olympics but were not allowed to participate because of racist exclusion.

1933 Katherine Mearls Rogan won her fifth consecutive long-jump national title. In 1928, Rogan set the U.S. record in the 40-yard dash at 5.4 seconds, and she is credited with establishing the 50-yard dash at 6.0 seconds in 1926. She also competed in the Olympics in Amsterdam in 1928, the first year women were allowed to compete in track and field.

1936 At the Olympics in Munich, Helen Stephens won gold in the 100 meters and the 4×100-meter relay. In 1935, at age 17, Stephens won four AAU championships: the 50 meters, 200 meters, broad jump, and shot put. In 1936, she was selected the Associated Press Female Athlete of the Year. Stephens continued to win AAU events in 1937.

1948 Alice Coachman's gold medal in the high jump in London made her the first African American woman to win an Olympic gold medal. After her Olympic success, Coachman became the first African American to endorse a product, Coca-Cola, appearing in advertisements and on billboards with Jesse Owens, the 1936 Olympic track and field hero.

1948 Audrey Patterson was the first U.S. medalist in the Olympic 200 meters. She won the bronze with a time of 25.20. This was the first year the event was held.

1948 The long jump was held for the first time at the Olympics.

1948 The shot put also became an Olympic event in London. It wasn't until 1960, in Rome, that a U.S. woman won a medal, when Earlene Brown captured the bronze.

1951 The first Pan American Games were held. Evie Hall coached the U.S. women's track team.

1956 Nell Jackson, a track-and-field star at the 1948 Olympics, became the first African American of either sex to be head coach of a U.S. Olympic team, when she was selected to coach the U.S. team at the games in Melbourne, Australia. In 1968, she became the first African American and one of the first women to serve on the board of directors of the United States Olympic Committee, as chair of the U.S. track-and-field committee. Jackson also coached the U.S. team in the 1972 Olympics. Jackson held the U.S. record in the 200 meters from 1949 to '54.

1956 Winning the silver, Willye White became the first U.S. woman to medal in the Olympic long jump, a new event in 1948. A U.S. woman didn't medal again until 1976, when Kathy McMillan won the silver.

1956 Aeriwentha "Mae" Faggs Starr, a sprinter, became the first African American woman to participate in three Olympic Games—1948, '52, and '56. She won gold in the 4×100-meter relay in '52 and bronze in the same event in '56. In 1948, at age 16, she was the youngest on the team.

1956 Mildred McDaniel Davis, holder of seven national titles, won the gold medal in the high jump at the Olympics. She won the gold at the Pan American Games in 1955.

1958 Earlene Brown was the first American woman to break the 50-foot barrier in the shot put.

1958 Lillian Greene-Chamberlain was the first national champion in the 880 yards and the first African American woman to represent the United States in international middle-distance competition—400 meters and 800 meters—before they became Olympic events.

1960 The 800 meters was reinstated at the Olympics in Rome.

1960 Wilma Rudolph became the first woman to earn three gold medals in track at one Olympics, by winning the 100 meters, with a time of 11.0;

the 200 meters, with a time of 24.0; and the 4×100-meter relay. Rudolph, whose bout with polio forced her to wear a brace on her leg as a child, became an international celebrity after the Olympics and was selected the Associated Press Athlete of the Year for 1960 and 1961.

1964 At the Olympics in Tokyo, Japan, the 400-meter race, the heptathlon and the pentathlon were held for the first time.

1964 Earlene Brown was the first American woman to medal in the shot put, winning the bronze. Brown was also the only shot-putter to compete in three consecutive Olympics—1956, '60, and '64.

1964 Edith McGuire finished the 200-meter dash in 23.0, winning the gold and breaking Wilma Rudolph's 1960 Olympic record. McGuire won the silver in the 100 meters and another silver in the 4×100-meter relay. Between 1963 and 1965, she won several AAU championships.

1965 The 1,500 meters was contested for the first time at the outdoor track-and-field championships.

1967 When Maren Seidler won the shot put at the national championships at age 15, she became the youngest athlete ever to win a track-and-field title.

1967 Madeline Manning became the first American woman to win an international championship in the 800 meters, when she won gold at the Pan American Games.

1968 Madeline Manning won the gold medal and set an Olympic record for the 800 meters, with a time of 2:00.9 in Mexico City. This was the first U.S. medal in the event.

1968 Wyomia Tyus became the first runner, male or female, to win consecutive gold medals in an Olympic sprint event, when she won the 100 meters in a world-record time of 11.08. She had previously won gold in Tokyo in 1964, with a time of 11.4. Gail Devers matched the consecutive golds in 1992 and 1996.

1968 At the Olympics, Barbara Ferrell won the silver in the 100 meters and gold in the 4×100-meter relay. In 1967, she twice tied the world record of 11.1 in the 100 meters. Between 1967 and 1969, Ferrell won several AAU championships.

1969 At the outdoor national championships, Kathy Hammond set the U.S. record in the 400 meters, at 51.65. She had broken the record four previous times.

1972 The 1,500-meter race and 4×100-meter relay were introduced at the Olympics in Munich. Also, the hurdles were extended from 80 meters to 100 meters.

1972 Willye White became the first American woman to compete in five Olympics, starting in 1956 and finishing in 1972.

1972 Kathy Hammond, a three-time national champion in the 400 meters, was the first U.S. woman to win an Olympic medal in the event, taking the bronze. The event had been held since 1964.

1972 Jane Frederick was the first woman to win the pentathlon at the U.S. nationals in five separate years—1972, '73, '75, '76, and '79.

1973 At age 15, Mary Decker (Slaney) set three world records: the outdoor 800 meters, indoor 880 yards, and indoor 1,000 yards.

1976 Madeline Manning became the first woman to break the two-minute mark in the 800 meters, with a time of 1:59.8 at the Olympic trials.

1976 Chandra Cheesborough, of Ribault, in Jacksonville, Florida, set the U.S. high school 100-meter record of 11.13, which still stands.

1976 Kathryn Schmidt was the first U.S. woman to throw a javelin more than 200 feet, setting a mark of 203 feet. At the Olympics in Montreal, she won the bronze medal with a throw of 196.8 feet. She also won Olympic bronze in 1972.

1976 Martha Watson, a graduate of Tennessee State, competed in her fourth Olympics as a long jumper; she also ran on the 4×100-meter relay team in 1972 and '76. In her career, Watson won eight national long-jump championships and set U.S. records in 1970 and '73.

1979 Maren Seidler dominated shot put for more than a decade. She won the national championship in 1967, '68, and from '72 to '80. Seidler set two U.S. records, in 1974 and '79, with a throw of 62 feet, 7¾ inches. The record lasted until 1987.

1982 Mary Decker (Slaney) became the first woman to run 880 yards in less than 2 minutes. She was also the first woman to receive the Jesse Owens Award as the outstanding U.S. track-and-field athlete.

1982 In May, the National Collegiate Athletic Association (NCAA) Division I women's outdoor track-and-field championships were held at Brigham Young University (Provo, Utah). UCLA won the first team championship and won it again in 1984.

1983 The first women's world track-and-field championships were held.

1983 In March, the first NCAA women's indoor track-and-field championship were hosted by the University of Michigan at the Silverdome, in Pontiac. The University of Nebraska won the team championship and won it again in 1984.

1984 At the indoor championships, Valerie Brisco-Hooks became the first U.S. woman to run the 400 meters in less than 50 seconds, when she posted a time of 49.82.

1984 At the Los Angeles games, Valerie Brisco-Hooks became the only woman to win both a 200-meter race and a 400-meter race in one Olympics. Her 400-meter time of 48.83 still stands as an American record.

1984 At the Olympics, the heptathlon replaced the pentathlon, when the javelin and 200 meters were added to make it seven events.

1984 In the first Olympic 400-meter hurdles, Judi Brown, of the U.S. team, won the silver.

1984 Chandra Cheesborough became the first woman to win gold medals in both the 4×100-meter and 4×400-meter relays. The time of 3:18.29 in the 4×400 was an Olympic record.

1984 Benita Fitzgerald won the gold medal in the 100-meter hurdles at the Olympics.

1984 In Los Angeles, sprinter Evelyn Ashford became the first woman to run the 100 meters in under 11 seconds, with a time of 10.97. A member of five Olympic teams—1976, '80, '84, '88, and '92—she won her fourth Olympic gold medal on the 4×100-meter relay team in 1992, at the age of 35.

1984 Leslie Maxie set a world junior record in the 400-meter hurdles, 55.20, which still stands.

1985 Indoor track events were held for the first time in NCAA Division II and III history. They have been held since 1983 in Division I.

1986 Jackie Joyner-Kersee, one of the greatest athletes of all time, set the heptathlon world record by scoring 7,148 points at the Goodwill Games in Moscow. Later in the year, she extended the record to 7,158 points at the U.S. Olympic Festival, where she won all seven events.

1988 Suzy Favor (Hamilton), of the University of Wisconsin, was the first athlete of either sex to win the NCAA outdoor 1,500-meter championship four consecutive times, taking the title in 1988–'91. She won 54 out of 56 races and 40 consecutive finals and won nine NCAA titles, a record that still stands. In 1990, Favor, a 14-time all-American, won the Honda-Broderick Cup.

1988 Jackie Joyner-Kersee set a world and Olympic record in the heptathlon in Seoul, with 7,291 points, winning the gold. She also won the gold in the long jump, with a mark of 24 feet, 3½ inches, becoming the first woman to win both an individual event and a multievent in Olympic competition. She went on to win gold again in the 1992 heptathlon and a bronze in the long jump, in Barcelona. In 1999, she was named *Sports Illustrated for Women*'s Greatest Female Athlete of the 20th Century.

1988 Sharon Hedrich won the first Olympic 800-meter wheelchair race.

1988 At the Olympic trials, Florence Griffith-Joyner, known as "Flo Jo," set a world record of 10.49 in the 100 meters. At the Seoul games, she earned three gold medals, winning the 100 meters, 200 meters, and 400-meter relay. In the 200 meters, she set a world record of 21.34. She also captured the silver medal on the 1,600-meter relay team. "Flo Jo" still holds the records in the 100 and 200 meters.

1988 In Seoul, Louise Ritter won the gold medal in the high jump, with a mark of 6 feet, 8 inches. In her career, she won 10 indoor and outdoor national championships. As a student at Texas Woman's University, Ritter won three consecutive Association for Intercollegiate Athletics for Women national championships, 1977–'79, and won again in '81.

1989 Lori Norwood was the first American woman to win the individual title at the world modern pentathlon championships.

1989 Dawn Sowell, of Louisiana State University, set three collegiate records that still stand: 100-meter, 10.78; low-altitude 100-meter, 10.91; and 200-meter, 22.04.

1991 Diane Dixon won her 9th consecutive, and 10th overall, 400-meter national championship, with titles in 1981 and 1983–'91.

1991 Jackie Joyner-Kersee won the World Championship in the long jump at 24 feet, ¼ inches.

1992 Kim Oden, of Nebraska Wesleyan University, won her third consecutive Division II championship in the heptathlon and her fourth consecutive in the high jump.

1992 The 10,000-meter walk was added to the Olympics in Barcelona.

1992 Barbara Jacket became head coach of the Olympic team. Under Jacket, U.S. women won four gold, three silver, and three bronze medals.

1992 Gwen Torrence won the gold medal in the 200 meters at the Olympics. She also took gold in the 4×100-meter relay and silver in the 4×400-meter relay. In 1991, Torrence won silver in both the 100 meters and 200 meters at the world championships.

1992 Jackie Joyner-Kersee became the only woman to have earned a gold medal in the heptathlon in two consecutive Olympics (1988 and 1992).

1992 Gail Devers, one of the most outstanding sprinters and hurdlers in history, made a remarkable comeback after recovering from a debilitating illness identified as Graves' disease. At the Barcelona Olympics, she won the 100-meter run and was on her way to a second gold in the 100-

meter hurdles, when she stumbled and fell. At the 1996 Atlanta Olympics, Devers successfully defended her 100-meter title and was on the gold-medal 4×100-meter relay team. A three-time Olympian—1992, 1996, and 2000—she was a world gold medalist in the 100 meters in 1993 and a world silver medalist in the 100 meters in 1995.

1993 Jearl Miles won the gold medal at the World Championships in the 400 meters with a time of 49.82.

1994 The Tennessee State University Tigerbelles became one of the most dominant college programs, under the leadership of coach Ed Temple, who started in 1950. In 44 years, the Tigerbelles sent 40 women to the Olympic Games, collectively winning 23 medals, 13 of them gold. Legends such as Wilma Rudolph, Mae Faggs, Chandra Cheesborough, Willye White, and Madeline Manning were all products of TSU.

1995 NCAA Divisions I and II began holding a combined indoor track-and-field championship.

1995 Connie Price-Smith won the silver medal in the world indoor shot put, the highest placement ever by an American in the event. It was also the first world championship (or Olympic) shot put medal for a U.S. woman since 1960. She was a four-time Olympian, in 1988, 1992, 1996, and 2000; a twelve-time outdoor shot put champion, 1988–2000; and a seven-time indoor shot put champion, 1991–2001. Price-Smith retired in January 2002 at the age of 39.

1995 Shiela Hudson set the U.S. triple-jump record of 47 feet, 3.5 inches, becoming the first to break the 46-foot barrier. She was a five-time U.S. triple-jump champion, with titles in 1990 and 1993–'96.

1996 Aimee Mullins was the first disabled athlete in NCAA history, and the only double-below-the-knee amputee, to compete on a Division I track team. She raced for Georgetown University (Washington, D.C.).

1998 Joetta Clark (Diggs) was the first woman to run in 20 Millrose Games. In her 20th competition, at 35, she placed second in the 400 meters.

1998 Windy Dean, of Southern Methodist University (Dallas), won her third consecutive Division I championship in the javelin throw.

1998 Christopher Newport University (Newport News, Virginia) won a record sixth Division III outdoor championship; the University of Wisconsin at Oshkosh won its fifth in 1997.

1999 Melissa Mueller was the first American woman to pole-vault to 14 feet, 8¾ inches, an indoor record that was later broken by Stacy Dragila.

1999 Regina Jacobs set an American record of 2:31.80 in the 1,000 meters. On July 21, 2000, in Sacramento, California, she set an American record of 14:45.5 in the 1,500 meters. She qualified for the Olympic team four times: 1988, 1992, 1996, and 2000. Jacobs won the silver medal in the world championships in both 1997 and 1999 and was a nine-time indoor 1,500-meter champion.

1999 The pole vault was added as a women's event at the world championships in Seville, Spain. Stacey Dragila won the gold, clearing 15 feet, 1 inch, tying the world record set earlier in '99 by Emma George, of Australia.

1999 Gail Devers won her third gold medal in the 100-meter hurdles at the world outdoor championships in Seville, Spain.

1999 Jearl Miles-Clark set an American record of 1:56.40 in the 800 meters on August 11, in Zurich, Switzerland. A three-time Olympian, she was a gold medalist in the 4×400-meter relay in 1996 and 2000 and a silver medalist in the event in 1992. Miles-Clark was outdoor champion in 1999 and was a three-time outdoor 400-meter champion.

2000 The pole vault became a part of all NCAA women's track-and-field championships, after debuting in the Division III outdoor meet. Laura Rosenberger, of Eastern Mennonite University (Harrisonburg, Virginia), was the first winner in indoor and outdoor competition.

2000 Louisiana State University, which had won 11 consecutive championships from 1987 to 1997, won its 12th Division I team championships in outdoor track and field. The University of Texas holds three outdoor championships and five indoor.

2000 Abilene Christian University (Texas) won its 12th Division II indoor team championship, and 8th in a row, a record. For 10 of the 12 championships (through 1999), Wes Kittley was the coach. Saint Augustine's College (Raleigh, North Carolina) is second, with three championships.

2000 On February 7, Regina Jacobs set a 1,000-meter record at the New Balance Invitational in Boston. She erased Mary Decker Slaney's 1989 record of 2:37.6 by clocking 2:35.29.

2000 In April, the U.S. women's 800-meter relay team set a world record, with a time of 1:27.46. This broke the East Germans' record of 1:28.15, set nearly two decades earlier.

2000 On April 29, Marion Jones anchored an American team in the 4×200-meter relay to a world record of 1:27.46, at the Penn Relays, in Philadelphia.

2000 On June 21, Monique Henderson, of Morse High School, in San Diego, California, set a national high school record for the 400 meters, at 50.74.

2000 At the U.S. track coaches first national invitational team championships, in Austin, Texas, UCLA's Tracey O'Hare set a collegiate outdoor record in the women's pole vault of 14 feet, 7¼ inches. O'Hare also set the indoor record on March 4, at 14 feet, 6 inches.

2000 Tisha Waller was the first American in 10 years to rank as high as number two internationally in the high jump. She was three-time outdoor champion, with titles in 1996, '98, and '99, and four-time indoor champion, with titles in 1996 and 1998–2000. In 1999, Waller won the bronze at the worlds.

2000 Marla Runyan became the first legally blind member of a U.S. Olympic team, finishing third in the 1,500 meters at the trials.

2000 Joetta Clark (Diggs) competed in her fourth Olympics, 1988–2000, in the 800 meters. She was indoor champion six times from 1988 to 1998 as well as a five-time U.S. champion, and at the University of Tennessee, Diggs won four straight NCAA championships.

2000 Jesseca Cross was the first American woman, and one of only two U.S. athletes (the other being Ralph Rose in 1912), to make an Olympic team in both the shot put and hammer throw.

2000 Suzy Favor Hamilton competed for the third time in the Olympics. She is the second-fastest American ever in the 1,500 meters, behind Mary Decker Slaney. Hamilton was a three-time outdoor 1,500-meter champion, with titles in 1990, '91, and '98; three-time indoor champion, with titles in 1991, '98, and '99; and two-time Pan American Games gold medalist. At the University of Wisconsin, she was an NCAA All-American 14 times and as a senior was awarded the Honda-Broderick Cup.

2000 The U.S. team won the gold medal in the 4×100-meter relay at the Sydney Olympics, making it the 10th time the United States won the gold in this event.

2000 On September 30, Marion Jones became the first woman to win five medals in one Olympics. She won gold in the 100 meters, 200 meters, and as a member of the 4×400-meter relay team, and won bronze in the long jump and as a member of the 4×100-meter relay team.

2000 The 4×400-meter relay team of Monique Hennagan, Jearl Miles-Clark, Andrea Anderson, and La Tasha Colander-Richardson won the Olympic gold medal.

2000 Kelly Blair La Bounty competed in her second Olympics in the heptathalon. She finished eighth in Atlanta. She was also a three-time U.S. champion.

2001 On June 3, Angela Williams, of the University of Southern California, became the first woman to win three straight 100-meter titles at the NCAA Division I outdoor championships, in Eugene, Oregon. Three other women have won two consecutive 100-meter titles: Nebraska's Merlene Ottey, in 1982 and '83; Indianapolis State's Holli Hyche, in 1993 and '94; and Louisiana State's D'Andre Hill, in 1995 and '96. In 1999, Williams set a personal-best time of 11.04, which broke the 23-year junior record held by Brenda Morehead of Tennessee State.

2001 On June 9, in Palo Alto, California, Stacy Dragila broke her own world outdoor record in the pole vault, clearing 15 feet, 9¼ inches. She has won the only two world pole-vault titles in history and has set 15 world records. In February 2002 Russia's Svetlana Feofanova eclipsed Dragila's indoor record with a vault of 15 feet, 6¼ inches.

2001 In July, at the World Veterans Athletic Championships in Brisbane, Australia, 65-year-old Carolyn Cappetta, of Concord, Massachusetts, set a world master's record of 65.69 in the 400 meters. She also set a world master's record of 2:46 in the 800 meters and another record of 4:56 in the 4×400-meter relay, winning gold in all three. In January, Cappetta set the U.S. record in the 200 meters—32.25.

2001 Dawn Ellerbe set the world indoor record for the 20-pound weight throw, at 77 feet, 5¼ inches; she also set the U.S. outdoor record in the hammer throw, at 70.46 meters. Ellerbe was a six-time indoor champion in discus, with titles in 1995, 1996, 1998, 2000, and 2001, and a four-time NCAA champion at the University of South Carolina.

2001 Erica Distefano, of the College of New Jersey, was the first Division III athlete to win the college high jump at the Penn Relays. Distefano broke her own school record of 5 feet, 9 inches, with a jump of 5 feet, 9¾ inches.

2001 Wheaton College (Norton, Massachusetts) won its third straight Division III indoor championship. The University of Wisconsin at Oshkosh also won three straight, in 1994–'96, as did Christopher Newport, in 1988–'90, and the University of Massachusetts Boston, in 1985–'87.

2001 Amy Acuff won the indoor championship in the high jump at the U.S. track and field championships and was on the Olympic team in 1996 and 2000. She was U.S. outdoor champion in 1995 and '97, a three-time NCAA indoor champion, with titles in 1994, '95, and '97, and a two-time NCAA outdoor champion, with titles in 1995 and '96 while at UCLA.

2001 Jearl Miles-Clark, 34, won the U.S. indoor 800-meter championship. She was fourth in the event in the 1999 world championships.

2001 Marion Jones won the 200 meters in the world outdoor championships in Edmonton, Alberta. In the 100 meters, she took the silver, after winning 42 consecutive 100-meter finals. Ukrainian Zhanna Pintusevich-Block won the gold.

2001 At the world outdoor championships, Anjanette Kirkland narrowly defeated Gail Devers, age 35, in the 100-meter hurdles, to win the gold medal. Devers was trying for her fourth 100-meter world title. Kirkland won the U.S. indoor championship in March. Jenny Adams won the bronze at the world outdoor championship.

2001 The 4×100-meter relay team won the gold medal at the world championships.

2001 Sara Reinersten, 26, lost her left leg at age 7 because of a tissue disorder, but it did not stop her from becoming a champion runner. At age 13 she set a world record for above-the-knee amputees in the 100 meters (18.06, which still stands). She also holds world records in the 200 and 400 meters and the marathon. So far, she has finished five marathons.

2001 Shelia Burrell won the bronze medal in the heptathlon at the world championships. Yelena Protihorva, of Russia, won the gold.

2002 At the Millrose Games in Madison Square Garden, New York, Regina Jacobs, age 38, won the women's mile for the fourth straight year—she is the first to do so.

2002 Louisiana State University captured its ninth woman's title at the indoor track and field championships, with 57 points. UCLA was second and Florida third. In Division II, Wheaton College in Massachusetts won its fourth consecutive title.

2002 At the NCAA Divison I indoor track and field championships at the University of Arkansas, three new collegiate records were set: Perdita Feliciena of Illinois in 60 meter hurdles, with a time of 7.90 seconds; Amy Linnen of Arizona in the pole vault, with a vault of 14 feet, 10¼ inches; and Candice Scott of Florida won the 20-pound weight throw, with a distance of 75 feet, 7½ inches. A technicality prevented Scott from claiming the record.

Middle- and Long-Distance Running

What a glorious moment: Joan Benoit Samuelson emerging from the tunnel into the Los Angeles Coliseum, running the final few yards to the finish line. As she waved her hat to the wildly cheering crowd, they knew—as the world watching on television knew—history was taking place. This unassuming woman from Maine had won the gold medal in the first Olympic marathon for women, in 1984. Samuelson forever proved that women could run 26.2 miles and not self-destruct.

1876 In what was billed as the first sports competition between the sexes, Mary Marshall defeated Peter Van Ness in two out of three 20-mile races in New York. Her prize was $500.

1966 In August, Roberta Gibb Bengay became the first woman to run the Boston Marathon. She ran unofficially, disguised as a man, and was later disqualified when race officials discovered her ruse. She finished in 3:26:02, ahead of more than two-thirds of the 415 men in the race.

1967 Kathrine Switzer, a member of the Syracuse University track team, became the first woman to register to run in the Boston Marathon. She registered as K. D. Switzer so she wouldn't be identified as a woman and wore a baseball hat to shield her hair and face. When it was discovered she was a woman, race officials tried to tackle her and throw her out of the race. Switzer went on to win the New York City Marathon in 1974 and finished first among U.S. women in Boston in '75.

1970 The Road Runners Club of America held the first championship marathon for women.

1970 The first New York City Marathon was held, with one female entrant, Nina Kucscik, of Huntington, New York, who dropped out after

15 miles because of illness. She came back to win the event in 1972 and '73. The first woman winner was Beth Bonner, in 1971. Greta Waitz, who immigrated from Norway, won the New York Marathon a record nine times, 1975–'80, '82–'86, and '88.

1971 Doris Brown set a world record in the 3,000 meters, won five cross-country titles, and was on the 1968 and '72 Olympic teams.

1972 Nina Kuscsik was the top woman finisher in the Boston Marathon with a time of 3:8:58 in the first year women could officially enter. She and eight other women competitors pinned on the letter "F" for female. Their numbers were the first ever issued to women in the 76-year history of the Boston Marathon. Elaine Pederson, of San Francisco, finished second, and Kathrine Switzer finished third.

1973 Mary Boitano won the 6.8-mile Dipsea Race on August 26, becoming the first female to win the race in its 68-year history.

1975 On June 14, Marion May, of Fairbanks, Alaska, became the first woman to win a marathon in open competition against men, at the Midnight Sun Marathon, in Fairbanks. The 21-year-old, in her first regulation marathon, led the 53 male competitors, finishing in 3:2:41.

1977 The first wheelchair athlete to compete in the Boston Marathon was Sharon Rahn (Handrich), who finished with a time of 3:48:51.

1979 Joan Benoit Samuelson won the Boston Marathon, setting a new American record of 2:35:15. In 1983, she won her second Boston Marathon in 2:22:43, establishing a world record that lasted for almost 10 years. In 1985, Samuelson set an American record in the Chicago Marathon of 2:21:21. In 1991, she finished fourth in the 95th Boston Marathon.

1981 In August, in New York, Ruth Rothfarb, at age 80, became the oldest woman ever to complete a marathon.

1981 In December, in Kansas, the first NCAA Division I women's cross-country championships were held at Wichita State University.

1983 Mary Decker (Slaney), one of the greatest middle-distance runners of all time, won the women's 1,500 (4:00.9) and the 3,000 meters (8:34.62) at the first world track-and-field championships. Slaney won 10 consecutive 3,000-meter events between 1982 and 1984.

1984 In Los Angeles, the marathon became an Olympic event for women. Joan Benoit Samuelson was the first gold medalist, with a time of 2:24:52. She took the lead after 14 minutes and stayed ahead of the pack the entire time. Her entry into the Los Angeles Coliseum for the final lap remains one of the most memorable scenes in women's sports history.

1984 Mary Decker Slaney set the American record in the 2,000 meters, 5:32.7, which still stands. Slaney also set an American record in the 1,500 meters, 3:57.12, in August 1985, which still stands.

1985 At this time, Lisa Larson Weidenbach is the last American woman to have won the Boston Marathon.

1987 Vickie Huber, of Villanova University (Pennsylvania), won the NCAA 3,000 meters at both the indoor and outdoor championships. She repeated her wins in 1988, and she also won the NCAA outdoor one mile and national outdoor 1,500 meters. In 1989, she won the Honda-Broderick Cup as the nation's outstanding female collegiate athlete.

1988 The Olympic 10,000-meter race for women was held for the first time in Seoul, South Korea.

1988 Sarah Fulcher finished the longest continual solo run ever, as certified by the *Guinness Book of World Records*, in her run around the perimeter of the United States. She finished the 11,134-mile run in 14 months, averaging a marathon every day.

1990 Kim Jones was ranked the number one marathoner in the United States by *Track and Field News*. In 1989, she placed second in Houston and third in Boston, won the Twin Cities, and placed second in New York. She was second in the Boston Marathon in 1991 and '93.

1991 Jean Driscoll became the first athlete with a disability to win the Sudafed Female Athlete of the Year Award. Driscoll, a paraplegic marathoner, won seven Boston marathons, setting five world records in the process, and also won nine Bloomsday races.

1991 California Polytechnic University won its 10th consecutive NCAA Division II championship in cross-country.

1992 Just shy of her 40th birthday, Francie Larrieu, a premier middle- and long-distance runner since 1969, finished third in the Olympic trials. In 1969, at age 16, she tied the American record in the 1,500 meters (4:16.8). Competing in distances of 1,500 meters to 2 miles, she established 36 U.S. records and 11 world records. Larrieu switched to long distance in 1984, becoming the national champion in the 10,000 meters. In 1986, in her first marathon, she finished second in Houston. Larrieu was a member of five U.S. Olympic teams—1972, '76, '80, '88, and '92.

1992 Lynn Jennings won her third consecutive world cross-country championship, having previously won the title in 1990 and '91. She placed second in '86 and third in '72. Also in '92, she won the bronze medal in the 10,000 meters at the Olympics in Barcelona.

1993 Lynn Jennings won the bronze medal in the 3,000 meters at the World Indoor Championships.

1994 The 3,000-meter race was replaced by the 5,000 meter run.

1994 Villanova won its sixth consecutive NCAA Division I cross-country championship, coached by Marty Stern through 1993 and by John Marshal in '94. In 1990 and '91, Sonia O'Sullivan, of Villanova, won back-to-back individual championships. Carole Zaja won back-to-back in 1992 and '93.

1994 Krista Johnson won the Chicago Marathon. She had won the Houston Marathon in 1993. In 2000, she placed second in the Olympic trials but did not compete in Sydney, Australia.

1994 Kim Jones competed in her fifth Boston Marathon, placing eighth. She placed second in 1993 and '91, fifth in '90, and third in '89.

1994 When Oprah Winfrey ran the Marine Corps Marathon in Washington, D.C., she raised interest in women's running exponentially. Her training had been a regular topic on her television show, and when she ran and finished the marathon, she attracted major media attention. Because of Winfrey, many women, as well as men, took up the sport.

1995 Lynn Jennings placed second in the 3,000 meters at the World Indoor Championships. In 1996, she took the silver in the 5,000 meters.

1996 Ultramarathoner Ann Trason is a legend and the world's most accomplished ultramarathoner. She holds several long-distance running titles, won the TAC/USA 24-hour race, completing 143 miles and setting a world record for 100 miles in 13:55:02. She also holds the world record for the 100 kilometers, at 7:00:47, and the 50,000 meters, at 3:20:23. Trason won the Comrades Australian 54-mile race twice. She also finished the Western States Endurance Run of 100.2 miles an incredible nine times and had seven consecutive victories (1989–96). In two of the races, Trason placed second, and in 1995, she was just five minutes behind the overall male winner, with a time of 18:40:01. At the International Association of Ultramarathoning World Championships she led the U.S. team to its first ever world title, breaking her own world record for the 100k by almost 9 minutes with her 7:00.47 time. She tied for first in the Cove Canyon Crawl 50k; set a track record at the Redwood Empire 50,000 meters; and was second over all in the American River 50 mile.

1996 Jean Driscoll became the first seven-time wheelchair-athlete winner of the Boston Marathon.

1997 State University of New York College at Cortland won its seventh consecutive NCAA Division III cross-country championship.

1997 The oldest woman to set a world record in long-distance running was Sue Ellen Trapp. In May, Trapp ran 235-plus miles in the Sugeres, France, 48-hour race. She was 51 years old at the time.

1997 Natala Skinner, of Sun Valley, Idaho, became the first American to win world championship titles in the 7.5 kilometers and the 15 kilometers in the same year.

1998 Kim Ariet, of Lewis College, won the NCAA Division II championship in both the 5,000 meters and the 10,000 meters for the second time. Christie Allen, of Pittsburg State University (Kansas), also accomplished this in 1992 and '93.

1998 In Utica, New York, the National Distance Running Hall of Fame was dedicated to honor the greatest runners in history. The inaugural class of five members included pioneer marathoner Kathrine Switzer and marathon legend Joan Benoit Samuelson.

1998 At the NCAA Division I championships, Amy Skieresz, of the University of Arizona, won her second consecutive title in the 10,000 meters. Katie Swords, of Southern Methodist University (Dallas), won back-to-back championships in 1995 and '96, and Carole Zajac, of Villanova University (Pennsylvania), did the same in 1993 and '94.

1999 Lynn Jennings established herself as one of the greatest runners of all time. For 15 years, 1985–'99, she won at least one national title, accumulating a total of 39. She holds 15 road titles in distances from 5 kilometers to 15,000 kilometers and holds the U.S. record of 31:19.89 in the 10,000 meters, set in 1992.

1999 Lisa Smith was the first woman finisher in the Marathon des Sables, a 150-mile race in the Sahara Desert. She finished 36th out of 600 entrants, making her the highest-placing U.S. runner ever in the event.

2000 Adams State College (Alamosa, Colorado) won its eighth consecutive NCAA Division II championship in cross-country.

2000 Regina Jacobs set the American record in the 5,000 meters, 14:45.35, at the Olympic trials, running the race shortly after finishing the 1,500 meters. She became ill and did not compete in Sydney. Jacobs qualified for the Olympics four times—1988, 1992, 1996, and 2000. She was the 1,500-meter champion at the Olympic trials in 1992, 1996, and 2000. Jacobs won the silver medal in the world championships in 1997 and '99 and is a nine-time indoor 1,500-meter champion.

2000 Elizabeth Jackson set the American record in the 3,000-meter steeplechase, 9:57.20, in Sacramento.

2000 Anne Marie Lauck, a member of the 1996 and 2000 Olympic teams, was ranked number two in the United States by *Track and Field News*. In 1996, she placed 10th in the marathon. In 1999, she finished second in the 10,000 meters at the USA outdoor track-and-field championships and 16th at the world championships.

2001 On February 18, in New York, Marla Runyan, who is legally blind, set an American indoor record in the 5,000 meters of 15:07.33. She broke Lynn Jennings's 11-year-old record of 15:22.64. In June, Runyan won the 5,000 meters at the outdoor championships with a time of 15:06.03. She finished eighth in the 1500 meters at the Olympics in Sydney in 2000—the highest a U.S. woman has ever placed.

2001 At the USA outdoor track-and-field championships, 37-year-old Regina Jacobs won the 800 meters and won her 10th national outdoor title in the 1,500 meters, becoming only the third woman to win both in the same championship. Marie Mudler was the first, in 1965, and Kim Gallager completed the double in 1984.

2001 Running in her first marathon, Deena Drossin finished seventh in the New York City Marathon with a time of 2:26.58, the fastest time ever posted by an American woman. In 2000 she set the U.S. road record in the 5k at the Olympic trials. She was also the 10,000-meter champion in 2000 and 2001, and she placed second in the 5,000 meters in 2000. Drossin, a five-time defending U.S. 8-kilometer cross-country champion, won the 4-kilometer cross-country championship in 1999. At the University of Arkansas, she was an eight-time NCAA all-American.

2001 Andrea Hatch, of Charlestown, Massachusetts, ran in her 24th consecutive Boston Marathon, the longest streak by a woman. Hatch finished in 4:49:38. Her personal best was in 1983, 3:10:01.

2001 In August, Erica Larson, age 30, won her third consecutive Pikes Peak marathon in 4:49.12. The first half of the run is a 7,815-foot ascent.

2001 Amanda McIntosh won the women's division of the Leadville Trail 100-mile race and placed eighth overall out of 407 male and female starters and 176 finishers. Her time was 22:16. The race goes through Colorado's San Isabel National Forest and ranges in altitude from 9,200 to 12,600 feet. Her first 100-mile race was the 1998 Rocky Racoon race in Huntsville, Texas, where she set a course record.

2001 Ann Trason, perhaps the most successful female ultra-marathoner in history, just keeps on running. At age 40, she won the USA track and field 50-mile trail championship at the White River race in Greenwater,

Washington and the Western States 100-mile endurance run for the 12th time. Between 1981 and 2001, she was named *UltraRunning Magazine's* Runner of the year 12 times.

2001 Ann Riddle won the USA 100k national championship.

2001 On July 14, Betsy Kalmeyer, age 40, from Steamboat Springs, Colorado, won the women's race of the Hardrock Hundred Mile Endurance run (a 101.7 mile course) in 29:58. In the race, competitors climb and descend 66,000 feet running, hiking, and crawling. She became the first woman to complete the course in under 30 hours, breaking her own previous record by two hours. She placed third overall, the highest female finish ever. Ruth Zollinger came in second at 30:40

2002 Regina Jacobs broke Lynn Jennings's world indoor record (9:28.15) in the two mile at the Boston Indoor Games with a time of 9:23.38.

2002 In February, Jacobs, at age 38, set a new world indoor record for the three-mile with a time of 14:44.11, in New York City. The old record was held since 1985 by Christine McMilken of New Zealand.

2002 The Boys and Girls of Brooklyn, New York, girls distance medly relay team set a national indoor record of 11:50.86, breaking the mark set in 1983 by Mepham High of Long Island, New York. Stand-out Stacy Livingston, ranked number one in the country among female high school middle distance runners, ran the opening lap. The team also set a record of 8:53.67 in the 4×800 meter relay.

2002 Nicole Teter set a new indoor record for the woman's 800 meter with a time of 1:58.71, breaking the record of 1:58.92 shared by Mary Decker (Slaney) in 1980 and Suzy Favor Hamilton in 1999.

2002 At the World Cross Country Championships in Dublin, Ireland, in the five mile race, Deana Drossin won the silver medal in 26:46 and Colleen de Reuck the bronze in 26:17.

TRIATHLON

TRIATHLONS, CONSIDERED to be the world's most physically demanding sport, evolved as training exercises for runners. The competition consists of three segments: swimming, biking, and running. The Ironman, the most famous of all the triathlons, takes place in Hawaii. This grueling race is made up of a 2.4-mile swim, a 112-mile bike race, and a marathon (26.2 miles).

1974 The first known swim, bike, and run triathlons were held at Mission Bay, in San Diego, California.

1978 The first Ironman triathlon was held in Hawaii, and 12 men completed the race.

1979 Thirteen men and one woman, Lynn Lemaire, crossed the finish line at the Ironman.

1981 Valerie Silk was named race director of the Ironman.

1982 The dramatic footage on ABC's television broadcast of Julie Moss crawling on her hands and knees to a second-place finish in the Ironman triggered a worldwide explosion of interest in the sport. The United States Triathlon Association was created.

1989 The International Triathlon Union (ITU) was created, with the representation of 25 nations in Avignon, France, at the founding congress.

1989 The first world championships were held in Avignon. U.S. triathletes Jan Ripple, Laurie Samuelson, and Karen Smyers finished second, third, and fourth, respectively.

1990 Karen Smyers, of Lincoln, Massachusetts, was the first American to win the ITU world championship. She also won the first of six consecutive national championships.

1992 Karen Smyers was named Triathlete of the Year by *Triathlete* magazine.

1994 In her first Ironman triathlon, Smyers finished fourth. Her time was the fastest ever for a woman in her first competition.

1995 The triathlon was included for the first time in the Pan American Games, staged in Mar del Plata, Argentina, and Karen Smyers won the gold medal. She also won her second world championship, in Cancun, Mexico, and later won the Ironman, becoming the only woman to win both events in the same year.

1997 Sue Latshaw became the first American and second woman to break the nine-hour barrier for an Ironman distance event, as she won the Ironman Europe in Roth, Germany.

1999 Karen Smyers was selected to be the flag bearer for the United States at the Pan American Games in Winnipeg, Manitoba. The 1999 season marked a comeback for the celebrated American, who missed most of the previous two seasons while recovering from injuries sustained in two training accidents, including a collision with a truck while she was on a training ride. She finished second in the Ironman despite having thyroid cancer.

2000 The triathlon debuted as an Olympic sport in Sydney, Australia. Joanna Zeiger, of Baltimore, was the top finisher at the U.S. trials and finished fourth in Sydney, missing the bronze medal by only 16.91 seconds. Michelle Blessing was named coach of the men's and women's Olympic teams.

2001 Siri Lindley, of Boulder, Colorado achieved the number one world ranking after winning two world championship titles and two World Cup races in July. After winning the ITU World Aquathlon Championship—2-kilometer run, 250-meter swim, 2-kilometer bike—she became only the second U.S. woman to win the ITU world championship (Olympic distance). Joanna Zeiger was the third-place finisher.

2001 On August 12, Karen Smyers won the Elite, the first triathlon held in New York City.

VOLLEYBALL

VOLLEYBALL PLAYERS weren't always expert setters and towering spikers who can hammer the ball at speeds greater than 60 miles per hour. In the early years, volleyball was a slow-paced game, often played at social outings—much different from today's game of power and athleticism. In 1964, volleyball became the first Olympic team sport for women. Six players on a team defend the court by always returning the ball across the net before it touches the ground, doing so within three hits or sets. The net is 7 feet 4¼ inches high. Each winning hit is worth one point, and the first team to reach 15 points wins the game. Winning two out of three games wins the match.

1895 The game of volleyball was invented by William G. Morgan, a physical director at the YMCA in Holyoke, Massachusetts.

1901 Senda Berenson, director of physical education at Smith College (Northampton, Massachusetts), introduced the sport of volleyball at Smith's Demonstration Day.

1903 The first *Volleyball Rule Book* for girls and boys was published by the Spalding Athletic Library.

1912 New rules were established: the net was raised to 7 feet, 6 inches; serve rotation of players was incorporated; and a two-out-of-three-games match was recognized.

1926 The Spalding Athletic Library published *The Red Cover*, a special series of rules for women. The NSWA also created a separate set of rules for women: the court size became 30 by 60 feet, and no more than three contacts per side were allowed.

1928 *Volleyball for Women*, by Katherine W. Montgomery, was published as the first textbook for women with complete instructions and photographs on how to play.

1928 The United States Volleyball Association (USVBA) was formed, along with a committee on rules for girls and women.

1947 The Federation Internationale de Volleyball (FIVB) was established with 14 members and served as the official international governing body of the sport.

1949 A women's division was included in the USVBA national championships for the first time, at the Naval Armory in Los Angeles. Eight women's teams were entered.

1951 The USVBA awarded all-American honors in the women's division of the national tournament for the first time.

1952 The world championships added a competition for women.

1955 The first time U.S. women competed in international competition was at the Pan American Games in Mexico City. The U.S. team won the silver, and Mexico won the gold.

1960s Volleyball became a popular team sport in junior and senior high schools and in colleges. Club teams also expanded throughout the United States.

1960 The Mariners, a club team from Santa Monica, California, won their sixth consecutive national title.

1961 The women's net was lowered to 7 feet, 4.25 inches, where it remains today.

1962 Two of the first colleges to add a women's division to their schedules were the University of Minnesota at Duluth and the University of Hawaii.

1962 The first world championships for women were held; Japan won.

1964 Volleyball was introduced as the first team sport for women at the Olympic Games in Tokyo. The United States did not medal. Japan won the gold, the USSR won the silver, and Poland won the bronze.

1964 The national championships served as the United States' first volleyball trials for both men and women.

1967 Harlan Cohen, an all-American, was selected to coach the U.S. women's team.

1970 At the world championships, Mary Jo Peppler was voted Best Female Player in the World. Peppler is often credited with being the first woman to stamp her identity on the sport. The split-second timing and agility on the court she possessed brought her teams numerous championships.

1971 The Association for Intercollegiate Athletics for Women (AIAW) hosted its first intercollegiate volleyball championship. Sul Ross State (Alpine, Texas), behind star player Mary Jo Peppler, won the first two championships.

1972 In Houston, Mary Jo Peppler and Marilyn McReary started a women's club team, E Pluribus Unum—meaning "out of many, one." The team won two straight USVBA national championships, with Peppler as player-coach.

1973 The AIAW hosted the first junior college/community college national championship.

1974 At the world championships in Tokyo, the U.S. team finished 12th.

1975 Mary Jo Peppler joined the professional Juarez team, of El Paso, Texas, making volleyball the first professional mixed-team sport.

1975 The International Volleyball Association, a mixed professional league, began paying women to play. Mary Jo Peppler and Kathy Gregory were two of the stars of the league.

1977 At the summer tournament in Varna, Bulgaria, the U.S. women's team posted its first victory over the Soviets.

1978 At the world championships in Saint Petersburg, Russia (then named Leningrad), the U.S. team finished sixth, its highest to date.

1978 The women's national team was provided a training facility at the U.S. Olympics training center in Colorado Springs.

1979 The U.S. team qualified for the Olympics in a regional contest against Cuba. Flo Hyman was voted MVP of the tournament.

1980 The United States had now developed a world-class team, but the Olympics in Moscow were boycotted.

1981 Flo Hyman was the first American woman to be named to the All–World Cup team. At 6 feet, 5 inches, Hyman displayed awesome offensive and defensive maneuvers that helped make her one of the best players in the world. At the University of Houston, she received a volleyball scholarship, was an all-American for four years, and then led the U.S. team to the silver medal at the Olympics in Los Angeles in 1984. Hyman was instrumental in attracting more African American girls to volleyball.

1981 The University of Southern California Trojans won the first National Collegiate Athletic Association (NCAA) championship, defeating the UCLA Bruins. In 1982, the Rainbows, from the University of Hawaii, won the second championship, defeating the Trojans, 3–2.

1981 At the first Division II championships, held at the University of California at Riverside, California State University at Sacramento beat Lewis University (Romeoville, Illinois) for the title.

1982 The U.S. team won the bronze medal at the world championships.

1984 At the Olympics in Los Angeles, Flo Hyman led the U.S. national team to its first medal, a silver, losing the gold to China. The team was backed by Bob Lindsey, who donated $500,000, and was coached by Arnie Selinger. Paula Weishoff was named MVP. Other star players were Rita Crockett, Debbie Green, and Elaina Oden, who had 84 kills.

1986 On January 24, Flo Hyman died while playing professional volleyball in Japan. Her Daiei team was playing a match in the city of Matsue, and after coming out of the game for a regular substitution, Hyman collapsed on the bench. Her death was caused by a rare disease known as Marfan's syndrome, which afflicts tall, thin people.

1990 The U.S. team won the bronze at the world championships.

1991 Caren Kemner was named Most Valuable Woman Player in the World by the FIVB. She was an outstanding player for the United States and had also played professionally in Brazil, Japan, and Italy. In 1990 and '91, she was nominated for the Sullivan Award. Kemner also was a six-time United States Olympic Committee Player of the Year.

1992 Portland State University (Oregon) won its fourth NCAA Division II championship. Portland State has played in a total of six title games. California State University at Northridge has appeared in seven championships, winning two—in 1983 and '87.

1992 The U.S. team won the bronze medal at the Olympics in Barcelona, Spain. Cuba took the gold, and the Soviet Union took the silver. Caren Kemner led the U.S. team with 127 kills and seven aces. Kemner was named Team USA MVP five times in her career.

1993 The first World Grand Prix Championships were held. The U.S. team won the 1995 championships.

1994 The USVBA changed its name to USA Volleyball and continues to serve as the national governing body.

1995 The U.S. team won the World Grand Prix Championships. Tara Cross Battle was named MVP.

1995 The U.S. team won the silver medal in the Pan American Games. Tee Williams, an outstanding player at the University of Hawaii, where she was NCAA Division I Player of the Year in 1987 and '89, and a member of the national team since 1990, was one of the standout players.

1995 Attendance at the NCAA championships exceeded 100,000 for the first time. The University of Nebraska defeated the University of Texas, 3–1, for the title.

1996 In Atlanta, Paula Weishoff was a member of the Olympic team for the third time. She had been a member of the national team since 1981 and was MVP in 1984 and '92. In addition to winning numerous U.S. medals, she played professionally in Brazil, Japan, and Italy.

1996 Washington University (Saint Louis) won its fifth straight Division III championship. The school won seven championships out of eight appearances under coach Teri Clemans.

1997 Stanford University (California) won its fourth NCAA Division I championship, becoming the first college team to win four national championships, with previous titles in 1992, '94, and '96. The seniors on the team were the first class of women volleyball players to win three championships in four years.

1998 California State University at Long Beach, with a record of 36–0, was the first NCAA women's volleyball team to finish the season undefeated and win the NCAA Division I title. Nebraska went undefeated to the national title with a 34–0 record in 2001.

1999 Misty May of California State University at Long Beach received the Honda-Broderick Cup as the collegiate woman athlete of the year. She was named co-MVP of the NCAA Division I tournament after setting a new NCAA tournament record for 20 aces in six tournament games.

1999 The United States Professional Volleyball League was formed, creating a professional touring team with the intent of a barnstorming world tour. The first match was held at the Alliant Energy Center, in Madison, Wisconsin, on August 28, against the Canadian national team. Canada won in three sets. The first official league season started in 2002. Two previous attempts in the 1980s and '90s to launch a women's pro league failed due to lack of funds.

1999 Pennsylvania State University won the NCAA Division I title by beating Stanford. This was the first championship for a school east of Texas and just the third for a non-California school.

1999 Bonnie Bre, of Penn State, was the first setter to be named to the all-American first team four times, 1996–'99. Bre started every match for Penn State in the four years she played.

1999 The University of California at San Diego appeared in its 10th Division II championships, winning 6—including 3 straight, in 1986–'88—all under coach Dong Dannevik.

2000 The U.S. team placed ninth at the Olympics in Sydney.

2000 The University of Nebraska went undefeated for the NCAA championship.

2001 Central College (Pella, Iowa) won its third straight NCAA Division III title. In 1999, the team had a 59-consecutive-game winning streak, equaling an all-division record.

2001 At the State Farm Classic, Nebraska defeated Pacific to win its 36th consecutive match. Nebraska's winning streak is fifth on the all-time NCAA list; Penn State is first, with 44 consecutive matches. In the first round of the tournament, Nebraska swept Hawaii, handing the team its first season-opening loss since 1980.

2001 Former USA Volleyball president Rebecca Howard was the first woman elected to the executive committee of the FIVB.

2001 The USA Women's National team captured the gold medal at the 2001 FIVB World Grand Prix in Macau, China. It was the first time since 1995 that the U.S. women had placed first in the event. They defeated home-standing China 26-28, 25-20, 25-21, 25-11. USA libero Stacy Sykora was named the tournament's best libero.

2001 Stanford won its record fifth NCAA Division I title, sweeping previously undefeated Long Beach State, 31-29, 30-28, 30-25. Stanford's Logan Tom had 25 kills and was named outstanding Final Four player.

WATER POLO

WATER POLO is played in a pool no longer than 25 meters for women, with two teams of seven players each. An inflated ball is batted between players, with the purpose of scoring a goal by getting the ball into a cage at the end of the pool. Players must constantly stay swimming and cannot touch the bottom of the pool.

1911 Charlotte Epstein and L. de B. Handley helped form the National Women's Lifesaving League, a swimming and water polo league in the New York metropolitan area.

1926 The first women's Amateur Athletic Union (AAU) national championship was won by the Los Angeles Athletic Club.

1931 The AAU decided the sport was too rough for women and canceled the championship for 30 years.

1961 Rosemary Mann Dawson, hired by the University of Michigan Athletic Department as its first female coach, revived the women's national water polo championships. The Ann Arbor Swim Club, led by Micki King, later an Olympic diving gold medalist, won the first three national championships.

1962 Chuck Hines started a girls' water polo program at the Des Moines, Iowa, YMCA. In 1965, Hines became the chairman of the newly formed AAU National Women's Water Polo Committee.

1966 The Santa Clara Swim Club, of California, won back-to-back indoor titles in 1965 and '66.

1969 From 1964 to 1969, the Northern Virginia Aquatic Club won seven national titles.

1975 Between 1971 and 1975, the Florida team won the majority of the national championships—with the Cincinnati Marlies winning the indoor championship in 1974.

1976 The U.S. national water polo team was established.

1977 Anaheim, which later became the Fullerton Area Swim Team, or FAST, coached by Stan Sprague, won the indoor national championship in 1975 and 1977 and was the outdoor champion in 1976. Merced, California, coached by Flip Hassett, won the 1977 outdoor championship.

1977 The first international women's water polo competition was sponsored by Canada. The YMCA team of Asheville, North Carolina, coached by Chuck Hines, represented the East, and Commerce, California, coached by Sandy Nitta, represented the West. The Netherlands won the tournament.

1978 U.S. Water Polo was formed, taking control of the sport from the AAU and YMCA.

1978 The Commerce International Women's Water Polo Championships were organized by Sandy Nitta and held in Commerce, California. The event was the largest women's tournament in the world and the first held in the United States. Sixteen teams competed, including 11 from other countries. Sainte Foy, from Quebec, beat the United States in the closing seconds to win the tournament.

1979 The Long Beach, California, team coached by Kelly Kemp, won the 1978 and 1979 indoor nationals.

1979 The first official Federation Internationale de Nation Amateur (FINA) Women's Water Polo World Cup was held in Merced, Cal ifornia, with the U.S. team defeating Australia, 8–7. Canada beat Holland, 7–3, which gave the United States a second-place finish, with a total record of six wins and six losses. Australia was third, and Canada fourth.

1980 Sandy Nitta, a 1964 Olympic swimmer, became head coach of the U.S. national team, a position she held through 1995.

1986 Water polo became an official world championship event in Madrid, after a 1982 exhibition event at the world swimming championships in Guayaquil, Ecuador. The United States won the bronze and won bronze again in 1991. The world championships are held annually except in Olympic years.

1996 A junior women's world championship sponsored by FINA was held for the first time.

1997 The Speedo Cup National Age Group Championship initiated a separate division for girls.

1998 Coralie Simmons, of UCLA, was selected Player of the Year for the second consecutive year.

1998 The International Olympic Committee added women's water polo to the 2000 Olympics in Sydney. Six teams of 11 players each were selected. Legendary U.S. player Maureen O'Toole announced she was coming out of retirement to compete in Sydney.

1998 In March, Guy Baker, former assistant coach of the men's national team, was named the first head coach of the U.S. women's national team. Baker was an all-American at California State University at Long Beach and, after graduating, served as an assistant there. In 1991, he took the head coaching position at UCLA. In his second year, he was named Coach of the Year by the American Water Polo Coaches Association.

Baker is the only coach to have won men's and women's national titles in the same academic year.

1999 Water polo made its debut in the Pan American Games in Winnipeg, Manitoba.

1999 Sandy Nitta was the first female coach inducted into the U.S. Water Polo Hall of Fame. She served as head coach of the women's national team for 16 years and organized the first women's international tournament in the United States. As head coach of Team USA, Nitta won three bronze medals in the world championships and three silver and one bronze in World Cup competition.

2000 Erika Lorenz, 19, of San Diego, California, was selected as the youngest member of the senior national team. Lorenz has represented the United States at the Holiday Cup in California, the Thetis Cup in Greece, and the Olympic qualification tournament in Sicily.

2000 Maureen O'Toole, regarded as the greatest female water polo player of all time, joined the national team in 1979 at age 17 and rejoined in 2000 at the age of 39, so that she could play in the Olympics. She was named MVP of the national championships 15 times, MVP of the world championships six times, and U.S. Water Polo Female Athlete of the Year five times. O'Toole played on 25 national and international teams for the United States.

2000 Coralie Simmons scored 12 goals in the first seven-game Olympic qualifying tournament.

2000 Water polo made its Olympic debut, and the U.S. team won the silver medal, losing the gold medal game to Australia.

2001 Water polo became an official championship event under the National Collegiate Athletic Association (NCAA). UCLA won by defeating previously unbeaten Stanford, 5–4. UCLA won the national title six out of the last seven years, winning the "national" competitions before they were sanctioned by the NCAA.

2001 In December the U.S. Junior National team beat Australia 10-9 in overtime to win the fourth FINA Junior Olympic championships.

2001 At the FINA World Championships the U.S. women placed fourth.

WATERSKIING

IN 1922, Ralph Samuelson, of Minnesota, invented waterskiing when he designed a pair of skis out of two pine boards and then was towed behind an outboard-powered boat on Lake Pepin, in Lake City, Minnesota. In the late 1920s and 1930s, waterskiing in the United States became an exhibition sport, and in 1939, it became a competitive sport with the formation of the American Water Ski Association (AWSA). At Jones Beach, on Long Island, New York, the AWSA organized the first annual national championships. The championships included the traditional three waterskiing events: slalom, a zigzag course of flags; tricks; and jumping, where distance is the key factor.

1939 The AWSA was established to promote recreation and competitive events.

1939 The first U.S. waterskiing championships were held in Jones Beach State Park. Esther Yates won the women's all-around.

1940 Willa Worthington Cook performed the first 180-degree solo swivel.

1942 The first water ski show was organized at Cypress Gardens, in Florida, by Julie Pope.

1949 At the first world water ski championships, held in Juan Les Pines, France, Willa Worthington Cook won the slalom, jumping, and overall titles. Cook was a great champion, winning numerous national and international competitions.

1949 Martin meters for measuring jump distances were introduced.

1950 Willa Worthington Cook was the first skier to master swivel skiing. A swivel ski is designed with a rotating binder to allow the ski to track forward while the rider does ballet maneuvers.

1950s In the late 1950s, Charlene Melbourne became the first female barefooter.

1952 In Lakeland, Florida, Mary Lois Thornhill set the jump record of 56 feet, becoming the first woman to hold the record.

1955 Willa Worthington (McGuire) Cook retired from active competition. In her career, she won eight national championships and 18 national events titles; she never lost in tricks at the nationals. Cook won a clean sweep of the overall, slalom, and trick events in 1949 and 1951. She also represented the United States at four world tournaments, winning the overall three times and accumulating five event victories.

1957 Leah Marie Rawls was the first woman to serve as director of the AWSA, a position she held from 1957 to '59. Rawls placed second overall in the 1957 world championships.

1957 The Johnson jump metering system of triangulation was implemented by the AWSA.

1959 The first masters water ski tournament was held at Calloway Gardens, Pine Mountain, Georgia. Nancie "Rideout" Robertson, competing against men, was the overall winner.

1962 The national water ski championships were broadcast on television for the first time.

1964 At the Florida State Open in Lakeland, Barbara Cooper Clack became the first woman ever to jump 100 feet.

1969 In a feat hard to match in any sport, Elizabeth Allan won all three events—slalom, tricks, and jumping—at the nationals, the world championships, and the masters.

1970s As the popularity of recreational boating grew, so did interest in waterskiing.

1972 Waterskiing became an exhibition sport at the Munich Olympics. Elizabeth Allan won the gold in slalom and the bronze in tricks.

1975 Janesville, Wisconsin, was host of the first national show ski championship with teams that included women.

1975 From 1962 to 1975, Elizabeth Allan dominated the sport, winning 42 national titles and winning the overall U.S. masters title, the most prestigious invitational event, nine times. Her eight world titles are a record.

1976 Barbara Fox became the first and only woman to drive the boat for a U.S. masters tournament. In 1977, in Milan, she became the first and only woman to drive a world tournament.

1978 Jean Matthison won the first barefoot nationals, held in Waco, Texas. Later in the year, she won the first world barefoot championships, in Canberra, Australia.

1979 The city of Monroe, Louisiana, was host of the first national intercollegiate waterskiing championships that included teams with women. Northeast Louisiana University won the title.

1982 At the world barefoot championships, women competed in jumping for the first time. Lori Powell won the gold medal.

1984 The Coors Light Water Ski Tour, the only standardized series of professional waterskiing in the world, began.

1984 The first Women's Grand Prix Pro Tour slalom championship was won by Camille Duvall.

1987 Austin, Texas, was host of the first kneeboard nationals, in August. Dixie Adrus won the open women's division, Jackie Kalls won the women's division, and Cherie Lumis won the girls' division.

1987 Deena Brush (Mapple) was the overall winner in the World Championships, U.S. Nationals, U.S. Masters, and the Pro Tour Grand Prix. She is the only person to be a member of the U.S. water ski team seven consecutive times.

1989 In West Palm Beach, Florida, the U.S. water ski team won its 21st consecutive world championship team title. The women's division overall winner was Deena Brush (Mapple), the only female ever to hold the world slalom and jump records simultaneously.

1991 For the first time since 1949, the U.S. team lost a world tournament, placing second at the world championships in Austria.

1995 At the Pan American Games, Deena Brush Mapple won a gold medal.

1996 In September, the world slalom record was set by Kristi Overton-Johnson in West Palm Beach. At the age of 8, she competed in her first nationals and at age 10 she became the sport's youngest competitor, vying against skiers up to 10 years her senior.

1996 Kristi Overton-Johnson won the U.S. nationals, the U.S. Open, and the masters.

1996 Waterskiing became an Olympic event in Atlanta.

1997 Waterskiing was recognized by the U.S. Olympic Committee as a sport in the Pan American games.

1998 Rhoni Barton was named U.S. Water Skier Athlete of the Year by the AWSA and was ranked number one by the International Water Ski Federation. This led to her being the 1999 U.S. Open overall champion and setting a world overall points record at the Sunset Cup in May.

1998 Camille Duvall was named the first woman coach of the U.S. national water ski team. Duvall won 48 world and national titles, reigning as the world professional slalom champion five times and the number one female water-skier in the world for 10 years in the 1980s.

1999 The AWSA became USA Water Ski. The organization sanctions more than 800 tournaments every year, ranging from small local events for beginners to national and world tournaments.

1999 Kristi Overton-Johnson won the world slalom championship.

1999 In July, the tricks world record was set by Tawn Larsen-Hahn in Wilmington, Illinois.

1999 Rachel George won the world overall and national overall barefoot titles.

1999 Tara Hamilton was named Wakeboarder of the Year by USA Water Ski.

2000 Camille Duvall was voted one of *Sports Illustrated for Women*'s 100 Greatest Female Athletes of the Century.

2000 Regina Jaquess held the junior world record in all three skiing events—slalom, tricks, and jumping.

2000 Ashley Lathrop was undefeated in all events in water ski racing.

2001 Lucille Borgan, at age 88, continued to compete at the national level and also serves as a judge.

2001 At age 17, Regina Jaquess made the U.S. team and qualified to compete in the world championships in Recetto, Italy, on September 24–29.

WEIGHTLIFTING

STRONG, PHYSICALLY powerful, having the solid tools to get the bar over one's head. This is the ultimate definition of a competitive weight lifter. Cheryl Haworth, holder of 35 U.S. weightlifting medals, established records that will be hard to beat. Women compete in two types of lifts—the snatch and the clean and jerk. The snatch is a simple movement lifting the weights from the ground to overhead. The clean and jerk is two movements, first to the shoulders, then overhead.

1975 The Amateur Athletic Union (AAU) began to sponsor power lifting for women. In 1978, the first international power lifting championship was held, with 68 women competing.

1977 Jan Todd bench-pressed 176¼ pounds, deadlifted 441 pounds, and lifted 424¼ pounds from a squat, to become the first woman to lift more than 1,000 pounds in three power lifts. In 1981, she became the first woman to exceed 1,200 pounds in the three-lift total.

1986 The International Weightlifting Federation incorporated women's events for the first time at the Pannonia Cup in Budapest, Hungary.

1987 The first women's world championship was held in Daytona Beach, Florida. Karen Marshall, of the United States, won the first gold medal in the 82.5-kilograms category.

1992 Lynn Stoessel-Ross was the first woman elected to the United States Weightlifting Federation board of directors. She was later reelected for three additional years as athlete's representative and also served on the Coaches Committee.

1997 Carrie Boudreau, of Cape Elizabeth, Maine, became the first U.S. woman to complete a 402.2-pound squat, 236.7-pound bench press, and 462.7-pound dead lift in the 123.5-pound weight class. These record-setting lifts at the AAU "RAW" Meet gave Boudreau her fourth world power lifting championship.

1999 Cheryl Haworth won the only U.S. medal, a bronze, at the International Weightlifting Federation's senior championships in Athens, Greece, on November 29.

1999 Women's weightlifting was a part of the Pan American Games for the first time. Robin Byrd Goad won the gold medal in the 53-kilograms (117 pounds) weight class, snatching 187.5 pounds.

1999 Tara Nott won a gold medal while setting four U.S records in the 48-kilograms (106 pounds) class.

2000 Weightlifting became an Olympic sport in Sydney, Australia. Tara Nott won the gold in the 48-kilograms class, and Cheryl Haworth won the bronze in the 75-kilograms-plus class.

2000 On March 12, at the USA Weightlifting national championships, 16-year-old Cheryl Haworth established three new records: 120 kilograms (264.4 pounds) in the snatch, 145 kilograms (319.7 pounds) in the clean and jerk, and a 265-kilogram (584.3-pound) total. She now holds all the U.S. records in her weight class. She was the youngest weightlifter to ever make a U.S. Olympic team.

2000 Tara Nott's lift of 181.9 pounds gave her the silver medal in the 106-pound class at the Sydney Olympics, but after Bulgaria's Izabela Dragneva tested positive for a banned diuretic, Nott was awarded the gold. The U.S. team had not won a gold medal in weightlifting in 40 years. Nott's snatch was 181.9 pounds and her clean and jerk was 226, giving her a total of 407.9 pounds.

2001 The U.S. did not send a weightlifting team to compete in the World Weightlifting Championships in Antalya, Turkey, because of security concerns following the September 11 terrorist attack. Jackie Berube paid her own way and finished fifth in the 128-pound class, lifting a combined 429 pounds, equaling the 192.5-pound American snatch record she had set earlier in 2001.

WRESTLING

Westling is growing in popularity for women of all ages, with more collegiate, high school, and club programs added each year. Women compete against both men and women.

In 1997, Federation Internationale de Leettes Associees (FILA), the international wrestling federation, reduced the number of weight classes for women competing at the senior levels from nine to six: 46 kilograms (101.46 pounds), 51 kilograms (112.48 pounds), 56 kilograms (123.43 pounds), 62 kilograms (136.69 pounds), 68 kilograms (149.5 pounds), and 75 kilograms (165.34 pounds).

1987 The first women's wrestling world championships were held in Lorenskog, Norway. France won the title. There were no U.S. entries.

1989 In Martigny, Switzerland, the United States entered the world championships for the first time. Japan won the team championship, and the United States finished fifth.

1990 The first U.S. national championships were held in San Francisco. Marie Zeiglar won the 97-pound division, Afsfoon Roshanzimir won the 103-pound division, Patricia McNaughton won the 110-pound division, and Jennifer Ottiano won the 116.5-pound division.

1991 In Tokyo, the United States placed fifth for the second time at the world championships. The team placed sixth in 1990 in Lulea, Sweden.

1992 In Villeurbanne, France, Tricia Saunders became the first American to medal at the world championships, winning the gold in the 110-pound division. The U.S. team placed ninth.

1995 The University of Minnesota at Morris was the first college in the country to sponsor a varsity team for women's wrestling.

1995 USA Wrestling created a 16-and-under competition in freestyle events.

1995 In Moscow, the U.S. team placed fourth at the world championships for the third consecutive time. From 1993 to 1995, the U.S. team won five medals—four silver and one bronze.

1996 The Cadet national championships in Las Vegas marked USA Wrestling's first age-group national tournament for women.

1996 At the world championships in Bulgaria, the U.S. team medaled for the first time, winning the team bronze, along with one gold and two silver medals. Tricia Saunders won the gold in the 101.25-pound class.

1997 Twelve-year-old Teresa Gordon-Dick was USA Wrestling's first female national champion in a co-ed bracket.

1997 At the world championships in Clermont-Ferrand, France, the U.S. team placed third, winning three silver medals.

1998 In March, the first United States High School Girls Wrestling Association tournament was held at Pioneer High School, in Ann Arbor, Michigan. Dena Glisan, of Oakland Mills, won the 121-pound class.

1998 In Poznan, Poland, Tricia Saunders won her third gold medal at the world championships in the 101.25-pound division.

1999 Under coach Rob Eiter, the United States won its first world championship, in Boden, Sweden. Three Americans medaled: Tricia Saunders won the gold in the 101.25-pound division, Sandra Bacher won the gold in the 149.75-pound division, and Kristie Marano won the silver in the 165.25-pound division.

1999 Tricia Saunders was the first wrestler to be named United States Olympic Committee Women's Freestyle Wrestler of the Year three times—1996, '98, and '99. Also in 1999, Saunders won her fourth world championship, having won previously in 1992, '96, and '98.

2000 At the world championships again in Sofia, Kristie Marano won her second gold medal in the 149.75-pound division. Marano also received the Women's Wrestler of the Year Award.

2000 From 1987 to 2000, the United States ranked fourth in total international medals, with 27: 6 gold, 18 silver, and 3 bronze.

2001 Brooke Bogren was named Outstanding Wrestler for the second straight year at the FILA Cadet women's national championships. Bogren defeated Debbie Sakai, of Mililani Town, Hawaii, in the 52-kilogram title round.

2001 The United States won its first Pan American women's championships. The United States won four out of the six weight classes, totaling six medals and 57 points: in the 101.25 pounds, Clarissa Chun won the silver; in the 112.25 pounds, Stephanie Murata won the gold; in the 123.25 pounds, Tina George won the gold; in the 136.5 pounds, Sara McMann won the bronze; in the 149.75 pounds, Kristie Marano won the gold; and in the 165.25 pounds, Iris Smith won the gold.

2001 Both Texas and Hawaii held state-recognized girls' high school tournaments, and USA Wrestling registered 2,600 females.

2001 At the U.S. National Championships, Tricia Saunders won the 101.25-pound event, Stephanie Murata won the 112.25-pound class, Tina Wilson the 123.25-pound class, Sara McMann the 138.75-pound class, Toccara Montgomery the 152-pound class, and Iris Smith the 165.25 class.

2001 Stephanie Murata won the silver medal in the 112.25-pound category, Toccara Montgomery won the silver in the 149.75-pound class, and Jenna Paulik placed fifth in the 165.25-pound class in the freestyle world championships in Sofia, Bulgaria. The U.S. team placed fifth over all.

ORGANIZATIONS, LEADERS, AND OTHER MILESTONES

1883 On June 16, the New York Gothams baseball team held a "Ladies' Day," inviting women to come at a lower ticket price or for free. Ladies' Day helped in promoting the acceptance of women spectators at public sporting events.

1888 The Amateur Athletic Union (AAU) was founded in New York City to oversee rules and tournaments for men's amateur athletics. By 1914 the organization began sanctioning women's competition, and in 1916, it authorized a few women's track-and-field and swimming events. By 1923, the AAU sponsored women's competitions in gymnastics, basketball, swimming and diving, track and field, and handball.

1916 The first national women's tournament held by the AAU was in swimming.

1920 An all-Philadelphia team in field hockey coached by Constance Applebee visited Great Britain. It was the first women's team to represent the United States in an international competition.

1920 The National Federation of State High School Associations, now known as the National Federation of High Schools (NFHS), was established. Based in Indianapolis, the NFHS is the national service and administrative organization for high school athletic and fine-arts activity programs. The organization has a long-standing involvement with the promotion of females in sports. In 1993, the NFHS established an equity committee, chaired by Dr. Sandra Scott, the first full-time executive director of the New York State Public High School Athletic Association.

1923 The AAU began to sponsor baseball, track and field, diving, and gymnastics for women.

1923 A women's division of the National Amateur Athletic Federation was organized to promote physical fitness among women and to protect female athletes from exploitation by promoters or other officials. Lou Henry Hoover, wife of eventual president Herbert C. Hoover, organized the division under the slogan "A sport for every girl and every girl for a sport." This division was called the Committee on Women's Athletics (CWA).

1930 The Sullivan Award was established. The award is given annually to an amateur athlete whose performance, example, and influence have done the most during the year to advance the cause of sportsmanship. The first woman recipient was swimmer Ann Curtis in 1944. It was 12 years before another woman, diver Pat McCormick, won the award.

1932 In addition to the CWA, the National Section on Women's Athletics (NSWA) of the American Physical Education Association established programs considered to be suitable for girls and women. The organization also published sport guides, prepared by the rules and editorial committees.

1949 The International Association of Physical Education and Sport for Girls and Women (IAPESGW) was founded and held its first meeting in Copenhagen, Denmark. The organization provides opportunities for professional development and international cooperation, with members on 5 continents and more than 40 countries. A scientific congress is held every four years.

1951 The first Pan American Games were held in Buenos Aires, Argentina. The United States and other countries from North America, South America, and Central America compete in the quadrennial games, held in the year preceding the Summer Olympics.

1955 The NSWA became the Division of Girls and Women in Sport (DGWS) under the auspices of the American Association of Health, Physical Education, and Recreation.

1967 The DGWS formed the Commission on Intercollegiate Athletics to establish a process for conducting intercollegiate athletics for college women. Soon after, several national championships were held.

1969 The National Association for Sport and Physical Education was established under the American Alliance for Health, Physical Education, Recreation, and Dance. It is the country's only national association exclusively serving teachers and researchers.

1971 The Association of Intercollegiate Athletics for Women (AIAW) was formed, with representatives from 278 colleges and universities. The AIAW was the first organization to exclusively govern women's college athletics, developing rules and policies as well as overseeing all tournaments and national championships. Carole Oglesby, a pioneer in women's sports, was the first AIAW president. At the time of her appointment, she was on the faculty of the University of Massachusetts. Women's sports programs began to receive more attention with a wider participation. By 1975, national championships were held in 19 sports. Oglesby taught at Temple University (Philadelphia) for 25 years, and many of the women working today in sports programs throughout the country are her former students. She remains active in many organizations that promote the betterment of sports and other opportunities for women.

1972 On June 23, the education amendments that include Title IX were enacted by the U.S. Congress. Title IX, the first federal law to prohibit sex discrimination at any educational institution receiving federal aid, states: "No person in the United States shall, on the basis of sex, be excluded from participation in, be denied the benefits of, or be subject to discrimination under any education program or activity receiving federal financial assistance."

1972 For the first time, *Sports Illustrated* chose a woman—Billie Jean King—for Sportsman of the Year.

1973 The AIAW sanctioned athletic scholarships for women.

1973 Dr. Dorothy Harris was named director of the Center for Women and Sports Research Institute, the first research center for women in sports.

1973 Terry Williams, a golfer for the University of Miami, was the first woman to receive an athletic scholarship to a major college. From 1974 to 1981, the number of athletic scholarships for women increased from 60 to 500.

1974 The DGWS became the National Association of Girls and Women in Sports, which remains the principal professional organization for women in teaching, coaching, and research.

1974 The Women's Sports Foundation was founded by Billie Jean King to foster the development of women's sports in America. With current membership exceeding 125,000, the foundation has played a primary leadership role in opening the door of sports for girls and women in the United States and internationally. The original headquarters were in San Francisco, and Eva Auchincloss was the first executive director. In 1978, Holly Turner became the associate executive director. The foundation published the first *College Athletic Scholarship Guide for Women* in 1975.

1976 The Broderick Award was established to recognize the outstanding collegiate woman athlete of the year (in Division I schools). The award recognizes excellence as much in the classroom and the community as in the athlete's sport. It was named after Tom Broderick, an athletic apparel manufacturer, who created the award.

1978 Lillian Greene-Chamberlain became the first woman and first American to serve as director of the Physical Education and Sports Program for the 161 member nations of UNESCO (United Nations Educational, Scientific, and Cultural Organization), headquartered in Paris. She held the position until 1988.

1978 The Amateur Sports Act was passed, prohibiting gender discrimination in open amateur sports in the U.S. The act also established the United States Olympic Committee (USOC) as the sole authority for U.S. representation at the Olympics.

1980 The National Collegiate Athletic Association (NCAA) voted to hold national championships for women in Division II and III schools. In 1981, it added sponsorship for Division I. The first tournaments were in basketball, cross-country, field hockey, gymnastics, swimming, tennis, volleyball, and track and field. The NCAA was formed in 1905, but prior to 1980, no women's programs were included.

1980 The first Women's Sports Foundation Salute to Women in Sports fund-raising dinner was held in New York City. At the dinner, the foundation announced the first inductees into its newly established International Women's Sports Hall of Fame: Patty Berg, Babe Didrikson Zaharias, Amelia Earhart, Gertrude Ederle, Althea Gibson, Janet Guthrie, Eleanor Holm, Billie Jean King, and Wilma Rudolph.

1980 Donna de Varona was elected the first president of the Women's Sports Foundation and remained in the post for 10 years.

1981 The AIAW lost a court battle to prevent the NCAA from taking over sponsorship of women's championships. Adherence to AIAW rules ended with the association's demise in June, 1982, when the NCAA took over.

1982 The U.S. Postal Service issued its first commemorative stamps to honor athletes. Images of Babe Didrikson Zaharias and prominent male golfer Bobby Jones graced envelopes across the nation.

1984 Sandra Baldwin became the first woman president of USA Swimming.

1986 The Women's Sports Foundation moved its headquarters to New York City. In 1993, it relocated to Eisenhower Park in East Meadow, on Long Island.

1986 Henley Gabeau became the first woman president of the Road Runners Club of America and is credited with helping to develop programs and new clubs for runners of all ages throughout the country.

1986 The first Goodwill Games were held in Moscow. Conceived by Ted Turner, the games were created to promote friendly relations between Russian and American athletes after the 1980 boycott of the Olympics by the United States and the 1984 boycott by the Russians of the games in Los Angeles. The second Goodwill Games were held in Seattle in 1990.

1986 The International Olympic Committee (IOC) appointed Anita DeFrantz to lifetime membership. DeFrantz, a champion rower who won a bronze medal at the 1976 games, became the only American woman and one of only five women on the 91-member committee. She was also the first African American woman to serve on the committee. In 1993, she was elected to the executive board.

1987 Under new executive director Debra Slaner-Larkin, the Women's Sports Foundation established National Girls and Women in Sports Day, celebrated in Washington, D.C. The foundation also created the annual Flo Hyman Award, given annually to an outstanding woman athlete for "exemplifying dignity, spirit, and commitment to excellence." The award is named in memory of one of the premier volleyball players and captain of the 1984 Olympic silver-medal team. Hyman died while playing professionally in Japan on January 24, 1986. The cause of death was Marfan's syndrome, a rare congenital disorder of the body's connective tissue.

1987 The Broderick Award became the Honda-Broderick Award. Honda established additional awards for athletes in 11 different sports, overall awards for Divisions II and III, and an inspirational award.

1987 Maria Stefan was named executive director and vice president of global business for the Sporting Goods Manufacturers Association, which represents more than 2,000 manufacturers of sports apparel, athletic footwear, and sporting good products. Stefan is recognized as a longtime advocate of developing and perfecting products for women that maximize their performance at any level of participation.

1988 Carol Zaleski became president of USA Swimming and was the first woman on the technical committee of the Federation Internationale de Nation Amateur (FINA). In 1992, she reached another milestone as the first woman to chair the technical committee.

1988 Phyllis Holmes began her term as president of the National Association of Intercollegiate Athletes, making her the first woman to serve as president of a national coed sports organization.

1990 Eve Atkinson was appointed athletic director of Lafayette College (Easton, Pennsylvania). She was the first woman hired to that position at a Division I school combining men's and women's athletic programs and a Division I-A football team.

1990 Elaine Steward was hired by the Boston Red Sox as assistant general manager, the first woman to hold this position in Major League baseball history. In 1998 Kim Ng was hired for the same position by the New York Yankees. In 2001 she joined the Los Angeles Dodgers as assistant general manager, and was replaced at the Yankee's office by Jean Alterman, the third woman to hold the position.

1991 Barbara Hedges of the University of Washington became the first female Division I-A athletic director. Division I-A combines leadership for women's and men's programs. Along with Hedges, five other women held the position of athletic director at a Division I-A school as of 2001: Kathy Beauregard, Western Michigan University; Cary Sue Groth, Northern Illinois University; Judy Macleod, University of Tulsa; Andrea Seger, Ball State University (Muncie, Indiana); and Deborah A. Yow, University of Maryland.

1991 The NCAA elected Judy Sweet as its first female president in January.

1992 Tina Sloan-Green, a champion lacrosse player and coach, founded the Black Women's Sport Foundation, in Philadelphia.

1993 Women in Sports and Events (WISE), a professional organization that connects women in the business of sports and special events, was started in New York City by Sue Rodin. WISE currently has six chapters in cities nationwide and continues to expand. The organization holds regular meetings featuring high-profile speakers and also hosts networking and social events. Every June, a Women of the Year Award luncheon honors three women leaders in the industry whose accomplishments are recognized nationally.

1994 Wendy Hilliard, the first African American Olympian in rhythmic gymnastics, became the first African American president of the Women's Sports Foundation.

1994 Donna Gigliotti became the first woman coordinator for international athletics at the U.S. Department of State. As a primary link between the U.S. government and the sports world, the coordinator builds alliances with the sports community and oversees the State Department's support of international athletic events such as the Olympic Games.

1996 Barabara Hedges became the first woman director of the National Association of College Directors of Athletics. In 1998, Hedges became the first woman on the National Football Foundation board of directors.

1996 Becky Oakes was elected as the first woman president of the National Federation of High Schools.

1997 Vivian Fuller was hired in October to head the NCAA Division I athletics program for men and women at Tennessee State, making her the first African American woman to direct a college program with a football team.

1997 Sue Hillman became the first female head trainer in professional football. After working at the Pittsburgh Steelers' training camp, she was invited to camp by the Steelers, the Detroit Lions, the Washington Redskins, and the New York Giants.

1997 Celeste Rose became the first African American woman to be appointed to the NCAA's senior management staff when she was named NCAA group executive director for public affairs.

1997 Anita DeFrantz became the first woman to be elected IOC vice president in the organization's 102-year history.

1999 In January, Julia "Judy" Levering became the first woman president of the United States Tennis Association (USTA).

1999 In March, Judy Rose, of the University of North Carolina, was appointed the first female member of the NCAA Division I basketball committee. The committee selects, seeds, and runs the men's basketball tournaments.

2000 In another women's first, Sandra Baldwin was elected United States Olympic Committee chair for the 2000–2004 quadrennium. She served as vice president/chair for the board during the 1997–2000 quadrennium.

2001 The oldest summer camp for girls—Wyonegonic, in Denmark, Maine—celebrated its 100th season. In 1902, when the camp opened, it offered outdoor activities such as hiking and canoeing, which was a new concept for girls. Soon, swimming and horseback riding were added. Girls wore long skirts and slept in tents.

2001 Two women held the post of state association executive director at a public high school athletic association: Becky Oakes, of the Missouri State High School Activities Association, and Nina Van Erk, of the New York State Public High School Athletic Association.

2001 On August 31, Ashley Martin became the first woman to play and score in an NCAA football game. Martin, a placekicker for Jacksonville State University (Alabama), kicked an extra point with 8 minutes and 31 seconds remaining in the first quarter.

2001 Rebecca Howard, former president of USA Volleyball and Jang-Ja Hong of South Korea became the first women elected to the executive committee of the Federation Internationale de Volleyball (FIVB) Board of Directors.

Bibliography

Hult, Joan S., and Marianna Trekell, eds. *A Century of Women's Basketball: From Frailty to Final Four*. Reston, Virgina: American Alliance for Health, Physical Education, and Dance, 1991.

Johnson, Anne Janette. *Great Women in Sports*. Detroit: Visible Ink Press, 1996.

Macy, Sue. *Winning Ways: A Photohistory of American Women in Sports*. New York: Scholastic Inc., 1998.

Markel, Robert, Susan Waggoner, and Marcella Smith. *The Women's Sports Encyclopedia*. New York: Henry Holt and Company, 1997.

Oglesby, Carole A. *Encyclopedia of Women and Sport in America*. Phoenix: Oryx Press, 1998.

Smith, Lissa, ed. *Nike Is Goddess: The History of Women in Sports*. New York: Atlantic Monthly Press, 1998.

Whoolum, Janet. *Outstanding Women Athletes: Who They Are and How They Influenced Sports in America*. Phoenix: Oryx Press, 1992.